Mosley: Right or Wrong?

Oswald Mosley

Mosley: Right or Wrong?
Oswald Mosley

Published by kind permission of the
Friends of Oswald Mosley (FOM London)

Copyright © 2019 Sanctuary Press Ltd

ISBN-13: 978-1-913176-12-9

Sanctuary Press Ltd
71-75 Shelton Street
Covent Garden
London
WC2H 9JQ

www.sanctuarypress.com
Email: info@sanctuarypress.com

Preface

Britain comes to crisis, a deep crisis of the whole system. It may be deferred or concealed for a period, but the coming of crisis sooner or later is now certain. It is crisis caused by the results of war, the liquidation of empire without the preparation of any alternative, the maintenance of an economic system designed for the last century, and the absence of any world policy in the age of nuclear fission.

At the time of my resignation from the government I stated this crisis would come, and have continued to do so ever since. A war and two armament booms postponed it, but will finally increase its severity. At every stage I have advanced a constructive policy to meet it, which has been continuously developed as new facts changed the situation. I have stood throughout in fundamental challenge to the rulers of the present system, with an alternative policy which events now begin to justify. This policy has been explained to large audiences who have been good enough to listen to me while I have been denied the facilities of press, television and radio. Their lively and generally friendly interest prompted me to write this book in a new form.

Human nature made this book. These are questions put to me in the course of a life which is continually exposed to question by my fellow-countrymen and also by fellow Europeans. They range from questions asked at public meetings in halls, or in the open air, to discussions both private and public in universities, professional circles, expert and amateur gatherings of all kinds. Most arise from an acute interest in real and vital political issues, others from more personal motives which are sometimes almost trivial. But they are the things which concern people in daily practice - people of all sorts. I have not altered the substance of these questions,

1

but have sometimes put them in more concise form. The answers vary considerably in style, depending on the type of person who asks the particular question. The way and technique of speaking should change with the audience, though never the principle and substance. It was certainly an education for me to encounter this wide enquiry, and it may interest others to share my experience even if they disagree with my views. It is encouraging to find so many people with such a well-informed interest in things which really matter. The proportion of people interested in serious things is large in Britain, and tends to increase. It is they who ultimately determine the greatness of a nation, for to them the mass of the people in every street and village will look for leadership in time of trouble and crisis. They must themselves be serious if they are to give guidance appropriate to this age. It is always the duty of any national leadership to know what these key people are feeling and thinking. And the method? Ask for questions.

Some of the more profound subjects which concern me and my friends are scarcely touched in this book, because they seldom arise in normal questions and debate. The idea of higher forms, for example, is only mentioned in the course of a short definition of the difference - in ultimate aims as well as immediate policy - between ourselves and the communists, and very briefly in one concluding answer. Yet it is the deeper debate on the real direction of the human journey which must surely underlie all current controversy. We must know where we are going, and I have attempted in other writings to suggest an answer to that rare but final question.

The immediate issues discussed in this book will soon touch the very life of our country. They will settle far more than the question of who was right or wrong in the past. They will present a challenge in the near future which we ask a great people to meet with a great response.

Oswald Mosley

Europe A Nation

The Union of Europe

Question 1. What is the position of Britain today?

Answer: Deadly serious. It is all the more serious because so few people realise the gravity of the situation. So many assets are gone, and so many opportunities have been thrown. away. Empire was hurriedly abandoned, and the leadership of Europe was even more lightly rejected. Our rulers sought the best of all worlds by balancing between Commonwealth, America and Europe. They ended by falling between the three because they lacked both sense of reality and creative policy. They shrank from all hard but necessary decisions, such as the resolution to enter Europe with the Dominions and to make other arrangements for their remaining obligations. They failed to devise any alternative, clear-cut and practical policy. The result was to miss all chances and to be left in the most precarious position. We live in prosperity for the time being on borrowed money, at the mercy of foreign speculators. We risk at any moment to be back where we began as a small island, but this time without the means to support ourselves. We face the gathering economic crisis which could be foreseen for years past. The situation is desperately serious.

But we still have the quality which took us out of this island to become the leading power in the world. It is the character of our people. Our scientists, our technicians, our managers and workers can still lead mankind. Political errors subject them to impossible conditions. Great policies can still win for them the great place which belongs to them. We may as a result of recent mistakes first have to pass through a period of severe effort and even hardship, but at these moments our people are at their best, when they see both reason for exertion and a clearly defined

3

objective. That is why it is the first duty of statesmen to show them the truths however bitter it may be.

In recent years our politicians have made the supreme error of seeking, in fact if not in name, to make Britain the 51st State of America; it was the only means they could conceive to keep their state solvent. America threw Britain back to Europe, which at present is dubious concerning the entry of our country whose leadership it sought a dozen years ago, because our present rulers still oppose the true union and the vital interests of our continent. Thus our nation is made the football of outside powers, and Soviet Russia may at any time take part in the game.

While these grave matters are still in debate, the first duty of us all is to come together in the firm resolve to put Britain back on the map. The old motto "Britain First" is what we need again today. No matter what the cost or sacrifice, we must now show that Britain can live in freedom from our present dependence, until we can resume our greatness in European leadership. We must fight back by rigorous methods to win with our trade even on the exposed markets of the world to which the policies of the old parties have for the time being condemned us, until our regained strength will enable us to implement the solution of our choice. We must brace ourselves to put Britain in a state of defence with the aid of our magnificent science, without reliance on any foreign power, until our constructive policies can obtain universal disarmament. We must again stand on our own feet and look the world in the face as a great power. This is the task to which all patriots should now dedicate themselves, regardless of their usual opinion in more normal conditions. Then the nation can decide which policy finally to adopt. For my part I shall stand, as always, for the entry of Britain and our Dominions into a united Europe. Then the rest of Europe will be proud to accept us again as one of the great powers of the world.

Question 2. Should we enter the Common Market and a United Europe?

Answer, Yes, certainly. I would go further: common government as well as common market. Ever since the war I have stood for the policy of "Europe a Nation". This means that the time has come for the European peoples to unite, just as we English, Scottish and Welsh united to make Great Britain a nation. It is clear that Europe a Nation is the next stage in human progress, and we shall meet with increasing difficulties until we face this fact.

Question 3. Did you develop the "Europe a Nation" policy since the war?

Answer: Yes, because the new facts made such a complete change necessary. But even before the war, in 1937, I wrote an essay called `The World Alternative', suggesting that the European powers should unite at least to as great an extent as the countries in the present Common Market, without in any way losing their separate national governments. Events have now taken us beyond that.

Today, to make a common market without a common government is rather like putting the cart before the horse. It will be found that you cannot really organize a common economic system without a common government. This is being proved every day with increasing force. The belief that a common political system will slowly develop from common economic arrangements is an idea of the last century; like all the thinking of our present rulers. Also the political division of the European countries is becoming a mortal danger. Small, separate European countries cannot live any longer between the great powers of Russia and America, without becoming dependents of one or the other. At present we are all dependents of America, and it would be worse to be dependents of Russia. That is why we must unite to form a European government.

Question 4. Will not this complete union of Europe mean that we lose our our national character?

Answer, No, certainly not. Did we cease to be Englishmen when we joined with the Scots to make Great Britain? And did the Scots become less Scottish because they joined with us English? Of course not. Having the same economic policy, defence system, foreign policy etc., does not make Englishmen want to wear kilts or eat haggis.

Other nations, too, have been formed from very different peoples, who have not lost their national character. A Norman and a Marseillais are both Frenchmen, but they are very different in character. A Prussian and a Bavarian are both Germans, a Lombard and a Sicilian are both Italians, a Castillian and a Catalan are both Spaniards; all are people with different characteristics, yet they belong to the same nations.

There is even less chance of our losing our national character when we join Europe. At first we shall feel more British than ever when we have to keep our end up at the council table. But before long we shall begin to look at things from the European standpoint, just as today we look at things from a British standpoint and not just from a narrow, English point of view. Then Europe will be made, and our wise, age-old European civilization will hold the balance of the world.

Question 5. Are not continental institutions less stable than British, and in joining Europe may we not be drawn into their troubles?

Answer: What you say in effect is this: my neighbour may set fire to the house next door, so I will sit tight in my house till the flames reach me. Sitting tight was all very well while the Channel was a protection, but we cannot be indifferent today to what is happening twenty miles away. The Channel is now a small ditch across which trouble can jump any day. The more unstable continental institutions may be, the more necessary it is for us to give some stability to them. What would happen to us if the continent went communist? Apart from their possession of rockets with a longer range than twenty miles and also far more effective means of invading us than existed in the last war, the communists could give us more trouble in that position than any we should have by going in first and forestalling them.

Is it not remarkable that so many people in Britain are so much concerned about what happens in Timbuctoo, but so little concerned about what happens twenty miles away in Europe? We simply cannot afford disaster in Europe under modern conditions.

Do not be so afraid of continental institutions. Europe is full of life and effervescence; it may wake us up a bit and that will do us no harm. But European civilization has stood for three thousand years and its greatest day is still to come. Let us be there on that day.

Question 6. How can we persuade Europeans to unite after such a long period of division and hatred?

Answer: Someone, no doubt, put a similar question at the time of the Union of England and Scotland. History supplied the answer.

Union only comes when it is a necessity, not before; then it comes despite the past. And it has now become a necessity for Europe to be a whole. These small, divided nations cannot live between the giants, America and Russia, without becoming dependents of one or the other. Our economies, also, cannot survive without union. That is why union has now become a necessity, and will soon be a fact.

"Sharp is the glance of necessity"! Until this moment great European thinkers and great men of action could passionately desire the unity of Europe, but in vain. Our generation will make the dream a reality, because we must.

Question 7. Should we lose our national sovereignty?

Answer: What? Do you really think we still have our national sovereignty? - we lost it long ago. We are now the helpless dependent of America. On the contrary, the only way to regain an effective sovereignty is to enter Europe. There, at worst, we shall be an equal partner, instead of being an old pensioner as we are at present. And if we enter Europe with our Dominions and our scientists, we shall have the means to play a leading part. For no other country in Europe has such an asset as the British Dominions. But remember they are only an asset when we have the means to develop them, and this we can obtain only as a member of a larger and richer community. Also, British science today is right at the head of Europe; for instance, we are far ahead of any other European power in nuclear development, and would be ahead of the world if we could back our science with the same resources as America and Russia. But we can obtain these resources only by ceasing to be an isolated island and becoming a member of the European community. In short, the way both to regain freedom from our present dependence, and to regain our greatness, is to enter Europe.

Question 8. What is your evidence for saying that we have already lost our national sovereignty, and can regain our greatness only in Europe?

Answer: National sovereignty in hard practice consists of two things: the first is to pay our way without dependence on an outside power, and the second is to conduct and develop the Commonwealth without such dependence.

Let us look first at our general situation. The Treasury reckoned in 1959 (Radcliffe Report) that we need £400 million surplus in our balance of payments to run the Commonwealth, let alone develop its resources at the necessary speed. We have never had such a favourable balance as that, or anything like it, since the war. In fact, during the last year (ending December 1960) we had a deficit of £344 million; i.e. a gap of £744 million between what we need and what we have. The present preoccupation of our politicians is not how to develop the Dominions, but how to avoid national bankruptcy for our island.

This is why, for instance, the financial expert Mr. Shonfield wrote recently in the Observer (16/4/61) concerning the position of Britain in terms almost identical to the statements of many other authorities: "An austerity budget ... Would convince foreign holders of sterling, who now apparently hold the fate of this country in the hollow of their hands...." In cold fact our "national sovereignty" at present is at the mercy of foreign finance.

Now look at the position of the Dominions. The Governor of the Bank of Canada said that by 1956 the whole Canadian manufacturing industry was "48% foreign owned and 52% foreign controlled. Much the largest part in this external control is played by the United States." (Times, 29/10/60). We could add many quotations from well-known people. Where is the independence today either for us or our Dominions?

If you have any remaining doubt, look at the ANZUS pact. This is an arrangement by America to defend Australia and New Zealand, from which Britain is excluded. Why? Because we are too small and too poor in the modern world to pay for either the defence or development of our Dominions.

Climb off the hobby-horse of past grandeur, and have a look at the modern facts. Our position and our assets have been thrown away, and we are back where we began, a small island. We have scarcely the means to pay our way, or support our population, and we could not begin to find the surplus by ourselves to develop the Dominions, unless we accepted a full siege economy quite as rigorous as that of the last war. These are now the undeniable choices for Britain: bankruptcy, a permanent siege economy, or entry with our Dominions into Europe.

Europe and the Commonwealth

Question 9. How did you propose the Commonwealth should fit into Europe a Nation? What would be the position of the Dominions?

Answer: The Dominions fit naturally into united Europe. Their economy is largely complementary to that of Europe. These great primary producers can supply what Europe lacks. All Europe can provide an adequate market for their production. But our island is not large enough to provide a market for the Dominion primary products. All fifty million of us are quite incapable of consuming the total wheat production of Canada alone. But if Britain and the white Dominions enter Europe in the reasonably near future we can strike a balance between European and Dominion production. If we delay too long the rest of Europe may develop other sources of supply. In fact, the Dominions stand to gain most by quickly entering the European economy, though it has been represented as a disadvantage to them. What is needed is an organised marketing system for British, Dominion and European agricultural products, such as we have already in Britain; a big task, but quite possible.

There is no real difficulty about the entry of Britain and the Dominions together into Europe. It would be an immeasurable gain to us, and to all Europe. The Dominions can secure in Europe not only a market for their primary products but also capital for their development. Europe in return can secure a good life for its expanding population in the common development of these great empty areas and their potential wealth. This can be the most fruitful arrangement of mutual benefit in history. But it needs clear explanation to the Dominions and a definite lead from Britain.

If any Dominions then hesitated to enter the European economy with us, they could remain linked to the mother country by the Crown, until they realised the advantage of participation. These advantages to the Dominions are so great that their entry would certainly not long be postponed.

Question 10. Cannot we solve our problems within the Commonwealth without going into Europe as you suggest?

Answer: Anyone who can do a bit more arithmetic than counting on the fingers of one hand, may see that we cannot develop what is left of the Empire, or Commonwealth, from our own resources. We have available for that purpose each year the difference between what we produce and what we consume. As stated already, we are now running a heavy deficit instead of the necessary large surplus. The figures suggest our present incapacity to pay our own way and exclude all question of developing the Commonwealth from current resources. Even if we went onto a siege economy, and put everybody back on rations, we could scarcely find enough from our own resources for a rapid development of the Commonwealth. We could just manage to live on such a basis, if we were driven to it for a period through being excluded from Europe by the follies of our government. But it would be a miserable life, and even then would permit only a very slow overseas development.

No, the only way to develop the Commonwealth with speed enough to replace the old system before a really bad crash is to bring in new and larger resources. British wealth and manpower for rapid development were dissipated by the war. They no longer exist. An old firm which wants to expand, but lacks sufficient resources, needs to bring in new partners. Shall we turn for partnership to Europe, or shall we be taken over by America? That is the real choice.

Question 11. What will be the result of trying to develop the Commonwealth without entering into Europe?

Answer: Those who live in this dream of the past - that we can still develop the Commonwealth single-handed - are in reality making a present of Britain to America. They may not know what they are doing, but that is what is happening. Those who thus lull the people by talking about the old Empire are playing straight into the hands of others who want to sell us to America because they would do very well out of the deal.

Those who talk of solving Britain's problem in the Commonwealth have lost in this emotional moment their usually outstanding ability to count. Otherwise they would see from the present balance sheet and what is already occurring, that it means in hard practice the Commonwealth is bought up by America. And Britain would end by being kept as an old pensioner, if we survive at all in any British shape. To live in the past means to lose the present and forfeit any hope of the future.

The choice before us is stark and clear. Partnership with Europe, or becoming the 51st State of America. By bringing the vast potential resources of the Dominions into Europe we can be the chief influence in the continent. If we stay outside Europe and lose the Dominions completely to America, we shall become an American dependency. Which would you rather be, - the head of Europe, or the tail of America?

Question 12. Do you not think the Americans want us to enter Europe in order to increase their influence over us and Europe?

Answer: The Americans are getting tired of paying for our upkeep, economic and military. Conservative and Labour governments have been content to live on America ever since the war. It is an ignoble position, unworthy of Britain.

The Americans naturally prefer having in Europe a going concern rather than a row of old pensioners living on American charity. But you are perfectly right to be on guard against the new Europe becoming a new and greater sphere of American domination and exploitation. This is very likely to happen so long as we have common market without common government. A large and viable area without any effective government of its own, is very likely to fall under the control of a powerful outside country with an integrated system and united government. This is another strong reason for having common government as well as common market. Europe a Nation can run its own affairs without dependence on any other country. Three hundred million Europeans in union can become the strongest and richest nation in the world.

Question 13. What do you think of the campaign waged by Lord Beaverbrook's papers against the Common Market?

Answer: Lord Beaverbrook's arguments were formidable, and shook severely the case of the Conservative government. I welcome them, as reinforcing my case. What Lord Beaverbrook succeeded in proving effectively was that the Common Market would not work properly without common government. But this is my point. It is plain sense to recognize that you will get chaos if you throw together a number of highly developed national economies without first establishing an effective central authority; a common government strong enough to lead and to organize. By its half-hearted measures conservatism can characteristically discredit a cause it belatedly embraces.

Every one of the difficulties enumerated by Lord Beaverbrook can be overcome through political union; very few without. He has performed a service in puncturing the illusion that a single market will work without a single government.

For the rest, it is a pity that he should not have realised: (1) That every argument he employed for the common development of the old Empire applies more forcibly to the common development of the new Europe, and all its overseas territories, by methods of modern organization. (2) That it is a disastrous confusion of thought and effective action to oppose the admission to our system of European labour, whose standards can rapidly be raised to our own by common government, while he wants to retain within our unorganized system all the much cheaper labour of the underdeveloped areas of the Commonwealth. (3) That the only final solution for British agriculture, which he rightly talks much about, is an organized marketing system throughout Europe, where the specialities of good British soil will find a better market than ever, and a frank recognition of the fact that farmers and farm-workers in Britain and Europe must receive a larger reward. This can only be supplied without harming industrial workers by mass production in city industries, which will also be made possible by a larger and surer market.

These are but preliminary illustrations of the overriding fact that men with healthy instincts in politics can realise their beliefs in practice only through the complete and effective union of Europe.

Question 14. What would you say are the chief points of difference between your policy and the moves made towards Europe by members of the old parties?

Answer: The two chief points of difference are: (1) We stand for common government as well as common market. We believe that to join the economies of the various European nations without the direction and authority of common government will either create chaos or so retard progress to the complete common market that crisis will hit us before Europe is ready. (2) We think it wrong to bring into the European system peoples who are on an altogether different standard of life. It is bad for them and bad for us; it can be fatal to both. We can level up living standards throughout Europe by the economic leadership of government, easily enough. But we cannot include very backward countries in this economic system, for reasons we will discuss later. This would lead inevitably to the disruption of our economy, and the exploitation and sweating of these peoples. It is far better to help them to make their own economy and to build their own civilization. Britain can enter Europe effectively with the Dominions, but not with these other parts of the Commonwealth. There are other points of difference, of course, between our policy and that of the old parties. But these two points are decisive, and it will be found that these realities have to be faced before Europe is made.

Question 15. You talk about the leadership of Britain in Europe, and others talk about the leadership of their countries. How can all countries lead at the same time?

Answer: Anyone who knows well the great European peoples is aware that each of them has particular qualities in which they are pre-eminent. The answer is that they will all lead in their own spheres. It is true for each of them to claim leadership in some respect. The qualities of the various European peoples are complementary to each other in remarkable degree. Bring them together, and you make something approaching a perfect whole. A nation of universal genius will be created. The poet's superb dream of the "Second Hellas" will be realised.

Question 16. Will not the conflicting economic and political interests in Europe make impossible or delay too long the complete union of Europe?

Answer: The European peoples have everything to gain from complete union. But we are in danger from the petty, haggling spirit of present governments. They are penny wise and pound foolish, always trying to outsmart each other over small things and missing the great advantages which they can win together. That is why we need a new spirit, a movement of the peoples towards union. Let it come up from the roots like a force of nature to meet the necessity and the opportunity. It is the duty of everyone of us to rouse the peoples' will to union. Then this great enterprise can quickly succeed if it is driven forward by popular enthusiasm.

Otherwise we may all be destroyed before the long process of commercial compromise and adjustment is complete. It is not the haggling of merchants each seeking his own advantage, but the fiery force of a new European idea which will fuse the divisions of the present nations into the union of a new and greater nation at a higher level. Europe requires a decisive act of faith and of will.

Economic Advantages of European Union

Question 17. What are the economic advantages of union with Europe?

Answer: First of all, a completely united Europe will provide a market of about 300 million people. It will also contain all the foodstuffs and raw materials we can possibly require. Certainly if we add our overseas territories, we shall not require anything from the rest of the world at all. It will, therefore, be a completely secure market insulated from the present chaos of the world. There will be no need either to buy or to sell on world markets unless we wish to do so. This decisive fact will alter the whole economic situation, and will at last enable government elected by the people to guide the economy in the interest of the whole nation.

Question 18. Would it be a large enough market, as well as a secure market?

Answer: A home market of 300 million people will be large enough for all requirements of industry, as well as being secure from dumping, undercutting, cheap labour competition, etc. For that sure market we can have mass production on a great scale. This will enable us both to raise wages and reduce prices, because (as everyone connected with industry knows) the cost of the article depends far more on the rate of production than on the rate of wage. You can have both high wages and low prices if the rate of production is geared to a large market. That is the first and outstanding advantage of the united European market. But, as we shall see, there are many other advantages.

Question 19. You propose to develop the European market through the "economic leadership of government using the Wage-Price Mechanism" - What do you mean by this?

Answer: In our view it is only necessary for the government to intervene at two key points: wages and sometimes prices. Within the new economic system of Europe and its overseas territories, government must ensure that similar wages are paid throughout similar industries. Otherwise there will be unfair competition within the new system. If a man or a woman in one part of Europe is doing the same work as a man or woman in another part of Europe, they must be paid the same rate for the job and must work under comparable conditions of welfare, etc. The result will be fair competition throughout. One firm may put another out of business by being more efficient, but not by paying lower wages.

Question 20. How can the new European system prevent depression?

Answer: Once this system of the wage-price mechanism is established, it will be relatively easy for a government to raise wages equally through such similar industries, as science increases the power to produce. It is essential to do this if we are not to have over-production and glut, with a return to slump and unemployment. Purchasing power must increase as productive power increases. This can only be achieved by the definite economic leadership of government in an area large enough to be independent of world markets and supplies, and therefore independent of the world costing system. We cannot raise wages, salaries, pensions, etc., enough to absorb the full production of modern machines in the home market, while we remain a small island dependent on selling sufficient exports on world markets to buy the food and raw materials we lack. Raising wages, etc. may in any case temporarily increase our costs, and if we are costed out of world markets we have a crash.

To avoid slump and unemployment by equating production and consumption we need a viable area, and the economic leadership of government. Europe and its overseas territories will form the viable area, because it will contain its own supplies and markets. Economic leadership within this area will solve the problem by raising the national income as science increases the means to produce. There will be no risk of being costed out of world markets, because we shall no longer depend on them.

Question 21. How would the Wage-Price Mechanism affect prices?

Answer: Price control should be necessary only where monopoly conditions prevail. The present power of monopoly to hold the community up to ransom is intolerable, and must be dealt with effectively to protect the consumers' interests, but without impairing efficiency. This can be done by controlling monopoly prices when necessary through the wage-price mechanism. A government exercising effective economic leadership can intervene whenever it is necessary to prevent some monopoly exploiting its position, without breaking up efficient industrial arrangements. Where no monopoly conditions exist the free play of competition on a fair basis will keep prices down, in fact will tend continually to reduce them.

Economic leadership by government through the wage-price mechanism means that government will intervene where it really matters, but nowhere else. That will be a change from the present method of government interfering when it is not necessary instead of taking action when it is needed.

Question 22. How will you bring down prices?

Answer: By mass production for the great and assured market of Europe. First give industry a large market for which to produce. That will be provided by the purchasing power of 300 million united Europeans. Then give industry a sure market for which to produce. That will be done by insulating Europe from unfair competition on the chaotic world markets.

Industry can then confidently install modern machinery, and

mass produce for a large assured market. As everyone knows, it is possible in mass production for industries to pay the highest wages and yet produce the cheapest goods in the world. That has been proved in many established experiments. Mass production equals high wages plus low prices.

Question 23. You have talked of public works when an undertaking is too big for private enterprise. What do you mean by this?

Answer: Public works are necessary in such cases. For instance, the opening up of many underdeveloped overseas territories may be a necessary activity of the state. Government must give economic leadership, but must not remain to conduct industry or control it. In such cases, the state should go ahead like a bulldozer clearing virgin forest. Diverse industries and services of private enterprise should follow behind like farmers cultivating reclaimed land and artisans building townships. The action of the state is essentially that of the pioneer when the initial task is too big for private enterprise. Our idea of the state is, therefore, exactly the opposite of bureaucratic socialism, which creates nothing, but takes over by nationalization what others have created. Our state is a leader creating new things; their state is a parasite living on what others have done and often ruining it in the process. Science will add limitless opportunities of creative state undertakings in spheres which are too big for private enterprise.

Question 24. You have talked also of public works in times of depression, when people do not use their purchasing power - what do you mean by this?

Answer: Yes, the second reason for using public works is to meet the situation if the people refrain from using their purchasing power, and thus cause slump. For it has been pointed out with force by some modern economists, for example by Professor Galbraith, that even if the purchasing power of the people is adequate to keep production in full swing, some change of habit may induce them temporarily to stop spending and may thus bring depression. At such periods we require public works under the economic leadership of government. The people's savings can be drawn into these undertakings on attractive conditions when they are in a saving mood.

I advanced such proposals in my speech of resignation from the government. Lloyd George was then advocating a similar plan, and I frequently discussed these points with him. The whole of this line of political thinking was then supported by the massive authority of Keynes's General Theory. But I believe in the future it will be necessary to go much further in this direction with measures far bolder and of altogether larger dimensions than we then conceived.

The public works just described will in themselves tend to take up slack in production when people are refraining from spending and the market inclines to contract. The opening up of all our overseas territories will make a big contribution, and there are other opportunities of useful work which will become necessities as the standard of life rises. For instance, I have suggested elsewhere the need to modernise our great cities, and something of the method. This necessary work would produce a large building boom in periods of slackening demand, with widespread economic repercussions.

New roads and other schemes like the Channel bridge, should be undertaken by the state. And in times of depression, not only economic works but amenity construction of every kind can be employed by the state when the people refrain from spending.

Also, when resources are sufficient owing to the vast production of the coming automation industries, we should never forget the duty of making the world more beautiful. It is nonsense to cut down production and cause unemployment and depression on the grounds that no market exists for the results. In a sanely organized system no question of overproduction can exist till we have made every street in every city of Europe a thing of beauty.

There are, of course, a great many practical things we have to do before the world reaches such a paradise, but we should never keep men in unemployment on the absurd ground that no use can be found for their labour. Once we have the economic leadership of government in an area containing the resources of Europe and our overseas territories, we can organize, through the stimulus of private demand, or the creation of public works, to keep every man and machine in full employment. This is the real use of public works. What our state will never do is to interfere with private enterprise in its own legitimate sphere, which is everything that can be done by private enterprise.

Question 25. How will entry into the suggested European system affect our balance of payments problem?

Answer: It will remove the trouble because we shall have an entirely self-contained system. Britain is a small island which is far from self-contained. Therefore we have to sell on the markets of the world enough to buy essential imports like food and raw materials without which we cannot live. But it is very difficult to sell enough on world markets for this purpose, because we face all kinds of unfair competition.

For instance, the Soviets have started to dump against us on world markets to smash the system of the West. They just make their own people go without until they have done it, and it is easy for a tyranny to do this. They keep goods back from Russian consumption and offer them at a price well below the lowest tender on world markets. No civilised government working within a free system can compete with this technique which the Soviets are beginning to develop.

Even a country like America is tempted by the inadequacy of its present system to sell below production cost, when it has a surplus which it cannot dispose of at home. They can do it because their exports are a much smaller proportion of their total production.

Then, as we shall see, modern simplified industrial methods are more and more employed for cheap labour in the East to produce cheap goods from machines which need only a few skilled technicians to serve them.

For all these reasons, and many others, it is becoming increasingly difficult for us to hold export markets. That is why we face balance of payment problems. That is why the government is always damping down the home market, wages, domestic purchasing power, etc., in order to drive industry into export markets. But industry cannot do what government wants, because export markets become increasingly difficult. We are like a dog chasing its own tail. That is why only politicians say: "Exports are fun". But all balance of payment problems are solved when we enter Europe. We shall need no export trade because we shall be large enough to be self-contained.

Question 26. What about internal competition within Europe?

Answer: Internal competition may knock out individual firms if they are not competitive, but it will not knock out Britain. A firm in Birmingham may put out of business a firm in Munich, or a firm in Lyons may put out of business a firm in Manchester, but whole nations will no longer go under because of their balance of payments problem. Such problems as between the European nations will have ceased to exist. Any individuals displaced from individual firms will be quickly re-absorbed into the expanding economy. For we shall have a continually expansionist policy as science increases the means to produce. The system of the wage-price mechanism, which I suggest, will secure both this continual expansion of the economy and entirely fair competition between individual firms. British industry can compete with any other industries under really fair conditions.

Question 27. Since we trade as much with America and the coloured Commonwealth as with western Europe, will not a change to a European system cause a considerable economic dislocation?

Answer: You omit the Dominions from your question. We propose their inclusion in our system. Broadly speaking the present trade figures are one-third with Europe, one-third with the Dominions, one-sixth with the coloured Commonwealth and one-sixth with the rest of the world including America. So our proposal develops the area which provides two-thirds of our present trade as an alternative to developing the area which at present provides one-third. We have to make that choice. Otherwise we shall not only suffer economic dislocation but ultimately the ruin of our system for reasons given elsewhere in this book. The development of Europe and our overseas territories (which are partly included against us in the above figures) can rapidly surpass in the conditions of a viable area and sure market our present precarious trading system, which rests on the fluctuating circumstances and cut-throat competition of world markets.

Question 28. How can you overcome difficulties of language, law and currency within Europe?

Answer: The language difficulties will be overcome by increasing education, like many other problems. Already English is beginning to become an almost universal language for practical purposes. Alternatively, a basic version of any of the main tongues could be adapted as a second language and easily learnt by every normal child.

But really to appreciate Europe and to enjoy the wealth of its culture, the main languages should be learnt. I should feel it as a deep personal loss to be deprived of the literature of France and Germany, and much regret that I cannot read easily in Italian or Spanish. Parents cannot better endow their children than by helping them to acquire several languages. In the future, extended travel facilities will greatly help this process; in fact, make it almost automatic. But today a knowledge of English and French will solve this problem nearly everywhere. The language difficulty is a problem of the infancy of our continent; it will be overcome. In the beginning we shall merely be in the same position as the multi-lingual states which already exist.

We should in any case codify our laws. Many eminent British lawyers already agree with this view. And while we are about it, we should bring it into line with the codified law of Europe. It is a job which sooner or later will have to be done, whether we enter Europe or not. It is no insuperable task, but will naturally require much consideration by the best lawyers of Britain and Europe. There is also no reason why wide variations should not occur in European law according to local preference; e.g. the difference between English and Scottish law.

A unified European currency can be instituted any time the European peoples so desire. There is no technical difficulty about it whatever. It would be a relief to the individual and an advantage for trade to get rid of the exchange rigmarole.

No, language is the only real difficulty. And that has the usual answer: live and learn, with a little work thrown in.

The New System

Question 29. Taxation - What is your policy?

Answer: The present burden of direct taxation crushes the individual and kills initiative. People cannot save enough to give their children a start in life. They cannot save enough to start their own business. They cannot save enough to safeguard their old age.

They cannot keep what they earn and use their own intelligence and energy to make more by producing more for themselves and their country. Direct taxation takes too much. It kills incentive to make more by producing more. Taxes must be drastically reduced. For any real government this is a "must". To reduce taxation we need action at four key points.

(1) We must cut out waste. Economy in administration is essential. This can only be secured by strong government. Weak government, subject to the present time-wasting procedure and the pressure of various interests, can never do it. A government elected by the people must be strong to act in their name and interest; this is one of the chief reasons for giving it power over finance.

(2) We must increase the rate of production and thus increase the yield of taxation. The same rate of tax in a community producing more wealth will raise more money. Greater production will enable taxes to be reduced without diminishing the funds available to government. The best means to reduce taxation is, therefore, to increase production. But production can only be increased for a larger, assured market, which encourages mass production methods. The European population will be that market. The greater production of wealth will permit a

proportionate reduction of taxation. The individual will then have more money in his pocket because more wealth will be produced, and a lesser proportion will be taken from him in tax. This is another great advantage of the European economy.

(3) All welfare services must be put on a contributory basis. In Britain at present the state pays for all kinds of benefits in which many people are not interested. Instead, people should themselves make contribution for the benefits they really want, and suffer no charge for those they do not desire. The Welfare State should become a real insurance and saving system to secure things the individual really wants. Both sides of industry should contribute to this welfare fund, but the state should not. The immense sums spent by the state, i.e. you, the taxpayer, must cease. This will enable the general level of taxes to be much reduced.

In some other European countries more money is spent in welfare services today than in Britain, but the contribution by the state is far less. That is why the burden of general taxation is less in these countries. We make a great mistake in letting the state pay for indiscriminate benefits, for which everyone has to pay in general taxation, but which many people do not want at all. We can save in this way large sums of money which can be used to reduce the general burden of taxes.

(4) We need a revolution in our system of taxation. Direct taxation must be replaced by indirect taxation, the original British system. The necessities of life like food, clothing, a reasonably sized home and essential furniture must be absolutely free from tax. Then everyone can live reasonably well, and can yet save from his earnings if he wishes.

Question 30. How will the necessary taxation be raised?

Answer: Apart from the basic necessities, many articles which are matters of choice rather than necessity must be taxed to replace the revenue lost by the abolition of direct taxation. The tax will, of course, be graduated according to the luxury character of the article. A large sports car will be taxed to yield a much higher proportion of its value than a modest family car. Things providing simple pleasures will be taxed at a much lower rate than all forms of ostentatious living. Yet as the wealth of the nation increases through greater production, many things today regarded as luxuries will be considered necessities and will be progressively freed from tax. And remember always that the greater volume of production will enable the general level of taxation to be reduced.

It is vital to restore the incentive to produce, to create and to save. This is one way of doing it, and it is the simplest. There are other and more scientific methods becoming available in the modern world. Again, an economy insulated from the world market and costing system will enable sober and careful experiments to be made in some very novel directions. In all such practical matters we must use the method which I have described as "dynamic pragmatism". We must always be ready to learn. We must be rapid in grasp of new facts and quick in new decisions, when situations change or new ideas occur. But the principle is firm and clear: it is to give to every man and woman the chance to create, to produce, to earn, and to keep what they earn for their own good purposes.

Question 31. What is your attitude to the Welfare State?

Answer: The people should be able to have all the benefits of the present Welfare State which they desire. But they should be able to choose what they want. They should make contribution to these benefits and to nothing else. The old and the sick who cannot make contribution would naturally remain on the present basis. But in the future, the whole scheme should be put on a fully contributory basis with contributions from worker and employer but not from the taxpayer. The present bureaucracy should be swept away.

This can be done by giving the administration of the contributory scheme to responsible trade union and employers' organisations. The trade unions of the future, for instance, could well take over most questions affecting conditions of work, unemployment pay, welfare, sick pay, holidays, compensation claims, legal representation, etc. Once trade unionism is taken into full partnership by government elected by the people, a fresh atmosphere and many new possibilities will be created. The people will be able to operate their own institutions within the general principles laid down by government. They will not need the restrictions, controls, inefficiency and expense of the present swollen bureaucracy. And within the trade unions as in every other sphere of national life, the testing days of the future will produce new leaders if the old leadership proves inadequate. New ideas and the new men they will produce can do all these things. The Welfare State can become a blessing instead of the burden, and often the absurdity, it is today.

Question 32. What is your monetary policy?

Answer: The first object of monetary policy is to secure a supply of money adequate to an expanding economy, neither more nor less than is necessary to a system continually increasing production. Extra money which is not matched by extra production means inflation. Less money than is required to match the extra production means deflation. Both are disastrous. The mass production evoked by the new European market will need a continually expanding supply of money to match the greater volume of production. The tendency of this mass production will be to bring prices down by making goods more plentiful, and in the early stages this will be good and necessary. But in the long run we shall need a stable price level to ensure steady progress.

I disagree strongly with the current opinion of the Establishment, that monetary measures alone will be enough to meet all the economic problems of this age. Keynes, in his General Theory and other works, made a great contribution to economic thinking from which we have all learnt much. But I have always held the view that in normal conditions Keynes would not be enough. Hence my whole thesis of the economic leadership of government through the wage-price mechanism described in previous answers. That economic policy, applied within a viable area, insulated from the world costing system, would permit a far bolder monetary policy than is possible in an island economy dependent on world markets.

Although many interesting new ideas are now available in the monetary sphere, no experiment is possible in the present island economy without risk of exchange disaster. But in an economy so large and viable as that of Europe and its overseas territory, sober and careful experiments could be tried in any of the new directions without undue risk. Apart, also, from new principles in monetary theory, a banking system operating within European territory, and designed to promote steady industrial expansion, could adopt such measures as a differential rate of interest according to some criteria of desirability from the national standpoint. For example, housing should not be charged the same rate of interest as the new dog-racing track, or many less desirable things which are now competing in the money market. We must always remember that it is the high rate of interest which is the main factor in the present high rate of rent. By this means alone the spiv and the speculator would be practically eliminated, although more direct measures would be taken against them if these measures and the general conditions of our stable system did not suffice. None of these developments are possible in an island economy tied to the world costing system. But all things are possible to the giant economy of the new Europe.

Question 33. What will be the position of the investor and the Stock Exchange?

Answer: There will be a much wider choice of investment in the stable but expanding economy of Europe, which will not be subject to the ruinous fluctuations now prevailing. People who invest their money in the constructive industries and services which create national wealth and amenity will reap a greater reward than they do now, because industry will be earning more. There will be larger earnings to distribute between salaries and wages, profits in the shape of dividends for such investors, and capital resources for industrial developments. It is easy to see how this will occur once we have the large and assured European market, for which industry may mass produce without fear of undercutting or dislocation by the fluctuations of world markets.

To take a simplified illustration: Supposing today an industry after selling its products and paying for overheads and raw materials, is able to divide ten units in the proportion of 6 to wages and salaries, 2 to dividend and 2 to capital resources for the development of industry. Suppose then the industry operates within the new European system and is able to double its production for that assured market: it will then have not 10 but 20 units to allocate in the same proportion, which will result in 12 to wages and salaries, 4 to dividend and 4 to capital resources for development. Wages and salaries alone would then be getting more than the total annual sum now divided between wages, salaries, dividends and capital resources. In fact, the advantage will generally be found to be greater because the overhead charges would not increase proportionately, and the same consideration applies to other factors in mass producing industries.

This over-simplified case I have given allows a higher proportion to dividend and capital resources than is usually the case at present, but it illustrates that all parties in industry must gain immensely from more production for a large and assured market. Wages and salaries in such a situation are quite certain to draw a larger sum than the total allocation to wages, dividend and capital development today. The conflict between labour and capital for the division of the present limited reward will be ended, and the investor will benefit by a larger return on money placed in an industrial development which will greatly enrich the community.

The genuine investor has everything to gain from a system in which the spiv and speculator are eliminated, not merely by law but by the end of the fluctuations and shortages through which profits are made at the expense of the community.

Investors will be able to buy and sell shares on the Stock Exchange in the far greater range and wider choice of genuine industries and services of an economy which will certainly and steadily expand. The Stock Exchange will not be subject to the daily, nagging intervention of government, but will be required to follow the rule of honourable, professional conduct which its leading members will find easier to secure when the day of spiv and speculator is ended.

Question 34. But should investment be allowed at all - would not social justice be better served by public ownership?

Answer: Let us face frankly and fearlessly the issue raised by this question. Either we have complete public ownership, or some system of private investment. Complete public ownership means that everyone is a servant of the state. It means government by universal bureaucracy. In short, it means communism.

Any system of freedom must allow people to save and to invest. If they save and invest in other industries than those in which they are employed, they are liable to be denounced as absentee shareholders, etc. The present system can lead to such abuses. In theory at any rate, the fate of great industries and the lives of their employees can be at the mercy of absentee shareholders who know nothing about them and are concerned only with profits. But at this point our policy of the wage-price mechanism would again operate, not only to make competition fair and to equate production and consumption, but also to prevent abuse and injustice. The economic leadership of government through this method can obtain a fair and proper balance between wages, re-investment and dividend. And remember that the life of the government depends on the vote of the mass of the people, and on its ability to persuade them that it is acting fairly.

Remember, too, that our industries in the new system will not be subject to world competition, and that similar wages will be paid in similar industries throughout the home market of Europe. An industrialist may be put out of business by a more efficient rival, but not by a competitor who pays lower wages. It is these conditions which make possible the raising of wages to the point where consumption balances production without destroying the competitive power of industry.

Present capitalism can never sufficiently raise wages without being priced out of world markets, or even being defeated by internal competition. Nor would socialist industries be in any better position if they operated within the international system, as the Labour Party proposes.

It is the viable area of the European system, insulated from world markets and world costing, which enables our method of the wage-price mechanism both to raise wages in order to provide a market for production, and to retain the incentive of profit which creates new enterprises. That is why we can give both workers and investors a fair deal, and, in so doing, can create a new economic system which will alike be free from the slumps and unemployment of capitalism and from the bureaucratic tyranny of communism.

Question 35. Will not the Wage-Price Mechanism require as much bureaucracy as socialism or even communism?

Answer: Obviously not, because government operating the wage-price mechanism will intervene only at the two key points of wages and prices. Socialism or communism means the complete control by the state or its institutions of every process of production, distribution and exchange. To intervene at two points of these immense processes clearly does not require the bureaucracy which the complete management of them all must involve. That is a proposition so evident as to be self-explanatory.

In fact, the "bureaucracy" required by the wage-price mechanism would be little more than the economic general staff with which government should long ago have been armed. The detailed organisation could be devolved to joint organisations of employers and trade unions. They could carry out the general instructions of government that similar wages should be paid and similar conditions maintained in comparable industries throughout Europe. A related organisation could also implement the price control policy in monopoly conditions.When it was necessary to hold a balance between interests, a government representative could be supplied to take the necessary decisions. Plenty of effective precedents for such administrative mechanism already exist in Europe.

The function of government's economic leadership would be rather to settle the general trend of industry, and for this purpose the power to determine wages in the various complexes of industry would be a most effective instrument to which industry would be very sensitive. It is quite unnecessary to conduct or control everything; this concept is the deep error of socialism or the communism with which it becomes identical in the final phase. Give government the power to regulate the wage relation between the various complexes of industry, the reward relation between wage and profit, and the relation of both to reserve and future development; you will then find that the people's government has quite enough power to lead the economic system in the best interest of the nation whose voters supply the mandate. Because the method is leadership, not bureaucracy, the number of officials required will be relatively small.

The contrast between the new thinking and the old socialist conception is another example of the simplification which comes as thought progresses and mind develops. Remember men thought of the complicated "penny-farthing bicycle" with two wheels of different size long before they thought of the ultimate simplicity of two similar wheels, and the modern jet airplane appears in basic principle to be a great simplification in comparison with the engines which first lifted men into the sky. In short, the complications, obfuscations and pedantries of the old Marxian thinking are as out of date as the universal bumbledom of socialist controls which end in communist tyranny.

Question 36. What will be the position of finance in your system?

Answer: Creative finance will have a bigger part to play than ever, and can reap great rewards if it plays that great part in the national interest. All the traditional abilities of British finance and those of other European centres will be required to develop new enterprises in Europe and its overseas territories. This can provide them with bigger opportunity and in the end - when basic needs are satisfied - with bigger reward than the present speculative scramble within a dying system. Provided they so operate within the European system, banking and finance will be free. There will be no need to control these forces, once we have removed their power to take money from the country, which we shall do by creating a self-contained system insulated from world markets. After that the energies of finance can only assist the country. It will get its reward from creative work, and not from wrecking trade, or government.

Question 37. Have you not often attacked international finance? - How can you prevent it from controlling or wrecking your system?

Answer: By removing the means to do it. By creating a system in which it cannot be done. I cannot emphasize too much this great advantage of our system. Everyone should understand that it is a decisive point. So long as the financiers can move money out of the country as they wish, they can control you. They can do it either directly or indirectly. They can do it as easily from New York, where you cannot put a finger on them, as they can if they are sitting in the City of London. You are at their mercy, so long as you continue the present international system of trade.

The only way to be free of their power is to change the system which gives them that power. This means getting rid of the present international system of trade and creating a self-contained system in European territory which is independent of it. We must in any case do this to save industry from the coming crises. We cannot remain in the island, small empire, half-European or sterling area economy whose international system places us at the mercy of international finance. By adopting our new system we shall remove for ever its power to destroy us. Then real, honest, constructive finance can get on with its creative task - the building of the European system - and can reap its just reward.

Question 38. Will not the financiers continue to control the economic system unless you nationalise finance or control them?

Answer: No. The financiers control the economic system for one reason alone: they can move money in and out of the country as they like. So long as you rely on international trade they are bound to have that power. In fact, international trade cannot be conducted unless they have this power to move money in and out. It is necessary to finance the trade. That is why neither the policy of the Labour Party, nor any other control system, can effectually control financiers so long as you have international trade. They always have the power under this system to move money out of the country, and consequently have the power to smash the government. It is not the government which runs them but they who run the government.

But as we have seen, our system is not dependent on international trade. As we shall not need it, we shall not need its financial machinery. We can therefore prevent financiers moving their money around without any danger to our economy. Constructive finance can then be free from control in promoting business within the European system. Government will control finance at the decisive point instead of finance controlling government. This will be a real revolution.

Question 39. Would exchange control be necessary in your system?

Answer: No exchange control will be necessary for normal transactions between individuals because the dangers of the present international exchange system would not exist. We should need neither exports nor imports in the viable economy of the European system, because it would contain all that we require.

Consequently we should not need the international finance which conducts these transactions. And we should not require the elaborate arrangement of controls which try to prevent the financiers moving their money as they wish, thereby dominating the system and making money out of economic disasters. We should be operating a self-sufficient system entirely free from international exchanges.

Today we have all the mumbo jumbo of exchange controls with a hoard of obstructive, oppressive officials, in order to prevent a sudden movement of finance wrecking the exchanges. Even then the controls are ineffective, because it is necessary to international trade that money should move back and forth; it is an inevitable part of these transactions. And directly there is any loss of confidence it does move, despite all the exchange controls. Then exchanges crash and governments tumble. All the control does is to hinder and to harry the individual who is doing no harm, and to let the big gangs who operate the racket go scot free to hold the nation up to ransom.

Question 40. Will an individual then be able to take his money out of the country?

Answer: Once we have established this system, an individual will be able to take all his money out of the country if he wishes, and can arrange it for himself. If, for instance, a man with a fortune in New York agrees to exchange his holding with a man who has a fortune in Europe, it will do no-one any harm if they do so. On the contrary, it would do a certain amount of good, if we thereby get rid of men who do not like our system and who would rather be in Wall Street, and if we attract those who would rather do a constructive job in the European system than speculate on world markets.

Even today the economic effect would be absolutely nil if a man in London exchanged with a man in Paris the purchasing power to buy a glass of beer in exchange for the purchasing power to buy a glass of red wine. And the economic effect would also be nil if the transaction were in millions. Such dealings between individuals would be absolutely harmless, and for purposes of travel, etc., could easily be handled by appropriate agencies. In such respects we should have far more freedom than now exists. The excuse of bureaucracy to interfere with these personal liberties is provided by the transactions of international finance which, in practice, bureaucracy is quite powerless to control so long as the present form of international trade continues. This is the now familiar practice of putting everyone in a strait jacket, because a lunatic system cannot exist unless the big rogues are at large.

Question 41. How will you stop financial corruption within the system, and other corruption?

Answer: By real enforcement of the present laws against corruption. Financial corruption could be stopped tomorrow if government were not afraid to enforce the law. Under the present system the financiers can break the government. What you need is a courageous government with popular support working within a new system which frees it from the control of finance. Our long and testing struggle can provide a government with strength and courage. Europe and the overseas territories can provide the new system. Once you prevent finance commanding government in a big way, it is easy to deal with the corruption which now abounds in a small way, by enforcement of the existing laws.

Private Enterprise, Automation, and Marxism

Question 42. Do you believe in private enterprise?

Answer: Yes, certainly. Private enterprise must always be the main motive of the economy. Most men work for themselves and their families, and want to do so in freedom. And why shouldn't they? The freer they are to work for themselves and the greater incentive they have to produce and to serve the community, the better for themselves and for the nation. The interests of the individual and the state in this matter are identical. Industry should be free whether it is large or small. There is nothing wrong with an industry just because it is large and has been built to that point by an exceptionally able man, provided its methods of competition are fair and rest simply on efficiency.

All men and women should have freedom to live and work as they like, and to enjoy the fruits of their labour in freedom and peace without interference or robbery by state or vested interest. We must reduce taxation in order to prevent the present interference and robbery by the state. But we must also have strong government to protect the individual against interference and robbery by vested interest, monopoly, etc.

Question 43. How is private enterprise thwarted today?

Answer: The individual is today oppressed in two ways. The fruits of his enterprise are taken by the state in taxation. The enterprise itself is often taken by great interests which crush out of existence the individual making his own business by his own intelligence and energy.

It is not enough for the state just to leave the individual alone and to refrain from excessive taxation. It is necessary for government to be strong enough to protect the individual from the big combinations of economic power which often bring individual enterprise to an end. These great vested interests are like the robber barons of an earlier age, whose plunder of the people was brought to an end by the strength and vigour of the Tudor kings. We need a similar spirit in modern government elected by the people to protect them from the predatory forces of the present period.

Freedom from oppression by government comes first, but freedom from oppression by vested interest comes second. And for this purpose the people need the power of their own government which they have created, and which they can change at will.

Question 44. In what respect does your concept of private enterprise differ from that of the Conservative Party?

Answer: The difference is decisive. Our policy creates the conditions in which private enterprise can operate. We give private enterprise freedom from unfair competition, freedom to produce for a large and assured market, freedom from oppressive taxation by the state and freedom from oppression and suppression by monopoly. Conservatism leaves private enterprise at the mercy of all these forces which destroy the enterprise of the individual today.

Question 45. What necessary things can be done by the Wage-Price Mechanism, while leaving industries free from controls and without the nationalization the Labour Party suggests?

Answer: With the wage-price mechanism we can (1) eliminate unfair competition by securing that similar wages are paid in similar industries throughout Europe; (2) equate consumption and production by raising purchasing power as science increases the means to produce; (3) ensure that the worker gets a fair proportion of the product of industry by progressively raising wages; (4) secure that a reasonable proportion also is used as capital for future development; (5) allow profit to be fair but not so great as to permit vast accumulations of hereditary wealth which distort and finally jeopardize the economy.

The simple power just to determine wages can secure all those things without the control of industry. Even the fair proportion for investment can be maintained without any more elaborate machinery. Government at any time can suggest that wages will be raised at the expense of profit, unless a reasonable policy is pursued at this point. The economic leadership of government through the wage-price mechanism enables a proper equilibrium to be maintained between wages, investment and profit without control of industry. Not only will equilibrium be maintained but a perpetual dynamism will be secured in the direction of industry on an upward path as science increases the means to produce and to achieve.

Question 46. In what main particulars does your Wage-Price Mechanism differ from the past or present policy of the Labour Party?

Answer: It was always a great mistake of the Labour Party to concentrate attention on the ownership of particular industries rather than the structure and direction of industry as a whole. That was one of the main reasons why I left their government and challenged their economic thinking thirty years ago. The justice of our reasoning at that time was implicitly recognized in one of the last speeches Aneurin Bevan made when he referred to the need of occupying "the commanding heights of economic power", rather than being so preoccupied with the ownership of particular industries. But, as usual in the Labour Party, this thinking was thirty years too late.

Our modern thought goes far beyond all that. We do not want to control industry, whether from one or two commanding heights or by nationalisation of some industries, because by leadership through the wage-price mechanism we can do what is necessary while leaving industry free.

Question 47. What is the guarantee the worker will get a fair deal?

Answer: The worker is sure of a fair deal through the action of government which depends on his votes. If the workers feel the government does not give them a fair deal, they can sack it by their votes, for they are in the majority.

But what will really matter to the worker under our system is the efficiency of industry. This will secure that his fair share is large, because the total production is big. Efficiency will come from industry which is free and competitive, but is assured fair and continually expanding conditions by the economic leadership of government and the development of science. That is why within the new system all questions of the ownership of industry will eventually become irrelevant.

Question 48. Does the Wage-Price Mechanism in any way treat wages and profits differently?

Answer: No. Let us get this matter quite clear. We treat wages and profits just the same. In both cases we secure that the rate and the conditions for the job shall be the same throughout the trade in question. One worker can make more than another worker if he works harder or is more skilful. It will be the only way he can make more, because piece work rates and hours of work will be the same in similar trades right through Europe. One employer will make more profit than another employer if he is more efficient. It will be the only way he can make more profit, because the charges he has to meet, wages, hours and conditions of labour will be the same in similar trades throughout Europe.

So wages and profits are both in the same position. A worker can earn more wages only by working harder or being more skilful. An employer can earn more profit only by being more efficient. We do not want to limit the amount the worker can earn, and we do not want to limit the amount the employer can make. On the contrary we want to encourage the worker by piece work to earn a lot, and the employer by efficiency to make a lot. They enrich the community as well as themselves by greater production. Hard work, skill and efficiency deserve reward, and there should never be a limit to it. That is cutting the rate, which is always wrong. Let all keep what they earn. The wage-price mechanism establishes a fair basis throughout, and both wages and profits are treated on exactly the same principle. But we set no limits for worker or employer in the reward for work, skill and efficiency. We believe in good reward for good work.

Question 49. Do you believe in higher payment for skill, differential reward?

Answer: Yes, certainly. Pay every man what he is worth, and do not be afraid of great rewards for great service. One of the dangers of the present system is that the differential reward for skill is disappearing. Skill and talent of every kind are liable to vanish if they are not recognised. And that would obviously be a disaster.

In the present industrial dog-fight nothing counts but the big battalions. As these do not usually represent the men or women of exceptional skill, outstanding ability is liable to go under, and eventually can cease to exist. Why work for years to acquire a special skill if it does you no good at all? This fatal modern tendency has got to stop.

The great majority of our people have had the good sense to know that a man should be paid what he is worth. It does not matter how big a reward a man or woman is paid, provided his or her skill is worth it. That goes for managers, leaders of industry, skilled workers, teachers, doctors and above all the presently neglected scientists - they should all get what their skill is worth. This is one of the vital matters which demand government intervention. It will never be done in modern conditions until government takes the lead.

Question 50. You have sometimes spoken of reducing the hours of labour as an alternative to increasing purchasing power?

Answer: Wealth or leisure - that could be the happy choice of the future in an organized European economy. Mass production for this immense and stable market of the new European system can greatly increase the supply of wealth.

Economic leadership of government, through the wage-price mechanism, will increase purchasing power as science increases the means to produce. Another desirable measure to meet the problems caused by mass production and automation in a large, well organized economy will be to shorten the hours of labour, and thus to reduce production while increasing leisure and well-being. Once we are organised men and women may choose between wealth and leisure. If they are sensible they will choose a good bit of both.

Question 51. What is your attitude to Marxism?

Answer: Briefly and crudely stated, there is something in Marxian premises, nothing in the conclusions. Marx discovered certain laws which work if men do nothing to interfere with them. But their operation can be completely changed by the will, energy and organisation of mankind.

Newton discovered the natural law of gravity, and its validity is quickly proved if you are idiot enough to step over a cliff and break your neck. But man has frustrated that law and reversed its effect, first by the balloon, then by aeroplane and finally by jets and rockets. Similarly Marxian dogmas like the "increasing immiseration" of the mass have been frustrated by trade union action for raising wages, social legislation, etc.

But some of the Marxian laws are still operating in the failure of present governments to raise mass purchasing power to a point where a market is provided for the product of modern machines, and in the drive to dispose of the consequent surplus abroad in the present scramble for world markets.

It is interesting to note that the British Left now advocates the disposal abroad by foreign lending and charity of that part of the British worker's product which he is not allowed to consume. In fact Labour Party policies now embody what Marx depicted as the final vice of a decaying capitalism.

It would, of course, require almost one tenth of the space used in Marx's own verbiage to cover the whole subject, and that space is not here available. It is enough now to say, that some of his laws operate if left alone. Yet the solution is not a communist bureaucracy and tyranny but the economic leadership of government in a free system operating within an area large enough to be viable. Thus we can overcome the Marxian laws by the continuous raising of the purchasing power of the mass of the people as science increases the means to produce.

For the rest, the answer to the Marxist "material conception of history" can be put in a nutshell which contains not the frivolity suspected in all short statements, but the final validity of an ultimate truth. If you see a donkey jump a ditch it is reasonable to conclude that he has seen a particularly luxuriant thistle growing on the other side. If you see a man jump a ditch it is equally reasonable to conclude that he may have another motive. This crude illustration which I have often used without effective refutation, is a simple way of saying that the main movements of men throughout the ages have been those of the spirit. It should now be only the very backward who are still enmeshed in this web of nineteenth century thinking. And the belief of these primitive peoples is greatly protected by having never read their prophet. In fact, most of his devotees among the imminent Marxian majority of mankind cannot read at all.

Question 52. What have you to say about the left-wing policy of solving our export difficulties by trading with Russia and developing the backward countries?

Answer: This suggestion assumes in us such a fine, fresh innocence that it is almost charming. It is the simplest and quickest way to ruin our country, and is largely according to Marx. It is the sure recipe for those who desire a crash, in order to install communism or the socialism which leads to it.

The first proposal to restore our export trade is such a simple booby-trap that a man of Marx's intelligence would scarcely have believed his opponents would be stupid enough to fall into it. Frame our economy to suit the Soviet demand for our exports, which at first would supply enough orders to encourage us and to secure the things the Soviets still lack for the moment. Then these trade relations could be broken on any excuse, and at any time that suited the Soviets. Finally we should be left high and dry, and in a really ugly position. For, in the meantime, we should not only have lost other markets but have jeopardised our chance of ever recapturing them, by distorting our economy to cater for the particular Soviet market.

The second suggestion to solve our export problems by concentrating on equipping the backward countries is much more sophisticated, and is on strictly Marxian lines. This is just what Marx thought capitalism would have to do in its last phase. Unable to find a market in the purchasing power of its own people, it would be driven to dump its surplus abroad. And in so doing, of course, it would accelerate its own disaster by bringing into existence fresh, cheap labour competition against it on world markets from the slave condition countries it has supplied with modern machinery. Naturally the Left wants us to do these things. They know that from their point of view it is the best and quickest way to bring the crash of the present system and the triumph of communism, or of the socialism which precedes it. But we understand very thoroughly their analysis, their arguments, and their tricks. Our thinking begins where theirs leaves off. We have designed a system to meet all the Marxian dilemmas, without incurring the alternative disaster of communist tyranny.

Question 53. Will automation aggravate the economic problem?

Answer: Yes, it is at once a challenge and an opportunity. It can either crash the system or introduce us to something approaching an industrial paradise. In effect, automation is merely an extension of the old rationalisation process - the progressive displacement of man's labour by machines. But there is this difference in principle; in the end, automation can mean not merely displacement but virtual replacement, because the machines will only require the service of a few specialists.

It is indeed difficult to see how this problem can be solved within the limits of the present system. For it accentuates precisely the dilemma from which the present system suffers: how to find a market in the purchasing power of the people for the goods industry produces. If more and more goods are produced with less and less labour, the system becomes less capable than ever of solving the problem. The logical end would be very few men producing a mountain of goods, surrounded by the unemployed without the means to buy them. No market, and crash on a bigger scale than ever must be the end.

Even the problem of foreign competition is aggravated in the early stages. It is true that in the end automation might be the means of defeating backward, low-paid labour by the output of machines serviced by a handful of highly paid specialists. In fact, the old orthodoxy of highly paid skilled labour defeating unskilled might then come back into its own. But, as Lord Keynes used to say, "in the long run we are all dead". And in the short run the effect of semi-automation, or rationalised industries, will give unskilled, cheap labour an even bigger competitive pull. Except for the work of a few technicians who serve the machines, and supervise, the work on the conveyor belts is reduced to dead simple but monotonous tasks for which such backward labour is particularly fitted. Every problem we have discussed is likely to be made graver by the arrival of some semi-automatic machines of this kind is the sweatshops of the East, and of Africa too, if present policy continues.

What, then, is the answer? - Always the same. Pull out of the competitive chaos of world markets. Establish a viable area large enough to contain its own foodstuffs and raw materials which is insulated from world markets. Within that viable area let the economic leadership of government establish comparable wages throughout comparable industries operated by similar

European peoples, and then raise wages, salaries, pensions and profits throughout as science increases the power to produce. Any further market which automation requires can be provided by massive state enterprises such as opening new territories or creating the cities of the future and their amenities. Within that system automation can be a key to a higher civilisation. Outside it, automation can be the open sesame to chaos.

Agriculture and Horticulture

Question 54. What is your policy for agriculture?

Answer: I was brought up in the agricultural industry in which my family had been engaged for generations. I went back to it after the war, and I learnt a lot in many ways. Though not very good for agriculture it was very good for me, because I am always in a bit too much of a hurry and I learnt again that you cannot push nature too fast.

The main products of British agriculture can hold their own in Europe or in most markets of the world. They are the very best available and people will pay a good price for them in the prosperity we can organise within the European market. But it must be an organised market. And here the lesson of a British Marketing Board can be applied throughout Europe. That method is one of the successes of recent governments, and I gladly acknowledge it.

Agriculture must know where it stands in market and price for a long time ahead. A marketing board system in the whole of Europe can do more to give agriculture a stable market and a fair price than can our island system, because it will be a much bigger market with much more purchasing power.

The British farmer can supply his vital foodstuffs in assured conditions with enough mixed farming to give a stable base. The British winners in that great market will be the beef and dairy products which come from the best grass in the world. Our farmers need not be afraid of entering into Europe. It is the chance of a lifetime. But we must organise the business properly, with marketing boards throughout.

Question 55. What does your policy do for the farmer?

Answer: Our policy gives British farmers what they have long desired - a fair price for the product without the need for subsidy with its quite unjustified stigma of inefficiency. So long as Britain is tied to competing in the world markets, everything has to be done to keep the price of exports low. If we have to compete with products made by cheap labour we cannot afford to pay high wages. Therefore government keeps the cost of living low by subsidising farmers to the tune of over £250 millions per year, so that the cost of food in the shops of Britain is lower than in any other industrial country. But once we have the viable economic unit of Europe and its overseas territory we shall no longer have to compete on world markets, and we can then have a high wage system. In the new Europe of the mass production and high wage system, the housewife can well afford to pay the farmer a fair price for the food she needs. Subsidies will no longer be needed, the farmer will get rid of the stigma he hates and the taxpayer will be relieved of a heavy burden.

It is true that some farmers at present look with considerable suspicion at proposals for closer integration of Europe. This is not surprising. They fear they will be asked to accept the same price for their products as the farmers of other European countries, while they still have to pay much higher wages than are earned by those working on the land throughout Europe. This merely shows the danger of doing things in a half-hearted way.

First, Europe must become a Nation, in which everyone is paid similar wages for similar work, and total wealth is increased by industry working for an assured and expanding market. Then the British farmer will have nothing to fear. On the contrary, he will be presented with greater opportunity. With his technical knowledge, high degree of mechanisation, heavy crop yields and wonderful climate for growing grass, he can compete on fair terms with anyone. Moreover a great new market is opened up. As the standard of living increases, 300 million people will eat more high quality food, which he is so good at producing.

For example, relatively few people in Europe have even tasted quality lamb, but they will probably want it once they can afford it. Our European system will insulate the farmer from unfair competition from surplus, usually subsidised, and from food at present dumped in Britain from countries all over the world. A European marketing system, based on the example of British producers' marketing boards, will organize the marketing of all produce. It will prevent the sudden unloading of local surpluses which at present cause so much chaos.

Thus we offer to the farmer a fair price for his produce, orderly marketing and a massive and expanding market. Is there any farmer who would not prefer this to the present precarious subsidies which depend on the goodwill of fickle politicians?

Question 56. What is your policy for horticulture?

Answer: The problems of horticulture are more difficult than those of agriculture. In part this is because government policy differs. The British grower, unlike the farmer, receives no subsidy. But like most industrialists, he has some protection by tariffs on imports which the farmer has not got.

Thus when Europe becomes a Nation, he will receive increased protection from countries outside Europe, but none from those inside. Competition from his fellow growers in Europe will be much fairer than it is today. All will pay the same wages and more or less the same price for fuel, fertilisers and other requirements. And there will be a large market, sharply increasing its demands for horticultural produce as the standard of living improves. Marketing will be improved, ironing out the fluctuations of price so common in the present chaos. But climate, which tends to be to the advantage of the British farmer, tends to be to the disadvantage of the British grower. This is particularly true of glasshouse production. Growers in other parts of Europe may be able to produce, in the open, plants which in Britain can only be grown in costly heated glasshouses.

We face this realistically. First we provide protection from those countries outside Europe. Then we ensure that costs of production, other than those related to climate, are the same for all growers throughout Europe. Next we provide orderly marketing. Finally we provide a huge and expanding market, with an increasing demand for high quality produce. If even under these conditions British growers find that they cannot compete with certain produce, they will be no worse off than they are today, when so many growers are selling their holdings and are fortunate if they can do so for building purposes. But we go further. If growers find themselves unable to continue to grow the produce they are equipped to grow, then government assistance will be available to enable them to change their holdings to some other form of production. It is only right that the people of this country, who will reap such advantage from forming Europe a Nation, should compensate any who suffer in the process. But few will suffer. The advantages we offer will outweigh all the problems of climate, and the British grower will seize his opportunities and reap his share of increased prosperity. He may be encouraged by the consideration that a market of increasing wealth and power of discrimination will attach more and more importance to the freshness which he alone can supply.

Science and Support of Scientists

Question 57. What is your attitude to science?

Answer: Our whole future depends on science and we should never forget it for one moment. Yet on the occasion of a recent government shuffle a leading Conservative daily wrote that the Minister for Science "will at last have something to do" as Leader of the House of Lords (Daily Mail, 28/7/60). Could you have a better illustration of the present attitude of press and politics, particularly politics, to science? It is, of course, exactly the opposite of the right attitude in the twentieth century. Science is not the least important but the most important subject of government. The Minister for Science should not be a man who only finds he has "something to do" when he is given the additional task of "leading the House of Lords" but a man whose every energy and waking hour are given to the most absorbing task of our day, which is a matter of life and death to Britain. As for making the Leader of the House of Lords Minister of Science in his spare time, it is like picking the experienced driver of a stagecoach as pilot for a jet-plane, and then giving him all who are most valuable to the nation as passengers during his first flight. In that one phrase of an ably conducted modern newspaper you can see very clearly the reduction of contemporary politics to absurdity and tragedy.

Question 58. Will you provide more money for education in science?

Answer: We should back science with everything we have got. We should educate young scientists and pay them properly, instead of letting them be tempted away to America. And it would not even require much sacrifice to do this. This could be done for a very moderate sum in terms of even the present national income.

Question 59. Will you provide more money for scientific research even if it means national sacrifice?

Answer: Yes, we should make much bigger sacrifices to keep ahead in research in every sphere, industrial, medical, space exploration; in the military sphere, too, until we get disarmament. A modern nation which cannot keep abreast in scientific research is finished.

The Minister of Science should be the corner-stone of the modern state. The whole attitude of politicians to science must change fundamentally. So long ago as 1947 I wrote that "statesmen should live and work with scientists as the Medici lived and worked with artists". The man of the future must be "part statesman, part scientist". If we had begun then to think in these terms, we should not be in Britain's sad and dangerous situation today. And even now these fossils who rule us have no idea of the age in which we live.

The Coming Economic Crisis

Question 60. Why are you so up against the Establishment — except for one brief period as a Minister, when you resigned, you seem to have been in opposition all your life?

Answer: Yes, it is quite true that I have opposed from start to finish the men and the parties who ruled Britain during my lifetime. The question is whether I was right or wrong to oppose them and their policies. There are enough clear facts now to provide an answer.

I began life as a young soldier in the first World War. We were fighting for our country in a war we were told was unavoidable, a war to end wars. What of the position then and now? Take a point just before the war, before I grew up - 1910. Let us look at what has happened between 1910 and 1960. It is only a period of fifty years, and there are many men now living who are over fifty.

In 1910, we were by far the strongest power in the world. In the naval sphere, which then gave us world leadership, we were twice as strong as any other power; we had a two power standard. We owned between a quarter and a fifth of the world's surface, and absolute order prevailed through most of that vast area. We were producing far more than we consumed. The surplus was lent to other nations to develop their territories. We had immense assets accumulated in foreign countries. As a country we were extremely rich though many of our people remained poor.

We had the biggest Empire the world has ever seen. The power of our wealth was relatively greater than that of America today. We were a world leader beyond compare since the greatest days of Imperial Rome. That is the position which our present generation of rulers inherited, these men I have always opposed.

Either they, or the men they tamely supported all the time, received from their fathers that wonderful heritage. What have they done with it? They have thrown it away.

I am not saying, of course, that in those days all was well, wisely or humanely conducted in the interests of the mass of the people. But it was an immense power for good or evil, a fine opportunity to keep the peace, elevate the condition of the people and lead the world along ever higher paths of civilisation. What have they done with that splendid chance? They have just fuddled and muddled it away, they have lost it in useless and avoidable quarrels in moments of feeble, petulant passion, or they have just scuttled and run from it like a rabbit who has inherited a lion's part.

Where are they today? Instead of still being twice as strong as any other power in the sphere that matters most, they are helpless dependents of the U.S.A. They even have to be occupied by American forces to save them from their late communist allies, whom their follies and blunders made the strongest power in Europe. So poor have they become that ever since the last war they have been obliged much of the time to live on American charity. The Empire has gone, and what is left is plastered with notices for us to quit. Some Dominions are drawn into the American financial system, and others are drawn into the American defence system, because our government has made us too poor and too feeble to provide either the capital for their development or the money for their defence. The only Dominion strong enough to stand on its own feet they have driven out of the Commonwealth with insults. Why?—in order to please former black colonies which detest South Africa and will reward them for this betrayal of their own kind by ever closer relations with the Soviet power.

In economics, they have thrown away most of the assets and all the opportunities. They stumble from crisis to crisis. Any slight breeze from across the Atlantic is a storm to the little boat which - metaphorically speaking - is all that they have left of the great battleship they once possessed.

They had not the courage to hold the Empire until it could be developed in orderly and planned fashion. They had not the wit or the guts to enter Europe and build an alternative system. They attempted a balancing act between Europe, Commonwealth and America, but fell between every stool. They were too timid to move, and too unstable to balance even themselves. There they lie, the men who were born with everything and now have so little. They are among the most pitiful, if not the most contemptible, figures in history. That is why I have opposed them and their small-time racket of an Establishment, all my life. Have a look at the facts - at what has happened - and judge for yourself whether I was right or wrong.

I do not suggest, of course, that we could have stayed in the same position we were in at the beginning of my life. But if we had avoided war, and had united rather than divided the Europeans, we could have moved into the modern world in a coherent, peaceful but far more creative fashion. We could have given the colonial peoples freedom yet remained ourselves rich and powerful, more than ever a world leader by methods I describe in this book.

The argument between me and the men of the old parties and their Establishment, is now over. I said they would ruin our country: they have done it. But I still say— and I will one day prove it, if you give me the chance — that our scientists, technicians and workers, and above all the will of our great people to live again and to be great, cannot only bring us back as other great peoples have come back, but can reach to yet further heights of the British spirit in European leadership.

Question 61. But are not the mass of our people now much better off than when we had the Empire and were a great power, certainly better off than before the first World War?

Answer: They are at present better off for three main reasons. The first is that science has immensely increased the power to produce. It may be argued that scientific advance developed largely under the influence of war, because nothing serious is done to help science under the present system except in time of war. But the scientific advance would have occurred under any sane system, conducted by statesmen of wisdom and vision. In fact, if science had been encouraged in the way I suggest, the increase in divisible national wealth would have been far greater.

The second reason is that trade union action and political pressure have secured for the people a larger share of the national income. It may again be argued that the upheavals caused by the wars into which the old politicians fell gave the people a strong position to get this larger share. But again, in any sane system, conducted by intelligent and humane men, the mass of the people would have had a larger share of a still larger income without the war and destruction.

The third reason for current prosperity is that the last war created a sellers' market during a long period, with an insatiable demand to make good the destruction it had caused. This artificial demand temporarily supported a system whose only escape from recurrent breakdowns of increasing severity is into war, which the power of modern weapons now makes too dangerous. The present prosperity is, therefore, precarious and transient. In one way it makes the situation even more dangerous, because it persuades the people to believe the politicians who tell them not only that "they have never had it so good", but that the present prosperity will last for ever without any change of system.

Question 62. Why did you always think an economic crisis is sooner or later inevitable?

Answer: The approach of economic crisis has been obvious for years past. I gave my reasons for thinking this in my resignation speech from the government. Each one of them is now slowly being proved true. The process has been interrupted by the war and two armament booms, the first preparing to fight Germany, the second preparing to fight the communist allies we had in the war against Germany. But despite the armament booms and a few new measures, all these factors are now beginning to operate again, and with increased force by reason of the postponements. The war also caused new and greater dangers to our economy.

When exactly it will come to crisis, no-one can say. If you see a ship with a great list to one side, you can say with certainty it will sooner or later capsize, but you cannot say when. That depends when a particular wave or gust of wind hits it in a particular place. The Stock Exchange too at such a moment leads the stampede by behaving like passengers who all make a dart for the side of the ship nearest the water.

My reasons for thinking the present island economy of Britain cannot endure are briefly the following:

We are still living with the same structure of industry and trade as we did when we were the only industrial nation in the world. A far higher proportion of our production than of any other nation goes in export trade, just as it did when the whole world was eager to receive our goods and ready to give particular advantages to us in exchange. Even a Conservative Chancellor of the Exchequer observed not long ago that this position has been passing away for over fifty years.

Now the special demand which follows a war - particularly a long and devastating war - is over, we are faced on world markets with the following factors of intensive competition. We will look first at the adverse situation on world markets which is the direct result of the war.

1. Previous competitors Germany and Japan, once prostrated by the war, have returned to world markets with far more intensive competition. We have made of Germany another England in industrial matters. Its agricultural base in its eastern lands has been taken away. It has, like us, a top-heavy industrial structure. Germany too must "export or die", and is working desperately and successfully to live in competition with us. We fought a

victorious war to prevent it expanding in the east and setting up the self-contained economy of its desires, which would have taken it away from world markets.

Japan is in a similar position. It, too, is a country with a top-heavy industrial structure, and must "export or die" in cut-wage competition with us. Its desire to expand in Manchuria and set up another self-contained system away from world markets was also frustrated. Our policy has produced a strong communist China and a Japanese competitor. That is why competition from Germany and Japan is more severe than before the war. It has to be, if all try to live in the system we have established. They are in the same boat as ourselves. But, as we shall see, there is not room in it for all of us, until we build together a bigger boat.

2. The Soviets were made by the war the strongest power in Europe. They now realise they can no longer defeat us in war, because they know the attempt will mean the destruction of the world, including themselves, but they intend to destroy us by deliberately accentuating what they call the "internal contradictions" of capitalism. They think our system will collapse in any case, but they mean to make it happen faster. So they are beginning to dump against us on the markets of the world, below even their production costs, at prices we cannot touch. That is their way to smash us, and it is only just beginning. We have scarcely felt it yet.

How do they do it? In the same way as they developed their science. They make their own people go short. They will not let them consume a large proportion of their own production, but reserve it for other purposes, just as the Pharaohs starved the Egyptians in order to build the pyramids.

Their first object was to develop science and produce weapons to match the west, and for this their own people went very short. Slums in Moscow and Sputniks round the moon, starve at home and show off abroad: that was the programme. Just look at the housing in Moscow, for example. Now they will use the same compulsory surplus, which their people are denied the right to consume, for another purpose. It will be used for dumping against us, and they reckon they will break our economy with this method. This kind of competition is new since the war. In fact the Soviet power was created by the war. What possible answer has the present system to this move of the Soviets to ruin our world markets? What answer is there, except to save ourselves in the self-contained system of Europe and its overseas territories?

3. Let us now look at the "normal" factors of the existing system which created all the unemployment in the thirties. They are likely soon to return with increased force. Every modern country is fighting for world markets. Every country is trying at the same time to sell more than it buys in order to have a favourable balance of trade. That is obviously a mathematical impossibility, and the result is that one country or another - whichever happens to be the weakest at the moment - is always going under. And the weakest country in the long run of the coming intensive competition is likely to be the country most committed to the business of "export or die", because of its large dependence on world markets.

None of these countries has yet found any means of enabling their own people to consume what they produce. Some like ourselves cannot, because we are too small to be at all self-contained. We must export and sell on world markets enough to buy the foodstuffs and raw materials we cannot produce at home. So we are always dragged back under the present system to the dog-fight for world markets. And our wages are held down to the level of that competition, which is very severe. If wages are raised beyond a certain point we are costed out of world markets and we all starve. That is pointed out to us all the time by present politicians. It explains why British wages, salaries, pensions, profits and general purchasing power cannot be raised sufficiently to enable our people to consume what they produce, thus providing a steady market which eliminates slumps and unemployment. That cannot occur until we are members of an economic system large enough to be independent of world markets, and viable because it contains all its own foodstuffs and raw materials.Europe alone can provide that system for us, now that the Empire has largely gone and we have been made too weak by war to develop what remains by ourselves.

4. The United States has not even yet solved the problem of enabling its people to consume what they produce. That is why it had economic crises and huge unemployment before the war, as its "technocrats" and others pointed out. Since the war it has temporarily solved the problem by giving away a very large part of its total production in world charity, by an armament boom, by a very skilful monetary policy on Keynesian lines which partially maintained the demand, and by a fantastic edifice of debt in a hire-purchase system which can crash at any moment, Yet despite all these measures, America has over five million unemployed at the time this book goes to press.

It is a question how long the American people will be content simply to give away their products in world charity, The danger of destruction in modern war may at any time produce a drive to peace which will end the armament boom. Even now the American papers carry headlines "Peace Scare" when Wall Street slumps. The hire-purchase monstrosity can crumble as soon as more debt is repaid than fresh money borrowed, when further unemployment interferes with instalment payments, when American demand is temporarily satiated in the manner Galbraith suggests. What will American industry then do with its enormous surplus of production? Surely a wave of cut-price goods will hit world markets, because American industry will dump its surplus production at any price it can get. What will happen to the fragile little boat of Britain's present economy in that tidal wave? Ever since the war any ripple on the American surface has nearly capsized the economy, which our rulers' policy has made completely dependent on Wall Street.

5. The sweated labour of the East is being more than ever exploited by western capitalism. Before the war cotton mills in India and woollen mills in Japan ruined Lancashire and Yorkshire. These mills did not grow like mushrooms on an autumn morning. They were erected by international finance supplying large loans for the purpose. The object was to make more money sweating the East than they could get from developing the West. These mills were supplied with modern, simplified machines. A very few highly paid technicians could supervise the machines and the oriental labour doing the job for a few shillings a week. That is why Lancashire has had to shift to other industries since the war. But the East is learning other industries as well, and international finance is supplying the capital to develop them. We have drawn attention for years to this fundamental problem. Modern, simplified, rationalised machines can be worked by illiterate, backward labour which has no trade unions, nor any possible means of self-defence. The mass of labour, sweated for a fraction of our wages, needs only a few highly paid supervisors and technicians. How can we compete against them when this method gets going on a great scale? We failed to compete before when it only affected certain industries. These industries were ruined.

6. We come now to another aspect of the same post-war problem: the method of sweating cheap labour is now spreading to Africa. This more than any other factor really explains the great racket of present policy. The first stage is agitation for the "freedom" of completely illiterate people, so backward they have not the faintest idea what politics or industrial organisation are about. The second stage is to set up black dictatorships which are often in the pocket of international finance. The third stage is the aim of this whole policy which is only just beginning. It is to set up the same sweat-shops as have operated so effectively in oriental industries, with such large profits to financiers and so much damage to western industry and workers. But in this case the workers are far more backward and helpless, once the protection of the old colonial paternalism is removed without anything prepared to take its place. They are mill fodder, sweat-

shop fodder without a hope in the world. Yet the whole process goes through in the name of freedom, love, brotherhood and humanity. What a racket - without equal in the annals of hypocrisy and political corruption!

What a threat to the life of Britain and the whole West! For the poisonous stream of sweated goods will enter the very arteries of Commonwealth. There is no protection against it under the present system.

All this is not theory but proved practice. It happened on a smaller scale in India, Japan, Hong-Kong and China. It was this process which ultimately threw China into the arms of communism. That is always the end, if you are foolish enough to allow it.

Have a look at all these things and then ask yourselves if our island economy can continue in prosperity for ever without any crisis? If your answer is no, have a close look at our constructive solution. In short, withdraw from the chaos of present international trading into a self-contained economy of Europe and its overseas territories, where government can equate consumption and production and maintain the ever-increasing standard of life which science makes possibles

This requires a new economic system in Europe which will be different both from American capitalism and Russian communism.

How to Make Peace and Obtain Disarmament

Question 63. What are your principles in working for peace?
Answer: Every sane man wants peace, particularly when modern war can destroy the world. The only question is how to get it. Here the first need is clarity. We risk at present just muddling into war, because we have not made up our minds what we really want. What do we want and what do we not want? That question has never yet been answered. We just try to find out what the Soviets want to do and then try to stop them doing it. That is not the way to peace, or to any settlement of the world.

My answer to these questions is clear. We want Europe and its overseas territories. They are vital to our life. We do not want Asia. We need nothing from America, but we cannot afford that the western hemisphere should be conquered by the Soviets. That would upset the balance of the world, and in the end endanger our lives.

From these principles follows a clear policy. We should defend Europe, its overseas territories and African regions. We should not hold Asia, and we should not fight for any part of Asia. We should retain our American alliance and be ready to fight if the life of America is threatened by the Soviets, provided America is still ready to fight if the life of our European system is threatened. But we would not fight for America if she involved herself in a war about Asia, and should clearly notify America and the world of this decision.

We should try to negotiate with the Soviets a world-wide settlement on this basis. The world would then be divided into three main spheres of influence. Our sphere would be Europe, its overseas territories and Africa, the American sphere would be North and South America, the Soviet sphere would be Soviet Russia and much of Asia.

Question 64. How would you go about negotiating peace?

Answer: I believe in summit conferences, with a different method. Meet the Soviet leaders in private and try seriously to negotiate a reasonable settlement with them. If they will not have it and just play the fool for propaganda purposes, get out at once into public debate. Invite them to come with us before the television and radio of the world. Then explain to all the peoples of the world what the differences are about. Let them have their full say, and let us have our full say. Let every method of publicity be used, television, ordinary radio in all languages, newspaper articles in all languages, every possible means of communicating the debate to the mass of the people.We should win if our propaganda were reasonable and our case the stronger. Our men would be capable of standing up to the Soviet leaders in public debate, because they would already have proved themselves in the hard test of seeing the communists off in our own countries.

Question 65, What do you think the outcome of summit conference held under your method would be?

Answer: We should by this method gain one of two objectives: either we should get peace through a reasonable settlement, or we should show up the Soviets as humbugs who talk peace in theory while they obstruct it in practice. They would lose the political battle for the opinion of the world. The Soviet leaders cannot afford to lose this conflict because it would mean that communism in every country became a dying force, and they rely on the communist parties to win the game for them now they cannot risk world war. So if we get the better of them in public debate we would quickly get them back to the council chamber for serious negotiations.

If our policy is clear enough and our proposals obviously reasonable, we can by this method drive the Soviet leaders towards peace. I believe we could in the end negotiate a reasonable settlement, because the communist leaders do not want a world war which will mean the destruction of everything including Russia, communism and themselves.

Question 66. What are the prospects of peace?

Answer: I think the prospects of peace are reasonably good, because no sane man can risk a war. But we must bring some dynamism into the winning of peace. We must stop the drift. We must stop the silly game of never moving except just to block the Soviets. We must be positive instead of negative. We are, of course, inhibited from great politics by being a small power. The great act of making a united Europe would change all that. All things are possible to Europe a Nation.

Question 67. Can you give a concrete example of how peace can be secured by United Europe which is not possible today?

Answer: Yes. Let us take one conspicuous example. Kruschev has offered at least fourteen times since 17th November 1956 in varying ways and various degrees to withdraw the Russian troops from occupied Europe if America would do the same. This offer was completely ignored by all European governments. Why?- Because the divided countries of Europe are too small and weak to live in face of Russia. They dare not live alone, and have to be supported and even occupied by America. But what a difference if 300 million Europeans came together. If we 300 million Europeans cannot look after ourselves in face of 200 million Russians without support or even occupation by America, we deserve to die. But, of course, we can. Our population is greater, our resources are greater, our science will be superior when it is properly supported, our technicians, our workers, our productive capacity will be the first in the world.

Question 68. Why do you think the withdrawal of both America and Russia from Europe would ensure peace?

Answer: Because the major risk of war will be removed. That risk is the proximity of the two young great powers, America and

Russia, without any sane, balancing force of an older and wiser civilisation between them. I believe Kruschev means it when he says he will withdraw if Americans do the same, because he is just as frightened at the prospects of a world explosion as everyone else. But if it were just bluff, we could quickly show him up by the method already described. We could either win the peace or destroy world communism. And he wants to keep the peace and communism.

Question 69. What about disarmament?

Answer: Again, every sane man wants disarmament. Whilst we have these great armaments we not only risk war and world disaster, but also spend on useless and dangerous things the resources we should spend on improving the life of the people. Once again the only question is how to get disarmament.

The real difficulty is hardly ever discussed seriously in politics or in press. This is the impossibility of knowing whether the other side has already destroyed its stock of nuclear weapons, if an agreement be reached to do so. It is outside practical politics to expect either side to trust the other. And how foolish we should be to trust the communists, when they let the world know in advance that they are ready to play any trick or lie to promote communism. Some men would take the word of a communist, yet would not accept the word of their best friend in business without a contract.

Question 70. Is there no means of knowing whether the other side has disarmed or not?

Answer: In the nuclear sphere it is difficult at present to know whether the other side is implementing an agreement to disarm. The reason is that an H-bomb can be hidden almost anywhere, for instance under the manure heap in any farmyard in Russia, Europe or America. There is no way of finding out except by turning over the manure heap and having a look. That would mean quite a lot of manure shovelling in all these countries, besides looking in all sorts of other possible hiding places. The problem is not easy. It is no use simply ignoring these difficulties. They are admitted in a parliamentary answer on 13th July, 1959: "Mr. Profumo told Mr. Henderson that there was no prospect of finding any satisfactory method of detecting the existence of concealed stocks of nuclear weapons. 'The only instrument I know of with which one could find a nuclear weapon in a crate would be a screwdriver'." (Daily Telegraph 14/7/59.) No-one in press or politics appeared to take the slightest notice. They just go on talking as if these realities did not exist. They are like the ostrich, head hidden in sand, whisking away the world's little troubles with the tail feathers. Until, of course, Fate, this tempted, takes the inevitable action.

Question 71. How would you overcome the present disarmament deadlock?

Answer: Despite this obvious difficulty we must not regard the prospects of disarmament as hopeless, because we can make a very effective start in other ways. We can stop all production and test of nuclear weapons once any effective system of mutual inspection is agreed; this will not be so difficult when Europe stands between America and Russia. We can also probably stop the production or effective assembly of the means to deliver H-bombs, not only airplanes and submarines but also rocket installations. These installations would either be developed jointly for space exploration or developed by individual nations only under international inspection to check their use for military purposes.

We can also reduce conventional forces, armies, navies and air forces to the level of police forces if this be agreed, because they cannot be concealed from mutual inspection. Invasion remains a great fear of the peoples, and occupation following a surprise rocket attack is a very real risk.

The only thing we cannot do within the present limitations of science is to ensure the complete destruction of existing nuclear stocks by mutual inspection. We have to wait until some machine is invented which rings a bell as an airplane flies over the manure heap which conceals an H-bomb. This may be a long way off. In serious language, we have to wait for new invention.

Question 72. What would be the net effect of your disarmament proposals?

Answer: All this is a very crude summary of a very complicated question, but it contains the essence of the matter. It adds up to this: We can, by negotiation, prevent any fresh production of nuclear weapons and reduce all conventional forces to police-force level. So far the only powers which have nuclear weapons are America, Europe and the Soviets. These three great powers could at least agree among themselves not to have any further production of nuclear weapons, and to prevent any other powers acquiring them. They could also secure the reduction of all conventional forces to a point at which fear of invasion could be forever removed. All this would be a great step forward toward peace and disarmament. There would be a much lesser risk of war if the only remaining weapons were in the hands of three powers, each of which knew that they would all be destroyed if the weapons were ever used. And if no more were produced they could gradually fall into desuetude, like other evil things.

Self Defence and Unilateral Disarmament

Question 73. Would you risk world war in defence of principles you regarded as vital to our life?

Answer: Yes, but the risk of war would immediately be much reduced if everyone knew what we would fight for and what we would not fight for. There must always in life be some principle for which you are willing to die. Had Englishmen and Europeans not held such principles, there would never have been an England or a Europe. If everyone knows the principle for which you are prepared to die, other people leave you alone in that respect - particularly when they know that war will mean not only your death but also the death of everyone else, including themselves.

Question 74. Cannot we disarm ourselves and avoid war as the Campaign for Nuclear Disarmament suggests?

Answer: This puts us at the mercy of Russia. All through history it has sometimes been possible to avoid death by accepting slavery. But you usually get the death before long as well as the slavery. To disarm unilaterally and step outside the western defence system puts Britain absolutely at the mercy of Russia, Moscow could ring up Whitehall any morning, and say that some British communist leader must take over and all must obey him. Otherwise the rockets would blast us from the face of the earth that afternoon. And we should have no answer but to submit, or to die with our hands in our pockets. Is any serious patriot going to put his country in such a position?

Of course, some very serious people would put Britain in that position. They are the communists. That is why they are the real, moving spirits in any agitation of this kind. They have always told us in effect that they put communism before Britain. The quickest

70

way to get communism is just this. It is not surprising on their record that they should stand for the disarmament of Britain, but it is surprising that anyone who loves Britain should assist them.

Question 75. Do you agree that Britain might supply only conventional forces and leave it to America to defend it with nuclear weapons?

Answer: This puts us at the mercy of America. It makes us a helpless dependent of a foreign power. Supposing one day America was no longer prepared to defend those who would not defend themselves? The old proverb says: "God helps those who help themselves". That is a very reasonable attitude. Even America might adopt it.

Supposing, too, Russia said one day: "We are going to take over this island, where a condition of serious disorder has arisen". (They could always cook up any excuse with the aid of their local communist parties.) Russia might continue: "If America is mad enough to interrupt this necessary work of humanity by shooting at us with nuclear rockets, every town in America will be flat the same evening". Can we always be sure that every American president in all circumstances would be ready to risk, or even to sacrifice, the life of America in an effort to save a distant people who would not save themselves? Surely no patriot can thus hand over his country in a helpless position to the mercy of a foreign power. It would be worth any sacrifice to preserve the life and independence of Britain. And if our defences are pooled in a united Europe expense can be less than it is today. Remember, too, that in this sphere the leading nuclear power in Europe is Britain. Our major means of defence will remain in British hands, because of our leading technical position.

Question 76. But can Britain have sufficient arms to deter Russia?

Answer: Yes, certainly, even Britain alone can have sufficient arms to deter Russian aggression. And together with Europe as a whole we could more than match Russian weapons. If Britain were alone, it is possible that Russia could almost destroy us, and that after the weapon muddle made by recent governments we could not do more than greatly damage Russia in return. But it is certainly not worth its while to destroy one island, and in exchange to have the whole of western Russia put out of action. Because it could certainly be devastated by the weapons we even now possess, which should always be held ready for the counter-attack The Soviets could not risk an exchange with us which would leave them so greatly weakened in face of their other opponents. Further, if we develop Polaris with Britain's naval tradition, and other weapons which are quite possible for us to acquire, we could hit back at Russia with an entirely destructive force.

In addition, of course, in the policy I suggest, we should be together with the whole of Europe and still allied with America for purposes of mutual defence. Yet I emphasize that even alone- if all deserted us which is most unlikely- we could still defend ourselves sufficiently to deter Soviet: aggression.

Question 77. Would Russia bother to attack us if we were not armed?

Answer: No, Russia need not bother to attack us. It could just take us over by threatening to attack a defenceless country. If we just sit here without weapons or defence of any kind, simply turning our cheek invitingly for the Russian smack, we shall get it smacked good and proper. And, of course, at the slightest threat of the smack there would be a very large demonstration in Trafalgar Square, with some very familiar faces on the plinth in front of a very large placard demanding that comrade So-and-So at once become Prime Minister. And Britain would then, very soon, become a communist country. We should not only have preferred slavery to death. We should not have had the manhood to exert ourselves to prevent both slavery and death. The only possible policy is to be strongly armed, together with the rest of Europe, whilst striving unceasingly for a negotiated peace and all-round disarmament.

Question 78. Are not present armaments bound to lead to war?

Answer: It is often said that the world has never had heavy armaments for long without war. This is true. But it is also true that the world has never before had a situation in which the use of armaments will mean the death of everyone. One side or the other, usually both, thought they would live and win. You do not hear of many fights in which each man knows in advance that both will be killed. That knowledge is a real deterrent.

The first step to stop war is to make it absolutely clear what we decide we must fight for. Because war, in present conditions, is only likely through accident or misunderstanding. So the first necessity is to make clear our principles and intentions. We hold Europe and its overseas territories, and we shall not let the western world be conquered by the force of communism.

Question 79. Will Russia allow the union of European countries which will make it an inferior power in face of the United Europeans and Americans?

Answer: Yes, because Russia knows that any attempt to impose her will on us by force would result in a world war which would destroy Russia, communism and everything else. If the Soviet leaders did not know this, they would impose communism on us by force today. When Europe unites, the Russians could only prevent it by force, and the use of force means world war and universal destruction. That is why the Soviet leaders no more dare move in this matter than at other times when the West does things they dislike.

Equally, we cannot interfere by force in the internal affairs of Russia without causing a world war which would destroy everything. In this matter we are all in the same boat. We just have to leave one another alone, and let each country have the system it desires. While each side is armed, neither side dare interfere. When we find the means for all-round disarmament, neither side can interfere. It is really not so bad as the alarmists make out.

But we must always remember that in the present situation wars can occur by accident. That is why we must always work for disarmament which will prevent the chance of accident.

Question 80. Do you think Russia and China will eventually fall out?

Answer: Some of the best judges of this situation think this will occur; for instance Germans who have long been prisoners in Russia, or who have travelled through Russia and China as businessmen, are mostly of this opinion. I have not this experience, but I would not be so sure that men united by the idea of communism will fall apart so easily as some think. Most of the leaders in Russia and China are like officers educated in the same staff college of the same army, or like cardinals from the same college in the same church. They may have acute differences or clash of interests, but a common faith and tradition is a very potent force to preserve unity despite such difficulties.

But in this matter we are considering great masses of people, and many of them very primitive people. The urge of China to expand into relatively empty spaces owned by Russia may bring a collision despite the common political faith of the leaders. Also the Russian leaders are now mostly Europeans and appear consequently to be much less seized than the Chinese by that strange oriental fatalism which impassively contemplates universal destruction in the dogmatic belief that what they desire will eventually grow from the ruins. Mr. Kruschev is not the type who says: Let us all die, because paradise will blossom from our ashes. In fact, that is not a European outlook. It is therefore possible that from the deep divergence of character an acute difference in policy may eventually arise.

At any rate, we should always be ready for this contingency and disposed to work for this result. If our European economic experiment is plainly succeeding at the moment when Sino-Russian differences come to a head, a good deal might happen. At such a conjuncture of history, the Russians who are a European people, and other Europeans in the U.S.S.R., might be peacefully and by agreement reclaimed for Europe. We should always at the same time strive for the best and prepare for the worst.

Question 81. What is your attitude to Japan?

Answer: Japan was an old ally of Britain, and it was only a long sequence of political errors which divided us.

The practical problem is this: the Japanese are a highly gifted people who entered the modern world late. Consequently great technical skill is blended with a capacity for very simple living. The industrial result is the most effective cheap competition in the world.

The question is how to find Japan a good means of life without the disruption of our markets. We shall be all right if we are insulated from such competition within the new European system. But what about Japan? How long would American capitalism stand for the invasion of its markets by the abnormally cheap goods of Japan's industry?

The final answer is to help Japan to develop its own economy. A natural expansion of Japan into Manchuria is now frustrated by the victory of Chinese communism to which western policy contributed so much. The alternative space for Japan appears to be a Pacific island system. This rock-firm people could then build both a political and psychological barrier to the advance of communism and a Japanese economy which would reduce its necessity for world markets. The Americans might finally be induced to favour some such solution, when they fully realise that their long-range rockets can command the strategic situation without advance bases. In any case we need Japan as a staunch friend, and should work for a solution which gives Japan as well as ourselves a good life.

America and the Uncommitted Nations

Question 82. What do you think of world government?

Answer: Well now, wouldn't that be nice? It might be safer and more pleasant if we had a world government with a world police force which everyone would agree to support, provided, of course, that it had a policy which we all thought tolerable. But the only world government we look like getting at the moment is a communist government, and that is a tyranny imposed by the force of a highly organised band of international bandits. If you think that an overstatement, just reflect for a moment on the fate of Hungary. In practice, the immediate prospect of world government is not nearly so good as it sounds.

The world government you mean-which is the world government with which you would agree-is out of the question at the moment because there are too many people who fiercely disagree with you. Convinced communists would be ready to die in order to resist your system-i.e., if you are orthodox conservative, labour or liberal in opinion. And as for people like me, we are every bit as ready to die in order to resist communism being imposed on us. So in practice world government is not as easy as it sounds. It is like the old question to the preacher who had eloquently described the happiness of Heaven compared with the troubles of this earth-Yes, very nice, but how do we get there? The lion lying down with the lamb would be a picnic in comparison with the problem of world government.

It is all too easy to reduce the idea of world government to absurdity. Yet the world government people have something when they say the world may die if we go on as we are now. And among them are many serious and distinguished people. We should not merely laugh at them or denounce them, but should produce a practical alternative.

Question 83. What do you think is the practicable alternative to world government?

Answer: If we reject as impracticable the present idea of world government we come back always to the idea of Europe a Nation. This is the first and practical step. If we can unite the European peoples into one government and defence system, the world will be effectively organised into three great blocs: America, Europe, the Soviets. In the immediate future only these powers will possess the decisive weapons. All effective power in hard, practical terms will rest in their hands. They will also have one great motive in common - only one, you will find in real practice - the motive of preventing the world being destroyed.

The practical way to set about the job is to divide the world into three effective spheres of influence by these three great powers. In the end I think this will shake down to Europe, the overseas territories and Africa in our sphere, Soviet Russia, China and much of Asia in the Soviet sphere, North and South America in the American sphere. If we can agree on something of the kind, under the compelling motive shared by everyone of preventing world destruction, there will really be nothing left in practical terms to fight about. We shall each have all the space, foodstuffs, raw materials and potential of economic development that we can possibly require. May I suggest, with all respect, that world government advocates who insist on this system or nothing and will not join with us in making Europe here and now, should reflect on a French proverb: "The best is the enemy of the good."

Question 84. If the three great powers, Europe, America and the Soviets, can so settle matters, what will happen next?

Answer: Then it is up to each of us to show that our system is the best. When it is finally recognised that we can no longer destroy each other without all being destroyed, the future will rest with the battle of ideas. The final world system will be the system which is proved the best in these three great experiments. The communists believe that their system is certain to win. We have an equal certainty that the system we propose for Europe will win. I am not sure the Americans are so sure. But if their system fails, they can learn from us or from the communists. And I think they will prefer to learn from us.

The long and the short of it is this. When war must destroy everyone, war can only happen not by design but by accident, by everyone going mad. The way to reduce this risk is to confine these weapons to a few capable hands which are at least sane, until we can get rid of them altogether. When war is thus excluded for all practical purposes, the conflict will enter the political sphere and will be settled by the battle of ideas. The outcome will clearly depend in the end on which of the rival systems is the most successful. That will be the system of the future. This is the peaceful way and the best way to settle this argument. In fact it is the only way to settle it without a war which will bring world destruction.

Question 85. What about the uncommitted nations?

Answer: The uncommitted nations have no modern arms, and they will not be able to get them if the three great powers decide to limit nuclear weapons to themselves. For the effective power will rest with the three great powers and not with the uncommitted nations. Yes, I am talking in terms of hard reality, not in terms of sentimental fantasy. We have already dreamed and babbled our way to the edge of catastrophe. It is time to face hard facts, and act.

Question 86. Would you abandon the Asian countries to Communism?

Answer: I would not fight for them, if that is what you mean by abandoning them. We simply cannot fight for everyone, everywhere. First of all this policy imposes on Britain, and would even impose on the whole of Europe, an intolerable strain. We have not the resources always to be ready to fight everywhere. Remember too, if we oppose the Soviets in every field - blocking their path in whatever direction they wish to move-we are asking for world war. The insanity, of course, is the baiting of red China by America in China's own off-shore islands. How would you like it if the Soviets tried to set up a puppet government in the Isle of Wight? This way madness lies, and certainly it means war if the madness lasts long enough. We must decide what we will hold, what we will fight for and what we will not fight for.

Question 87. Would you then abandon India to Communism?

Answer: Again, I would advise that Britain should not fight for India or any other Asian country for reasons just given. But we could in such circumstances give India very powerful assistance if the propaganda battle were properly organised on our side. Russia cannot afford a too obvious aggression. The reason is that the future will be settled by the battle of ideas, now that the great military machines are paralysed by fear of mutual destruction. That idea will lose which is associated with aggressive violence and the subjection of other peoples by force. The exposure of Russian or Chinese aggression against India in a really skilled world propaganda would do a good deal more to save it from conquest by communism than the military forces which the present government of Britain has maintained at its disposal.

I would not leave the safety of Britain to any moral appeal, because the temptation to settle the fate of the West by taking a defenceless Britain might be too great for Russia. But India is a less decisive field of action, and in any case Indian statesmen from Gandhi to Nehru have believed in moral rather than in physical force.

Question 88. What will happen to India?

Answer: India is more likely to be taken by subversion from within, than from without with nuclear weapons. Indeed, this can very likely happen. Suppose this occurred while we were nominally committed to fight for India as at present? Suppose that India votes a communist government into power? Would America and Britain send armies to suppress communism and the elected government by force? The most advanced State in India has already once voted communist. This is the way the communists mean to take India, by the usual combination of political agitation and street violence.

In practice, Russia and China are very unlikely to outrage world opinion by invading India, when they are quite certain -in their Marxist fashion-that they will get it in the end by their kind of political agitation. We have nothing to lose and much to gain by making it clear that we will stand up for the freedom of any country in the propaganda battle of the world, but will limit the use of arms to occasions when our own vital European interests are at stake. It is quite new in British policy, this idea of running round the world looking for wars to get into. It has so far proved disastrous, and if we so continue it may mean the end of us all.

Question 89. What will happen if America goes it alone in fighting for Asia?

Answer: Even if America in that event were defeated, I am quite sure a properly organized European Nation would be strong enough in terms of power to survive. After all, Europe has a population of 300 million of the most advanced people in the world facing 200 million Russians. We can be stronger in every respect; in science, technology, productive power. But, of course, our survival would depend on mankind's surviving at all the effect of nuclear explosions in the event of a war between America and Russia. That is why we should use the utmost influence to prevent it. That is why the balancing third force of a United Europe is so important. If America were attacked we should follow the right principle of standing by our friends, because America stood by us. Also by continuing the American alliance for the purposes of mutual defence, we make it less likely that either will be attacked. But I emphasise that we should warn the United States quite clearly that we would not fight if they looked like beginning the war by interfering in Asia.

Africa and Race

Question 90. Supposing the Soviets got a foothold in South America, or in some of the black states of Africa?

Answer: The United States has already declared a Monroe doctrine for the American continent and Europe could equally declare a Monroe doctrine for Africa. We should say to the black states: "We give you every liberty except one, the liberty to kill us." But having made the declaration we must have the courage and resolution to enforce it. And in taking strong action, if necessary, we can be reasonably sure of two things: (1) That if the Soviets were not prepared to fight for what they regard as their vital interests in Europe, e.g., Berlin, they will not risk world war for darkest Africa. (2) That the remote territory of Africa is the most difficult place for the Soviets either to fight a major war or to sustain a minor war.

Question 91. How will a Monroe Doctrine for Africa work out in practice?

Answer: In practice this will mean that we interfere in the affairs of the black states only if they permit themselves to become military bases for the Soviets, or accept weapons from the Soviets which can be dangerous to our life. If we thus intervene in the black states of Africa, or America intervenes in similar conditions in South America, we should withdraw immediately we are satisfied that the Soviet military installations have ceased to exist. If these countries go communist without conceding Soviet bases or creating dangerous weapons themselves, we should simply throw round them a cordon sanitaire and prevent them making trouble in our territories. Within the areas in question, this would probably lead quickly to collapse of the communist regime. If not, it would not greatly matter provided they were not in a position to trouble their neighbours.

Question 92. What about the black states which might be friendly to us?

Answer: We should, of course, in black states friendly to us encourage and give all possible assistance to a leadership which could emerge in the true traditions of their peoples, and which with our aid could evolve with reasonable speed to a standard of life and way of living more comparable with our own. Our policy would be warm friendship and the helping hand to black states who wished to work with us, but a rigorous enforcement of an African Monroe doctrine to prevent the development of Soviet military bases or dangerous weapons in black states which went communist.

Our policy is the exact opposite of the old-party habit of betraying our friends and fawning on our enemies in Africa. An attitude I first stated long ago would here be appropriate: "Stand by our friends, and stand up to our enemies."

Question 93. Do you think that a Monroe Doctrine for Africa would assist peace?

Answer: Yes, because it is an essential part of a policy I have already described. The best chances of eliminating the present risk of war by accident or muddle is a clear declaration of our intentions. The practical method will be the division of the world into three main spheres of influence. Once this principle is clearly established the use of force from outside will only be effective if it is on a scale to launch world war. And that no-one dare risk. In practice, too, I am reasonably sure we can get a working agreement not to interfere in each other's sphere once the Soviets see we really mean business. The Soviets do not want a world war; they are confident that the western system will collapse, and that communism will take over without war. We are equally certain that our system will prove superior to communism.

That is why I believe it is possible to get a practical division of the world into three different spheres of influence within which the great experiment of three different systems may be worked out. A Monroe doctrine for Africa is an integral part of this policy.

Question 94. What is your attitude to the race problem in Africa?

Answer: We believe in the division of Africa into two regions for white and black. They would live side by side, we hope in friendship and mutual help, but without mixture into one people. Africa is a near-empty continent with a population density of about 20 to the square mile as contrasted with about 200 to the square mile in Europe and about 700 to the square mile in England. There is plenty of space for both the blacks and the millions of whites in Africa, living in two areas where in ample room they can develop their own civilisations. Is it not really madness, for no compelling reason, to oblige these two very different peoples to live and develop together? It has brought us nothing but trouble, and in the nature of the case it can lead to nothing but trouble.

Question 95. How would you divide the white and black peoples?

Answer: The blacks under our plan would have most of Africa comprising some of the richest lands. The division would be according to climate, rather than natural wealth of which there is plenty for all throughout Africa. In the end we shall be faced with this division of Africa, or with white evacuation. We say that we need a substantial region in Africa for the future expansion of the European population.

We have a right to it for four reasons: (1) Europeans were settled in large areas of Africa before the Bantu tribes moved into these territories. (2) Africa has for centuries been an important sphere of interest for European countries, and modern strategic and economic necessities compel the maintenance of a considerable area under European government in this relatively empty continent. (3) It is an absurdity which can finally lead to tragedy that our people in the overcrowded continent of Europe, with a population of about 200 to the square mile, should be denied all effective access to a neighbouring continent with a population of about 20 to the square mile; a huge, virgin territory of vast wealth potential which awaits development. (4) All the achievements of civilisation which lifted Africa from jungle life to relatively high standards prevailing in some parts of that continent today were the creation of the Europeans.

We will give the blacks all possible help in their own areas to develop in friendship with us. But we will not destroy the work of Europeans who have made Africa their home. Recent events have proved how easy it is for Europe to hold what is necessary in Africa, if the will to live is there. Without will and resolution, in Africa as elsewhere, all will be lost.

Question 96. Is not the division of white and black immoral and unfair?

Answer: The Archbishop of Canterbury when he returned from South Africa said of apartheid: "If it were entire separation .... two separate countries, with separate cultures and customs and governments, there would be much to be said for it." (Times, 22/4/53). This is precisely the system which I have always wanted. Have not recent events greatly supported this view? Why hold on to black colonies which want to be free and have an overwhelming black population? Why not bring our own people out with compensation if they wish to leave, and make it clear to any who wish to remain that they will be under black rule? Then we can make it clear in the reasonable area of Africa we mean to retain for white government that the blacks in that area will in the same way be under white rule. When an Englishman goes to America to make money, he does not complain that he has no vote in American elections, or civil rights. Equally once we have separated things out in Africa neither white nor black will have any complaint at not having votes or civil rights, if they choose to remain in each other's territory.

Question 97. What are your reasons for saying the present and recent black colonies cannot be fitted into a European-African economy?

Answer: There are two main reasons. (1) Their economy is not complementary to the European economy. They produce things which are already to a large extent in world glut. There simply is not room in a European-African economy for the products of all the black colonies of Europe. Their inclusion will consequently be a cause of incessant friction and trouble between the European peoples. It is far better to let all the present and recent black colonies of the European countries form their own civilisation with a diversified economy, and ourselves to produce in white Africa with white labour such primary products as they supply us today. The black colonies can, with the help of white technicians, in due course cease to be entirely primary producing countries, and can develop a mixed economy of their own on a far more stable basis. The factor of costs in producing our own raw materials with white labour will no longer be prohibitive when we are insulated from the world cost system.

(2) If the black colonies are included in the European economy they will render impossible any system which consciously and deliberately advances to a higher standard of life. In fact their inclusion must wreck a European economy in the long run. At once the worst elements of the old capitalism would try to continue their present practice of setting up sweat-shops worked by cheap black labour. The poison stream of sweated goods would enter the very arteries of the new system. It would thus be impossible to establish a basis of similar standards of life in similar industries throughout the whole economic system, on which we can build an ever higher standard of life as science increases the means to produce. A host of controls would be necessary to prevent the cheap labour undercutting white labour everywhere, destroying the white wage standard and bringing the economy to ruin. In fact, even the most complete system of controls would probably fail to prevent it, and we should find ourselves back in conditions similar to the chaos of present world markets.

People so different cannot be organised within the same economic system. It is far better to let white and black, with their totally different way of living, develop separately. This is the only way to make the economy work at all, certainly the only way to advance with science to an ever higher standard of life.

The miserable business of living on cheap black labour will bring us nothing but trouble if continued into the future. We shall, in the end, have to choose between Europe and the black countries. The dangerous delay of British government in entering Europe has been due to a hesitation between the black colonies and Europe, which can prove fatal.

Question 98. Do you not think that the present policy of multi-racialism in Africa has a chance of success?

Answer: What is multi-racialism? Has anyone yet managed to define it as a practical system? No-one has yet denied it, because it is in reality an organised humbug, a series of small tricks, a delaying device rather than a policy with a clear ultimate aim of far-seeing statesmanship. It is suggested to the negro that he will one day have democracy and self-government. When he asks what this means he is offered some form of minority representation with a loaded franchise, which means in reality the whites still rule. This practice is invariable in every area really important to the white interest, and it becomes ever clearer that the concessions to the blacks are really intended to buy time and not to end in black rule. The black has learnt the slogan "one man one vote" from the old parties of Great Britain. He sees through the humbug and demands one man one vote.

All this petty deceit, this playing of small tricks comes to an end. We have finally to decide what we will hold and govern, and what we will give up. Much honour and some blood will be saved if we do it now.

Above all, the power of a United Europe can be decisive in this matter. If the Europeans decide together what they will hand over to black rule, none can deny either their will or the justice of settlement which leaves most of a still empty continent to future black development. For under our proposals the total area of Europe, white Africa and the Arab lands would certainly be less than the area left for black development, although today our European population alone is almost twice as great as the black population of Africa. Can it fairly be said that this is unfair to the blacks?

Question 99. But has not the method of British government been a proved success in states already developed to the point of black government?

Answer: Do you call it a success to establish a black dictatorship which keeps most opposition M.P.s in jail while elections are rigged by the public beating up of their supporters? Do you call it a triumph for democracy to have widespread personal corruption in these governments, which compete for funds from America and Russia by playing off one against the other? This occurs in some states.

Question 100. Why are things developing in this way in some new black states?

Answer: Because some of the leaders in these countries have been in touch with Moscow during the period of their tutelage under British governments. Is not this the real difference between the Congo and the ex-British territories? When the Belgians had hurriedly to evacuate the Congo, the country relapsed at once into anarchy and the new leadership immediately and openly approached Russia. In British territories, which are freed after a long period of preparation, the leadership is often communist-trained during the process. Consequently the black leadership has the political sense for an initial period to do two things: (1) To establish a black dictatorship which at any time in the future can turn the country over to communism. (2) In the meantime to soak the British people for money on a very big scale. They get a good deal of money out of us and out of the Americans by the simple process of playing on our fears that they will go communist if we do not pay up. Why not, instead, have a firm, clear policy?

Question 101. Will you summarise your policy in regard to Africa?

Answer: Yes. (1) Maintain white government in a considerable area of Africa which will preserve its long established European homeland. (2) Give all the true black states freedom after a brief period of preparation. (3) Prevent only intervention by the communist powers with arms. (4) Then leave the black states free to develop their economies, and for this purpose to get money where they can from America, Russia, or anywhere else. From us they can obtain technicians but not money, because we need our money for British and European purposes. (5) If they go communist, throw round them a cordon sanitaire to prevent their infection of our areas. Under these conditions very few communist regimes will long survive in Africa, because Russia will not long pay for a game that will not advance her cause. (6) The white will have no vote in black areas, and the black will have no vote in white areas. No-one expects this right in the country of another people.

Question 102. Isn't the "wind of change" blowing too fast for us to secure peacefully African living space by the time you achieve power?

Answer: The "wind of change" was largely blown up by a few foolish speeches, and has since blown back on its authors with considerable force. To some extent the situation is now more favourable to our plans than before these events occurred. For the incompetence of black rule, the impracticability of multi-racial society, and the pro-communist tendencies of rulers in the precariously established black states have all been demonstrated in the situation which these follies have precipitated. It has also been proved that a handful of white police or troops can procure order against almost any odds anywhere in Africa, if will and resolution still live. Many myths have been dissipated by these recently proved facts.

It is true that the present Conservative government has surrendered every interest of white civilisation, wherever possible. But even they have not dared yet to insist on the surrender of South Africa and all Rhodesia to black rule. The connection between this great southern block in Africa and north Africa should not present much difficulty to a resolute European government. In fact, the breakdown of some hasty experiments of present government may even facilitate it.

We want always to deal fairly; but it is fair to retain much of the continent whose civilization we have created. It is also not only fair dealing, but a prime duty, to preserve order where the lives of white men, women and children are at stake. Recent events have shown that the alternative is the evacuation of Africa and its reversion to jungle and savagery, unless communism intervenes to fill the vacuum. Communism will take over if we quit. But if we stay Russia will not fight a world war for remote Africa when it would not fight for its prime interests in Europe.

Once will returns, we shall find Africa at worst a police operation in which some of our young men can show their best qualities. For they will require not only courage and stamina, but kindness and toleration, in their coming task. In fact, before long, our help may be asked again in the area of Africa we propose to leave. You will find the "wind of change" can turn right round and blow the other way. It depends quite a lot on what is blowing-panic or courage.

Question 103. What form will practical assistance to the black states take?

Answer: American money and European technicians can be combined for practical assistance. America at present depends on finding an outlet for its surplus production. There is no policy yet in prospect to find this outlet in the purchasing power of its own people in the manner we suggest for the viable area of Europe and white Africa. America will finally be alone in the unhappy position of "export or die". It can at least temporarily resolve the problem of overproduction for its limited home market by the capital development of black Africa. But the administrative side will have to be conducted largely by European technicians, because America almost entirely lacks experienced personnel for this purpose.

Mosley: Right or Wrong?

Above all it is necessary to strip this large subject of confusing emotion and to get down to the practical problem: What plan is best for the general good? An effective plan can be based on the following facts.

(1) We can solve our own economic problem within the viable area of Europe and white Africa. The capital resources necessary for this task will be great, as large parts of Europe are still very poor. For a long time to come, therefore, we can supply additional funds to help black states only by impoverishing our own people. This is both wrong and politically impracticable. In fact it is not morality but masochism, if the problem of black poverty can be solved in any other way. A government should not put itself in the position of a father engaging in charity to the point of making his own family hungry.

(2) America long before the war had a surplus production problem, which is likely to become even more acute in the near future. It has no present idea of solving the problem by finding any means to enable its own people to consume what they produce. The U.S. economy is, therefore, dependent for survival on the classic capitalist device of discarding surplus production on the exterior markets of the world. This process used to be called "imperialist aggression" and is now called Christian charity, but the result in cold terms of economics is much the same. In any case it appears at present to be the only means of avoiding the usual over-production crisis in America, and it is warmly approved by the British Labour Party which sees in the development of backward areas the only means of prolonging the life of world capitalism-albeit by the method which Marx chiefly denounced as making worse the final crash.

(3) The black states need, for a period, outside assistance with capital equipment. After that they should be able to develop their own self-contained economy in the large and rich areas available to them.

If these three facts have any validity, is it not plain sense that in this situation Europe and white Africa should use our badly needed resources for our own development, and that America should use its embarrassing surplus for black development with the aid of necessary European technicians? After the period required for equipping the black states, America will again be confronted with its recurrent problem of over-production in relation to the available market, and in an aggravated form because exterior markets will close everywhere as backward countries become self-sufficient.

But America could thus win a breathing-space to think again, to develop politically and to reorganise its economic system. And by the success of our Europe-Africa experiment we can show America the practical way to avoid the communism which would otherwise most certainly confront it. Always provided that we do not first ruin ourselves by the two fatal processes which all our old parties recommend: (a) impoverish our own people by supplying to the black states the meagre resources we urgently require to build our European system, (b) render impossible the building of any stable economy in Europe and its overseas territory by including in our system peoples with an altogether different standard of life, who will be exploited to undercut and to dislocate our market with the chaotic results we observe beginning on world markets today. White and black can be combined within the same economic system only by the slave organisation of communism, to which this unnatural combination would quickly reduce us in common ruin.

Question 104. Do you foresee a troubled future for the African continent?

Answer: No. A peaceful future, directly you have a firm, clear policy. Once we have divided Africa into two regions, white and black, it will be obvious that we are prepared to give the blacks a fair deal. It will be equally clear that they have every liberty except the liberty to kill us. That position will be accepted for the simple, real reasons that we have the power to enforce it and that the use of this power is clearly just. We will then not only develop friendly relations with the black states, but will give them every practical assistance. The African leaders will develop their own true traditions in friendship with us when it is clear that communism cannot be made to work effectively in Africa.

Question 105. What do you think of the United Nations in Africa?

Answer: The policy I propose will be preferable to the present arrangement, whereby these countries are developed by British or European capital - which we badly need for purposes like re-housing our own people - and then American capital takes over the business our money and effort has created. This is now done under the guise of the United Nations intervening to remedy the anarchy caused by the weakness of present European governments. The method will mean in the end that we work and pay, and America picks up the business. The only safeguard so far against this dishonest process is the ineptitude of U.N. administration. It is far better to have the whole matter from the start on a clear cut basis. Africa will then be left in the peace of two friendly peoples living side by side and helping each other's future development. The final aim should be a complete replacement of black labour by white in the white area, and the replacement of white technicians in the black area by black technicians directly they have been trained. This will occur naturally - without any compulsion - as the two experiments succeed.

Question 106. Would not the replacement of black labour by white in Africa upset the economy of Africa?

Answer: It is feared it would do so in present circumstances because white labour costs more than black, and would therefore raise production costs. But sufficient capital to mechanise industry in the white area of Africa should more than offset the higher cost factor in white labour. Skilled labour with machinery can produce more at lower cost than unskilled labour without machinery. That has been proved over and over again. But for countries without great capital resources suddenly to replace black labour with white labour would just cost them out of world markets. This is the present dilemma for relatively small countries like South Africa.

Question 107. Do you not argue that black labour can be exploited by unscrupulous capitalism to defeat white labour if it operates in the same economic system?

Answer: Yes, certainly. Let us get this matter quite clear. (1) At present South Africa cannot replace black labour by white because the increase in production costs would cost their goods out of world markets. But no such increase in production costs would occur in most cases, if they were supplied by Europe with modern machinery. White men working machines can produce at least as cheaply as unskilled black labour without machines. (2) But if capitalism supplies cheap black labour with modern simplified machinery, this labour can defeat the more expensive white labour working the same machines. Only a few white technicians are required to supervise the work of these blacks. The black cost of production is lower and could destroy the white economy, if included in it. That is why South Africa, like the Dominions, should be included in the white economy of Britain and Europe, not in the black economy of the other parts of Africa. The point that cheap black labour can be supplied by capitalism with modern, simplified machines to undercut white labour on world markets goes to the very root of my economic thinking which postulates (a) an economic system insulated from world markets, (b) a division between white and black civilisations.

Question 108. Cannot Trade Union action in Africa level up black standards to white and so prevent the under-cutting competition you fear?

Answer: This is the same old illusion which wrecked the policy of the European socialist parties. For over a century British and European workers have been told that all the backward peoples of the world could be organised together in the second or third International and marched off in quick step to the millenium.

The workers are still waiting. In fact the workers of Lancashire and Yorkshire got tired of the wait and went off to other industries when they found the cotton and woollen trades were ruined by the cheap competition of India, Hong Kong, Japan and China. Neither the Second nor the Third International could save them politically, nor could international Trade Unionism save them industrially. In fact, the Third International which is, of course, communist, is now used to complete British ruin by dumping the production of Soviet slave labour against us in the markets of the world.

The Soviet system is the only one which so far has solved the problem of getting people with very different standards of life to work together in the same economic system, because that system is slavery. You produce what you are told to make, and you are given what the boss decides. This goes whether you are a first-rate scientist or an illiterate savage. It works in its fashion, but at a cost western man rightly will not pay.

Meantime all real progress is held up in the West by the old left-wing fantasy that international action can solve the problem. Again and again while they have talked in their international organisations, capitalism has got on with its job of making fat profits by sweating cheap labour to undercut western labour. And by the nature of the case, it is plain that this is bound to happen. Just take a journey through Africa and have a look at the potential labour of the new range of sweat-shops in the new field of exploitation. No objective and honest observer could believe for a moment that they could be efficiently organised in trade unions for generations to come. And meanwhile the West would be ruined by the undercutting of cheap labour.

The only way to deal with the problem would be by a system of universal control with the whole system conducted by an omnipotent bureaucracy: in short, communism, and this is precisely what the communists are doing. Apart from the tyranny which western men would not stand for a moment, the universal bureaucracy is wasteful and inefficient to an extreme degree. State action is, of course, necessary to develop nuclear science; it is the same in all countries. The Soviet tyranny is able to get spectacular results, precisely because it has the power to deprive its public of the ordinary amenities of life so that ampler resources can be used for scientific development. But the rest of the Soviet system, dealing with normal development and consumer goods, is a slow moving tyranny. In short, if we do not want communism, the only way to deal with the backward peoples is to assist them to develop their own civilisation and not to mix them into our own economy. Let like be with like. But let all help each other.

Question 109. What can a United Europe do in Africa that the individual nations cannot do at present?

Answer: A United Europe can solve the problem in Africa. We could act in two ways: (1) Supply the machinery and capital equipment which would enable white labour to replace black labour without raising production costs. A United Europe could also certainly find labour which would be willing to work, for example, in African mines, with the help of the modern machines it is skilled enough to operate. (2) Our system in the viable area of Europe and white Africa would be independent of world markets and of the world costing system. We could therefore raise the reward of the primary producer without any fear of being costed out of the world markets we would no longer require.

In fact, it will in any case be necessary to raise the wages and salaries of those engaged in the primary industries and basic services in order to provide a market for new automation industries.

Question 110. What will happen if we continue present policies in Africa?

Answer: American capital would rule Africa through the United Nations with much cant of humanity and brotherhood.

The result would be the setting up of sweated industries with backward labour which would compete disastrously with all European countries on the world markets to which we are now all tied.

This form of African development would entail a yet more fatal aggravation of the pre-war tendency of western finance to seek greater profits by sweating the East than it could get from developing the West.

We have already considered this question in connection with the entry of the black Commonwealth into Europe. We can enter Europe with the white Dominions but not with the former black colonies. Their inclusion would upset the whole economy of Europe and white Africa. It is necessary for us, and certainly better for them, that the black countries should develop their own economy and civilisation. For this purpose they should be free to get their money and their assistance where they wish provided they do not interfere with us. Once again live and let live.

Question 111. Have you not said that United Europe could put through an alternative policy in Africa-what is it?

Answer: Yes, I have suggested that an alternative policy would be possible to a completely united Europe. But I do not think it is so satisfactory as the policy I have just proposed, for reasons which I will give.

In 1954, I suggested that either of two completely different policies might succeed in Africa; if pursued decisively and vigorously. The first was the complete division into two regions, white and black, which I have just described. The second was a complete union of Europe and the whole of Africa, with a universal franchise resting on a high educational qualification. Anybody, white or black, would get the vote, on merit. This could work for two reasons:

(1) It would remove the present fear of white minorities that

they will soon be ruled by a majority of illiterate savages. The white population in a United Europe-Africa would out number the non-white by almost two to one. The majority would be far greater if an education test were introduced to the franchise, which incidentally might also be of considerable advantage to white civilisation.

(2) All sense of inequality or inferiority would be removed from the mind of the coloured population by this measure. They would be in a position of complete equality with the white, and would receive the vote on the same educational qualification. It is obviously a solution which the entire Union of Europe alone could make possible.

I do not think it is so satisfactory as the complete division into two nations already described, for the following reasons:

(a) Things have now gone too far. The prolonged hesitation and protracted muddle, the refusal ever to face facts and take decisions in time, the delaying devices to obviate action, the small deceits to replace great policies have destroyed confidence with both white and black. Separation is best when trust and respect have ceased, and it becomes in the end inevitable.

(b) A strength in government would be necessary to lead and to direct an economic development in a mixed civilisation which would exceed what would normally be regarded as tolerable. Government would have to intervene far more directly and frequently in economic matters than it would need to do in a civilisation composed of similar peoples on a comparable standard of life. Otherwise, precisely those conditions of economic exploitation would again arise which have already been described as threatening the existing civilisation with destruction. Such action is possible, but it would lead to a degree of government intervention which would be inimical to the growth that is fostered by freedom.

(c) To make a mixed civilisation work, a social conscience would be necessary which has recently been systematically impaired and will take some time to restore. The great values of the Europeans and those of the true black races, their traditional pride in their own people and stock, can return and can restore mutual respect. But all this will take time, because a new spirit in human affairs can only work slowly at first. And time presses. So it appears at present that on all counts complete separation into different regions - living side by side in friendship, but without mixture - will be the most satisfactory solution.

But it is well to note that in this matter as in many other spheres more than one solution is possible. It is nearly always the case in human affairs, and in politics in particular. Very often there are several solutions of political problems, often varying widely from each other. In my experience, the real difficulty in Britain is not to find solutions but to get anything done at all. It is not that the problems are so difficult to solve; the trouble is inertia and a deep resistance to all change until it is too late. What I described as our "dynamic pragmatism" can always find a solution, often several solutions. What we have to create in Britain is that energetic spirit which does things in time, which can only be born of a new movement created by the people for this purpose.

Question 112. What is your attitude to the Arabs?

Answer: Warm friendship. We have many sympathies and interests in common. We should support to the utmost the union of the Arab peoples under outstanding leadership, instead of seeking their division. They are our natural friends and allies in face of communism, for the true Muslim can no more be a communist than can the true Roman Catholic.

It was a tragic error to throw so much of Arab goodwill away to Soviet Russia. This situation was a product of the old-world mind which failed to realise that the arrival first of submarines and aeroplanes, and then of A-bombs and H-bombs, meant that the Suez canal was no longer a strategic route for Britain in time of modern wars. Our Mediterranean policy should then have been reversed (as I said at the time) and have been based on the union of the European powers on these shores, and the alliance of all the Arabs with us in face of the threat of Soviet Russia. Our rulers preferred the obsolete game of the European powers jockeying each other for advantages which no longer existed, and of alienating the Arabs in the defence of interests which equally no longer existed.

Today nothing divides us from the Arabs, except the necessity to have a dependable bridge between Europe and Africa, and a good life for the million Frenchmen and other Europeans who have long made their homes in that area. We should say to the leading Arabs: No man ever obtains 100% of his desires, but we can offer you 90%. By that we mean European support for your union, your economic development and your defence against communism, in return for our bridge between Europe and Africa and a good, secure life for our Europeans. No realist would refuse that outstretched hand, and realism now prevails in the Arab world.

The Racial Question

Question 113. What is your attitude to the colour problem in Britain?

Answer: This problem has been artificially created and is causing great hardship to many of our own people. I believe that the only solution is to send the coloured people home with fares paid to the West Indies, where a change in British policy can give them good jobs with good wages. The change in policy is simple, it is to buy sugar again from Jamaica and to cease to buy it from Cuba. We can also buy bauxite from them, and encourage other diversified industries. The cost of their return journey will be negligible on our national budget, and the change in economic policy can be an advantage to us as well as to them. The West Indies have some claim to special consideration because the present situation was caused through the ruin of the Jamaican sugar industry by what is usually called the Black Pact to buy sugar from Cuba. This was done by the Labour Party in 1951. But the policy has been continued ever since by Conservative governments. The result was to drive many starving Jamaicans over here in search of work and to create the chief element in the colour problem in Britain, which in all cases is easily soluble by a similar policy of fair treatment. All blame should attach to the British governments which were responsible.

The Jamaicans were the first victims, and the next victims were the British people among whom they were forced to live. Our people in these areas were already suffering from severe overcrowding through the long neglect of the housing problem.

Also many gangsters and racketeers, vice-peddlers, brothel keepers, etc., took advantage of the chance to mingle with the innocent mass immigration and enter Britain to ply their illicit trade in the more profitable market of a larger and richer country. The government is afraid to deal with the constant disgrace of the black-run brothels, clubs with all-night juke boxes playing, etc., which ruin decent neighbourhoods, because they fear it would be regarded in the black colonies as discrimination against negroes and might result in resentment to the point of losing the black colonies.

So a policy which began in a blunder and continued in cowardice has inflicted a real hardship on many British people, who have seen the quiet and respectable neighbourhoods in which they lived all their lives ruined by an influx of people with an entirely alien way of life. The only solution to the problem is to send these people home in a decent and humane way to the good jobs and fair wages which our policy can afford. The repercussion of this policy must be faced, and they are met by our general policy in regard to the negro question.

Question 114. Would not a United Europe and common citizenship mean a flood of immigrants into Britain from areas of Europe where wages are low?

Answer: No. Because immigration would be controlled until there were no longer any low wage areas. After that point there would be no such immigration, because men would stay in their own areas if they could get the same wages. You would not find Italians leaving the sunshine of their native land to live in the London fog once they got the same wages at home. They only want to come under present conditions because they suffer from unemployment and low wages.

You will remember in previous answers that our wage-price mechanism will level up wages and conditions in similar industries throughout Europe, and on that sound basis will then raise wages, salaries, pensions and the general condition of life as science increases the means to produce. You will have no movement of population from one country to another seeking work once you have established that system. Until then, immigration will be controlled.

Question 115. What about the immigrants who have come to Britain during or since the war, some of them very undesirable?

Answer: As stated already our government will ask the people to vote them power to return coloured immigrants to their own land in a decent and humane way by paying their fares back and providing them with employment at good wages at home. The main problem is that of the Jamaicans, and this is easily solved by buying from that island materials we require and cannot produce ourselves. When the black colonies have their independence and their own civilisation, it is fair to treat them as foreigners whom we merely wish well and desire to help.

In regard to European immigrants who are here already, government now has power to send back any who are undesirable to their own countries if it chooses to exercise that power. We would not apply this measure to all of them, because many Europeans are a welcome addition to our civilisation, but we would certainly apply it to a good number.

Most of those causing trouble in Britain today are not really Europeans at all. Some of the worst cases come from countries which are still nominally in the Commonwealth. Government should have power to return to their own countries any undesirable immigrants who have come here since the war, whether they are from Commonwealth or other countries. It is unfair to let the accident of the special condition of those years become a permanent burden and affliction to our people which can change the character of our civilisation. Our concept of European Union does not involve a rootless cosmopolitanism in culture any more than in economic matters.

Question 116. How would you deal with the question of coloured students and coloured immigrants who have been here a long time?

Answer: Coloured students could continue to come here for education and will be made welcome. We are not drawing a colour bar; we are simply looking after our own people and getting them a fair deal. We cannot allow the present housing problem and the coming unemployment problem to be made worse by a mass of coloured immigrants, but we will do everything possible to provide the traditional educational facilities to those who come here temporarily as students.

Coloured people who have been here a long time, who have been good citizens and have developed roots in this country will also not be sent away. For this reason we propose that all coloured people of this character who came here before the last war, should be allowed to stay if they wish. They are too few to create any serious problems. And on the whole they have been good citizens of Britain.

Question 117. What are your views about race?

Answer: Let me state quite simply that in my view a man should be as determined to preserve his own race as to preserve his own family. Then we will have a look at what science has to say on the subject.

The first thing to note is that races are different - I say different from one another, mark you, not superior or inferior to one another. The elementary fact that races are significantly different is now sometimes challenged by people who have not made the slightest study of the subject. Let us look at a few authorities. First Darwin, who wrote in *Descent of Man*: "There is however, no doubt that the various races, when carefully compared and measured, differ much from each other-as in the texture of the hair, the relative proportions of all parts of the body, the capacity of the lungs, the form and capacity of the skull, and even in the convolutions of the brain. But it would be an endless task to specify the numerous points of difference. The races differ also in constitution, in acclimatisation and in liability to certain diseases. Their mental characteristics are likewise very distinct....."

The famous T. H. Huxley, in *Man's Place in Nature*, . stressed the range in variation of the brain between different races. A similar point was made by "the founder of the science of comparative ethnology", Sir E. B. Tylor, wrote as follows in Anthropology: "Anthropology finds race differences most clearly in stature and proportions of limbs, conformation of the skull and the brain within, characters of features, skin, eyes, and hair, peculiarities of constitution. and mental and moral temperament .... In comparing races, one of the first questions that occurs is whether people who differ so much intellectually as savage tribes and civilised nations show any corresponding difference in their brain. There is, in fact, a considerable difference."

Mendel's theory of genes, on which all modern genetics is based, shows that the wider an outcross, and hence the greater the diversity of genes involved, the smaller will be the probability of ever recovering the original stock. The eminent modern geneticist, Professor C. D. Darlington, F.R.S., M.A., Ph.D., D.Sc, commenting on Galton and Mendel states that "Galton had uncovered the process of racial differentiation in its simplest instance much as Mendel had uncovered the process of recombination in its simplest instance."

The same author in his book The Facts of Life writes: "All races ... all mating groups and all social units composed of mating groups have their own genetic characteristics. They are all different ... It is absurd to pretend that water and vinegar are equal. Water is better for some purposes, vinegar for others. Vinegar is harder to get but easier to do without. So it is with people. The future of mankind rests with those genetically diverse groups ... which can practise mutual help and show mutual respect. Neither of these habits can be assisted in the long run by make-believe of any kind, certainly not by a make-believe of equality in the physical intellectual and cultural capacities of such groups."

Finally Professor Darlington summarised certain practical aspects of the question in the following remarkable passage, in The New Scientist (14th April, 1960): "Is there not then a third system, one of wider outbreeding, of real crossing, such as black-by-white . . ? The answer is: no. Such crossing represents not a system but a change of system, a change from relative inbreeding to outbreeding . . . And the original types from which you started will never reappear: one can never recover the parental strain from the offspring of a wide cross . . . If you change from outbreeding to real crossing, you are liable to run into trouble".

How can it possibly be argued in face of such authorities that no significant differences exist between races and that crossing of races can be undertaken without risk? The eager propagandist of this opinion merely "erects the small flag of his impertinence on the massive fortress of his ignorance." He does more, he seeks to condemn his own kind to extinction.

Question 118. Surely modern science has established that race differences are only skin-deep-you have quoted only one modern scientist?

Answer: Modern science has established nothing of the kind, and it is not difficult to show this. In addition to classic biologists-if I may so describe them-it is correct that I have so far quoted only one modern scientist, although I will now quote more. The scientist already cited is Professor Darlington, an Englishman whose integrity is well known to all, and whose reputation is world-wide. In this matter we have to be very careful to distinguish between science and propaganda. In the last war, it was suggested for political reasons that all men were the same. This has become a fashion of thinking, or rather of propaganda, in the post-war world and many of its institutions. I do not mean to suggest that all scientists who take this view are insincere; certainly not. But I do suggest that much present thought in this respect is wishful and emotional. We must base practical policy on facts, not on wishful thinking- either way.

I contend that the facts show that races differ from one another, and that it is natural to want to maintain the integrity of your own race and also to preserve the genetic and cultural variety that exists throughout the world. This view is supported by what is legitimately described as the classic view, which I gave in reply to the last question. But it is fair to say that some scientists contravene this view. Physical differences between races are usually admitted; controversy concerns the explanation of their origin rather than their existence. But there is still argument about the extent to which racial inheritance affects the mind, and consequently the creation and maintenance of distinctive cultures.

Certainly there is controversy among scientists on this subject. But the point surely is this: while this controversy continues in scientific circles without so far any suggestion of a conclusion which shakes the traditional view, it is really a suicidal insanity to discard the proved nature process of millennia-proved in the sense that it has produced from very primitive beginnings such a result as European civilisation-in a fit of emotionalism, evoked by war and post-war propaganda in people who have not even given as much study to the subject as I have been able to do in the course of a very active life devoted to other affairs. In certain academic circles I was recently accused of having "mugged up" the subject. The subsequent discussion revealed that I could certainly exonerate my emotional critics from any charge of that kind.

So let us now look at the result of a few more researches by scientists, not a single one of whom could be charged with having any political sympathies with me. First, the 1946, 1947 (Mayo, Ferguson and Crane) and 1959 editions of the Encyclopaedia Britannica all emphasise the differences between races. A leading British biologist, Professor C. H. Waddington, C.B.E., M.A., Sc.D., F.R.S., writes in his Introduction to Modern Genetics: "Man is a very variable animal. An Australian aborigine, a Chinaman and a West European differ as much from each other as do many related species of monkeys." Professor Juan Comas, D.Sc. (of the Mexican School of Anthropology) states that: "Negro and white are in no respect identical either physically, intellectually or emotionally." This appears in the UNESCO symposium, The Race Question in Modern Science (London,

1956). In the same work, Dr. G. M. Morant says: "It seems to be impossible to evade the conclusion that some racial differences in mental characters must be expected." And even Dr. Ashley Montagu (Rapporteur to the UNESCO committee that drafted the Statement on Race) admits in *Man: His First Million Years* that anthropologists are "by no means agreed" that differences in mental capacity do not exist between certain human groups. Indeed, the recent studies by experts like Shuey, Porteus, McGurk etc., do strongly suggest that there are innate mental differences between races, just as there are marked anatomical contrasts which none can deny.

In the new edition of You and Heredity (revised with the help of many scientists), Amram Scheinfeld writes: "What is now apparent . . . is that the relative differences, and a few of the absolute differences, go considerably beyond the surface traits which anthropologists in former years regarded as about the only important characteristics distinguishing races. Recent researches have shown that there also are significant average differences, even among ethnic groups," in blood types, disease inheritance and certain kinds of bodily functioning." Let us now take a look at the opinion of scientists of a different outlook.

The editor of a periodical which deals with race and allied subjects, and is supported by distinguished scientists from many countries, recently complained of the bogus "anthropological" arguments used "to advocate or justify Black and White crosses" and "castigate European peoples for their backwardness in showing a desire for racial miscegenation."Dr. R. Gayre, also observed: "What can occur without ill effects within one stock, does not provide any grounds for reasoning as to what can occur when two distinct stocks are crossed ... we do not think, in view of the natural phenomenon of associative mating, that the British or any other peoples, Black or White, are behaving unnaturally if they show some hesitancy to enter freely into hybridisation with strains vastly different from themselves". (*The Mankind Quarterly*, January, 1961.)

The well known eugenist, G. C. Bertram, M.A., Ph.D.. in his study West Indian Immigration, comments: "Viewed with distant dispassion, peaceful happiness is not typical, even of race juxtaposition, let alone race mixture, in many areas of the world." He justly summarises different opinions on the matter, but concludes that "most must surely find themselves unable to feel convinced that there are positive advantages to be gained from an increased mingling of African and European genes (that is to say 'blood' in popular parlance) within the population of the United Kingdom. Indeed, many are convinced already that the disadvantages of large scale mingling are heavy. Quite apart from the absence of any genetic advantages likely to accrue from this miscegenation, the growth of a host of social disadvantages and tensions would seem highly probable."

Dr. J.C.Trevor B.Sc, M.A., Ph.D., in Chambers Encyclopaedia says that whether race-crossing is biologically or socially desirable is still "a hotly debated question". In face of this great weight of evidence, provided by classic scientists before propaganda intervened, and modern scientists of repute and integrity, can anyone claim that "science has established race differences are only skin-deep"? Anyone who thinks this is just riding the hobby-horse of his or her wishes, and the unscientific answer is: come off it.

Question 119. Can science make any real contribution to this question of a mixture of races, since scientific evidence derives chiefly from experiments on plants and animals?

Answer: Let us agree that insufficient evidence exists in the human case on which to found a proven theory. That is all the more reason for not undertaking an irrevocable experiment in respect of which no adequate evidence exists. The onus of proving the benefit of a change to miscegenation rests on those who propose it. And, as you say, insufficient evidence exists in the human case; though so far as a mixture has been tried in practice in the coloured populations of Brazil and South Africa, it does not encourage us to think that the extension of the experiment will lead to a solution of human ills at a higher level.

Plenty of evidence exists over centuries in the animal case, and it seems conclusive. Darwin himself linked the human and animal examples. He wrote: "Some writers who have not attended to natural history, have attempted to show that the force of inheritance has been much exaggerated. The breeders of animals would smile at such simplicity; and if they condescended to make any answer, might ask what would be the chance of winning a prize if two inferior animals were paired together." After all, let us remember that - whether the practice of vivisection be desirable or not - much of the progress in medical science has come from experiments on animals. And we have in agriculture a far larger volume of evidence in the matter of breeding, accumulated from the experience of centuries into a fairly exact science. The results, in brief and very crude summary, are that in-breeding is dangerous over a long period, but can produce remarkable results. A moderate out-cross with a similar stock is the right corrective to in-breeding and is, in time, essential. A wide out-cross, however, is nearly always fatal; in fact, a cross between widely varying strains is in general principle always fatal.

The really decisive point is that if the race-crossing experiment be tried on a great scale, you cannot put it right again. Science seems entirely clear, from experiments which apply equally to human beings and animals, that the fatal step is irrevocable. Is it not the very depth of intellectual frivolity, and an immoral act, to interrupt the long and successful progress of human evolution and diversification, on the strength of a theory which - to understate the argument - has no evidence to support it?

Question 120. What are the practical effects of your views about race?

Answer: It is right to be proud of your race and to want to preserve it, just as it is right to be proud of your family and to want to preserve it. Race exists just as much as family exists, and in much the same way. It is simply a wider form of relationship. Of course, a lot of nonsense is talked about race as about most of the great truths of nature. It is exaggerated nonsense both ways.

I am a practical man and was brought up originally in the very practical trade of agriculture, in which my family was engaged for many generations. Therefore, I know the difference between the Ayrshire breed which specialises in milk production, and the Aberdeen Angus breed which specialises in beef production. If you tell us there is no such thing as difference in breed and that all these animals are just the same, all farmers will begin to laugh at you. And we should equally laugh at you if you lost a lot of time fiddling about in dusty archives to prove that they were both orginally descended from some buffalo in central Europe centuries ago, which had little beef on it and yielded even less milk because it was so busy escaping from the wild animals which were chasing it around.

What matters is that over a long period of time and for a variety of reasons, animals developed in this world with very different characteristics, animals which, above all, can do different things. And still more is this the position in the case of human beings, who for a very long time have had very different environments and experiences from one another in addition to being different breeds. The great third factor of education is added to heredity and environment in human affairs, and the consequent evolution of a culture increases rather than diminishes difference. It is unnecessary to remind ourselves of the vital fact that men have human intelligence and will, which have enabled them to progress much faster in their different directions - differentiation and diversity as the scientists call it.

Of course human beings are different from one another and have different capacities, and so have different races. If you don't agree with that get into the ring with a professional boxer if you are a university professor, and get into the laboratory and try to do the professor's work if you are a boxer. All these nonsensical theories about everyone being the same are quickly exploded by a little practice. Races are different from each other. That is the first basic fact to recognise

Question 121. Do you think some races are superior to others?

Answer: Superior is a term I never use. Different, is the word I use. What is superiority? It is a loose and generally ridiculous term. All men may be equal in the sight of God. But when it comes to hammering in a nail, mending a broken motor or doing a sum in higher mathematics, a lot of men can do the job much better than I can. On the other hand there may be some things I can do better than they can. Our capacities are different, that is the long and the short of it. Therefore, who can judge what is superiority? - even if such a thing exists in any absolute sense?

So let us face the fact that men are different, and not muddle ourselves with silly talk about superiority. Such attitudes lead in turn to the opposite error of pretending that all men and races are just the same.

I do not know in this matter which type I find the more ridiculous: the albino rabbit claiming to be a Nordic superman because he looks like a Scandinavian whose family has spent some generations in the Tropic of Cancer, or the masochistic denigrator of all western values, who on the one hand tells us that negroes are just the same as we are because they have white palms to their hands, and on the other proclaims that their primitive simplicity is so superior to us that he kisses their feet in an agony of self-abasement.

What these neurotics really mean, of course, is that they feel the primitive is preferable to their own particular brand of exhausted decadence, and in this matter, for once, they are right.

Question 122. Are you against mixed marriages; if so why?

Answer: Certainly I am against mixed marriages, because I am proud of my own race and want to preserve it. We British are, of course, the product of a mixture of peoples, but always peoples very close to the original stock; never what the scientists call a "wide outbreeding" or a "real crossing". When I express opposition to mixed marriages I am not referring to marriages within Europe but to marriages with quite different peoples. Not only do I think this process bad for us, but also bad in the wider interests of mankind as a whole. The plan of nature for thousands of years has been to develop different races with character of their own, and on the whole the plan has succeeded very well. All these diverse threads of humanity make up a brightly coloured scheme in this beautiful, interesting and fascinating world of endless future possibilities. Apart from not wanting the disappearance of my own race, I do not want all races eventually amalgamated in one dull, grey mess. And I notice that many people who desire this end are already in their own personalities precisely in that condition of grey mess. They appear to hate all life, vitality and brilliance in human existence, and want to reduce everything to their own sad condition. Let us rather all develop along our own lines and in our own civilisations, certainly respecting and helping one another but not mixing together in a way that would destroy identity and character.

Question 123. Would you seek to forbid mixed marriages by law?

Answer: No. It would be enough to let our people know the facts. Very few of them want mixed marriages. All the propaganda in favour of such ideas has had very little effect; the healthy instinct of the mass of the people is too strong. Tell our people the truth and revive the old pride in being British. That would be enough.

After all, for generations our people ran the biggest Empire of mixed races known to history. It never occurred to them to go in for mixed marriages except in isolated instances, until war-time propaganda (for obvious reasons) began to suggest that all people were the same and that any idea to the contrary was wicked. To desire mixed marriages is not normal to the British. Nor is it natural among the Negroes. The leaders of the great negro communities like the Zulus are very averse to mixed marriages. They are proud of their stock and want to preserve it.

There are, of course, exceptions, but in general it is only the trash on each side which wants to mix. It is against nature. Healthy strains do not desire it, only the exhausted who seek some form of biological renewal-in this case by the wrong method, because the out-cross is too extreme.

Our Movement will awake a new social conscience. Also it will end the present compulsory mixing of the people by government policy which permits and even encourages a flood of coloured immigrants into areas already overcrowded by reason of the long neglect of housing. This will meet the problem without any forbidding of mixed marriages by law. The more healthy instincts we can awake in our people and the less we repress by law, the better.

Question 124. Would things not be more peaceful if we were all one race?

Answer: Why should they be? The Europeans are all closely related, yet they have fought each other far too long. The escapists' answer that things would be more peaceful if we were all the same is no more valid than the statement that things would be more peaceful if we were all dead. It is the answer of the death wish which is the chief characteristic of contemporary decadence. It is always possible to solve the problems of life by escaping from life.

Question 125. Can racial differences never be overcome intellectually and socially?

Answer: Yes, of course they can at a certain level of intelligence, education and character. The first gulf which is overcome by intelligence is what was called class. It ceases to exist already at a certain level of intelligence. The next is the gulf of generation. That, too, is overcome at a certain level of intelligence or of character. The third and last gulf to overcome-the hardest task-is the gulf between races. Of course, it is surmounted already by men of very great intelligence. For instance, few of the world's leading scientists in discussing their own subjects, would be preoccupied by the thought that they came from different races. But having an intellectual discussion together is a very different thing from marrying each other. Also very few people have reached the level of such intellectual intercourse, and it will be at least some time before they do. If you now try to mix those who have very different ways and standards of life, you make trouble. You make such a row that you postpone the day when more people of different races will be able to get on well together on the social and intellectual planes.

Question 126. Would you describe yourselves as a racialist party?

Answer: No, because racialism is usually taken to mean that one race dominates others, and we believe that all races should be free to develop their own civilisations. We believe in the principle: "Live and let live". We believe in preserving our own race, but not in persecuting other races. We shall preserve our own race by two methods: (a) by preventing immigration to this country which creates overcrowding and other social problems, (b) By publishing the facts which science reveals: that races have different characteristics, and that the mixture of extremes is detrimental to both races involved. If our people are given this knowledge, no laws on the subject will be necessary.

Question 127. Then you did not at any time agree with Nazi racial policies?

Answer: No, I did not agree and have expressed myself clearly on the point in public on a number of occasions. Our policy in this respect as in others was very different. The reason was that our problem and our aim were both different. Our problem was to conduct a great Empire consisting of many different races, and our aim was to hold it together and develop it. The Nazi Party's declared policy was to unite all the German peoples in Europe, and their aim was to bring them together in an area adequate to their economic survival. Our policy on racial matters was therefore naturally different from their policy. And now that the war has broken up the Empire and made the conduct of what remains in the old way impossible, we do not change the British tradition in racial policy. We would discourage mixed marriages, but would not repress them by law. We can trust our people under the right guidance not to make them.

Our British contribution should always be balance and sanity in such matters. There was an element of hysteria in the Nazi approach to these things, which ended in disaster. The racial theme was exaggerated and pushed to extremes. (I speak now of peace time, and not of war atrocities which I deal with in another answer). An exaggerated and hysterical view of facts which are true in themselves can lead to an inhuman situation in which things are done which frustrate the very idea it was desired to promote. It is right to be proud of your own race and to try to preserve it, but not to lose all sense of balance and proportion on the subject.

Question 128. Do you consider your attitude on racial matters to be more in line with British tradition than that of the other parties?

Answer: Yes, because the British tradition is calmly and firmly to preserve our own race in practice, without falling into hysteria on the subject under the influence of any extreme or unproven theories.

It is interesting to note that the most respected leader of the Conservative Party - Mr. Disraeli - came very near on the other side to believing the same principle as the Nazis. He wrote: "All is race; there is no other truth". If my recollection is correct, you will find it in his book Tancred. He was, of course, a Jew whose family came from Sicily; a foreign import if ever there was one. Some Jews, like the Nazis, have always taken an exaggerated view of this matter. Race is important, but it is not everything. Such Jews are right - as we are right - to discourage mixed marriages and to try to preserve their own kind. But I would not go so far as Disraeli in saying that "all is race", strongly as I am against a mixture of races. It is indeed curious that the most revered of all Conservative leaders - who gave them practically every idea they possess, and whose now obsolete principles are still printed on the back of their membership card - should have taken this view of the racial question. It is becoming tragically comical now that the Conservatives are so busy importing negroes and similar far-away strains from all over the place into Britain and compulsorily mixing them with our people. Mixed-up kids, the Tories. They will certainly leave us with a lot of problems to straighten out.

Attitude to the Jews

Question 129. What is your attitude to the Jews?

Answer: I am not an anti-Semite. Anti-Semitism is hatred of all Jews on account of their race. I attack some Jews on account of what they do, but I never attack any Jew on account of his birth. I never attack any man on account of his race or religion. If a Jew does something against the interests of Britain or of Europe, he should be attacked like anyone else. He should not be attacked because he is a Jew, but equally he should not be immune from criticism because he is a Jew. This is a consistent principle from which I have never departed, before or since the war. I cannot, therefore, be called an anti-Semite, who is a man who attacks all Jews on account of race or religion. Our clear-cut principles differ from anti-Semitism for reasons which anyone can understand.

I have challenged opponents who have searched through all my speeches and writings to quote one case in which I have attacked Jews on account of race or religion, and they have failed to do so because no such quotation exists.

Question 130. How then has the idea got around that you have some special quarrel with the Jews?

Answer: The idea started in the early 1930's for the following reason. The Jews were then engaged in a quarrel with the anti-Semitic German government. Hitler condemned all Jews because they were Jews, which we never have done. Jews in England feared that we would develop on the same lines. They were mistaken, because as stated in previous questions we were a British Movement faced with British problems, and therefore had totally different policies in many respects from a German government faced with German problems. Also we felt

117

differently and developed differently in many ways. We were entirely a British Movement.

But some Jews in Britain feared that we should develop in this manner, and attacked us in many different ways ranging from financial pressure of every kind, victimisation of our members in industry, etc. to the point of some Jews attacking our members with razors in the streets. During the first two years of our Movement's existence I never criticised Jews at all. In fact, I was quite unconscious of any such problem. But when these things happened, I hit back and denounced the perpetrators with some vigour. That is how the quarrel occurred.

Question 131. Did you accuse some Jews of trying to involve us in a war against Germany in the thirties, and again more recently, of trying to involve us in war over Suez?

Answer: Yes. On principle I have always opposed the sacrifice of British lives in any quarrel which is not vital to the life of Britain. It seemed to me that certain Jewish interests were attempting to drag us into war with Germany, not in a British quarrel but in a Jewish one, so I denounced them with even more vigour. I was not alone in this view; for instance the British ambassador to Berlin was reported as saying that the hostility to Germany did not represent the will of the British people, but was the work of Jews and enemies of the Nazis (see Documents on German Foreign Policy, D. vii. 200).

According to the same constant principle I attacked the financial power of some Jews in 1956 at the time of the Suez adventure in the following terms: "Britain has been dragged towards war for the second time in no British quarrel but a Jewish quarrel. For the second time we have been dragged towards war by international Jewish finance .... We are certainly not anti-Semites who are against all Jews just because they are Jews. No man, woman or child can help how they are born, and Jews are as much entitled to a fair deal as anyone else. But I am resolutely opposed to Jewish financial interests which involve Britain in alien quarrels, and I will expose them always when they act in a way contrary to the interests of my country. Union Movement is the only force in Britain which dares to stand up to them. I oppose them not on the grounds of race but on grounds of what they do. And then only when they do something which injures Britain or Europe."

I will always attack any interest, Jew or Gentile, or any man, Englishman or Eskimo, who in my view attempts to drag Britain into unnecessary wars which will lose British lives in quarrels which are not our own. But throughout these events I have held to our principle of never attacking all Jews and thus becoming an anti-Semite. I criticised Jews only for quite specific and definite activities against our country's interests.

The deep quarrel concerning the second World War is now over, because the issue is over. I retract nothing, because I believe I was right about the war. But I do not continue feuds or quarrels when the reasons for them have ceased to exist. Both sides have suffered, and both should forego revenge. It is ignoble, and can again bring disaster.

Question 132. Do you attack International Finance in general, or Jewish Finance in particular?

Answer: I attack international finance in general, not Jewish finance in particular. Before the war I attacked Jewish finance in particular, and, for reasons just given, again since the war at the time of Suez. These issues are now over. I attack the principles of international finance in general, not individuals of the various races and faiths who are engaged in the business. Our policy brings the power of international finance to an end, not by discriminating against Jews but by changing the system. Our policy once for all brings to an end the evil we combat-international finance. We fight bad principles. We do not persecute individuals.

Question 133. Will the laws affecting finance and other matters apply impartially to Jew and Gentile?

Mosley: Right or Wrong?

Answer: Yes, certainly. Let us be quite clear on this matter:

(1) We attack no man for what he is born, only for what he does.

(2) We are not anti-Semites, who think Jews are bound to do wrong because they are born Jews.

(3) We establish a system which brings to an end the power of international finance, and also terminates the internal corruption of the financial power.

(4) These laws will apply equally to Jew and Gentile. Those who do not obey the law will stand trial and will be subject to a jail sentence if they do not first leave the country; they will be "inside"-or outside. The wrongdoers of the present system will obviously leave because they will prefer pursuing their practices elsewhere to going to jail. No Jew should complain of this, unless he means to break the law which will apply to all. And no anti-Semite should complain because, to the extent his view will be true, this policy will solve his problem.

(5) We welcome the co-operation of all in Europe - whether Gentile or Jew - who will work genuinely for the construction of the new nation, according to the law and method of the new system.

This is a policy of clear principle and plain sense which will be supported by the British people, who rightly detest persecution. And it solves the problem because it establishes the new European system, which alone can free us from the dominion of the big Wall Street operators in the great international of finance. That is why - having established principles which we believe can save Britain and Europe, which are both just and decisive of the main problem - we treat any Jew like anyone else. These same principles can at last terminate to a controversy which has long vexed mankind, and in a manner which humanity can approve.

Question 134. Do you condemn anti-Semitism?

Answer: Yes, certainly. It is a stupidity as well as an evil. How ridiculous to see a man blathering away about the Jews until he is blue in the face, without any idea in his empty head how to deal with the problem of international finance. He tries to substitute a mean and foolish persecution for a decisive policy. We bring the evil practices of international finance to an end without any persecution of anyone.

It is particularly ridiculous when these professional anti-Semites reject Europe and try to confine us to this island and the remnants of the Commonwealth. That system is completely dependent on international finance, now more than ever. Such a policy condemns us for ever to be the slaves of a system which finance controls. The rule of international finance is now exercised more effectively from New York than from London. Moreover there are as many Gentiles in the business as Jews, or more. Are the anti-Semites going to flap across the Atlantic and lift the big operators (Jews only) out of Wall Street, where they are protected by American rockets? On the one hand to give the impression that all Jews are to be persecuted and on the other hand to have no idea what to do about the real problem of international finance is to plumb the depths of sheer silliness. That is why anti-Semitism is the opposite of our policy. We seek great ends by decisive means. We despise and reject those who seek ignoble ends by ineffective means.

Question 135. Did you not oppose the pre-war boycott of German goods, just as you recently opposed the attempted boycott of South African goods?

Answer: Yes. To organise a boycott of a country's goods is to impose a blockade, and a blockade is an act of war. It is therefore very likely at some point to produce a shooting war. Nothing is more likely in the end to promote violence and bloodshed. Yet it is the professional pacifists who are often the prime movers in the boycott business.

Apart altogether from the morality of trying to change a country's political system from outside by force, who are the first to suffer from the results? The first victims are inevitably those whom the boycott is supposed to help, the weakest members of the community thus attacked. If the boycott of South Africa succeeded, the people who would suffer most would be the poorest blacks, who would lose their employment and could not much be assisted by an impoverished economy. The Union government could carry on indefinitely on a siege economy, and those in the weakest position would suffer. So would the interests of peace.

We had the same kind of thing on an even greater scale in the thirties. Then a previous leader of the Labour Party appeared with the Chief Rabbi to demand a boycott of German goods in order to help Jews who were having a bad time in Germany. It cannot be denied that some Jews were so suffering. But equally it cannot be denied that such agitations contributed to the outbreak of war, because to the extent they were effective they were liable to produce a determination in the government so attacked to break out from isolation and blockade at any risk and any cost. And none will claim that the subsequent war did the Jews in Germany any good. On the contrary, they suffered terribly.

The lesson of it all is surely this: if you want to help people in another country, the last way to go about it is to promote boycott, blockade and other methods which lead to violence and even war. The Jews who were killed during the war might have been alive today if that problem had been solved, among others, by a constructive policy of European unity which found the space and means for all to live in peace and plenty.

It was this view which at that time led me so strongly to attack the Jews who appeared to me to be driving to war in a profoundly mistaken policy. And this was the only occasion on which I came near to criticising Jews as a community, because they then appeared to be acting as an organised community. Whoever so acts must take the consequence of collective action.

To denounce an act of war is not to approve any oppression in a country which for a variety of reasons some of my opponents have tried to strangle economically. We get nowhere if we ignore the facts in these matters. And it is a demonstrable fact that many enemies of the pre-war German government grossly misrepresented its policies, just as certain powerful interests distort the facts about South Africa today.

Some people who conduct these agitations do so, of course, for evil motives, but many among the agitators have the good intention of helping those in other countries who they believe, rightly or wrongly, are having a bad time. They should realise that the effects of their action are precisely the opposite of what they desire. And they should make the effort of working out constructive policies, instead of indulging in a destructive emotionalism which may make them feel good but can do nothing but harm to those they seek to aid.

Question 136. What is your attitude to Israel?

Answer: I adhere to the policy of a Jewish national home, which I suggested in *The Alternative* (published in 1947) as follows:-

"For over two thousand years the Jews have asked for a national home, and sought again to become a nation .... To this end I propose the partition of Palestine and the placing of Jerusalem under a super-national authority which will afford Christian, Arab and Jew impartial access to their Holy Places. It is plain that even the whole of Palestine would not afford an adequate home to the Jewish population, even if it all were available without outrage of justice in the treatment of the Arabs. Such statesmanship would, therefore, in any case, be confronted with the problem of finding additional living room for the Jews. It is, naturally, desirable to provide such accommodation as near as possible to the Home Land of Palestine. But this consideration is not now so pressing in view of the rapid facilities for travel provided by modern transport.... No insuperable difficulty should be encountered, therefore, even if the main bulk of the Jewish population had to live at some distance from the traditional national home. Palestine would remain a home to them in the same sense that the Dominions regard England as home."

And I have emphasised repeatedly that this entire problem must be solved in a manner that humanity, as a whole, will approve.

Unfortunately, comprehensive settlements, which combine morality with foresight, are not customary in the world of the old parties, and the Jewish state of Israel was born amid the savage brutality which occurs when such governments yield to force what they refuse to reason. The consequence has been a legacy of cumulative hatred, perpetuated by western incompetence and aggravated by Soviet arms-dealing. But we still seek a progressive and peaceful solution for the future.

First, we must eliminate all possibility of another armed conflict in that area, especially in view of the increasing availability of atomic weapons. We should make it clear that we shall not permit any Arabs to cut two million Jewish throats. And equally we cannot allow aggressive expansion of the Israelis into neighbouring lands; they already have a million dispossessed Arabs on their conscience and our hands. It is quite possible to keep order in these easily accessible regions, without plunging about in the minor military operations that have previously disgraced a British government, slow to defend the interests of our own people but hysterically eager to act on behalf of others.

A united Europe, co-operating with a friendly and helpful America, would have little difficulty in developing new lands and organising any required sorting out of populations. Large-scale migration may well be inevitable, if friction between various unsuitable peoples is not to degenerate into chaos and bloodshed; this has become pressing in Africa. As I wrote in The European in December 1953: "There is plenty of room for both Jews and Arabs in the great area of the middle-East; all that is lacking is union, will and energy to accomplish the task. Whatever policy emerges must be based on reason, justice and the consent of the leading minds in both the Jewish and Arab peoples; all parties and opinions have behind them errors in this sphere which must never be repeated. Let us never again clash with the conscience of the world."

Relationship with America

Question 137. Should we not unite just with northern Europeans, and have looser ties with the whites elsewhere in the world?

Answer: This would mean the division of Europe. No plan could better suit our enemies. "Divide and rule" is the principle of international finance, which has divided us and ruled us, after the virtual destruction of Europe by fratricidal war.

We need urgently the complete union of Europe. It is now an economic, military and political necessity for the survival of our people. Three hundred million Europeans can save themselves and hold the balance of the world. To separate Britain, northern Germany and Scandinavia from the central European countries and from the Latin civilisation - from which derives our common heritage in every sense of that noble word - would merely aggravate the division of Europe, and increase the triumph and power of our enemies. And any other form of European division can only contribute to the same result.

It is a proposal which would split and weaken Europe, and tie us up with America. It would make the rule of Wall Street more secure in a loose white community, where any government of European people would be powerless and finance would be yet more powerful. This suggestion would replace the union of Europe with a rootless cosmopolitanism dominated by a finance whose rule is destructive of our welfare and alien to our values. This is the point where crackpot racialism and international finance make common cause.

Question 138. Are we not much closer to the northern Europeans than to the rest of Europe?

Answer: The suggestion is nonsense on historical, cultural, political and even ethnological grounds. European history and culture derive from Greece and Rome-in southern Europe. The notion that ethnic differences can be defined in this crude way is equally artificial. Englishmen of mixed Saxon and Norman descent, like myself, are more nearly related to northern French, to southern as well as northern Germans, and to the Lombards of Italy, than we are to the descendants of the original inhabitants of this island, whom our rude and rough ancestors chased into the local mountains. Similar considerations operate within all the main countries of Europe.

To apply this pointless theory logically you would have to divide existing nations. Just fancy, for example, suggesting to the French that their country should be split in two. What a way to unite the white race! You would end by finding many Europeans in the south who were nearer to us, in strict ethnological terms, than people in our midst. The fact is that the related families of Europe are so interwoven that you could never sort them out in this manner, even if anyone were foolish enough to try.

Such fallacious arguments can only contribute to the weakness and division of Europe and therefore assist the victory of communism. By driving his unfounded theories to the point of discarding our close relatives, the racial extremist would fall under the Mongol domination which further fratricide would make certain.

Question 139. Are we not nearer America than Europe?

Answer: Some will feel this on account of the language. Others (like many Labour leaders for all their boasts of brotherhood) instinctively dislike the free way of life in Europe, about which they know little.

My own feelings are expressed in the phrase: "With Europe we have everything in common except the language, with America we have nothing in common except the language." This was a deliberate exaggeration in order to concentrate attention on the point I desired to make; a device occasionally permissible in controversy if it helps to explain what you mean. What I meant was that for centuries the great interacting cultures of Europe had freely exchanged the wealth of their philosophy, literature, poetry and plastic arts. Shakespeare means as much to the educated German as Goethe means to us, or as Racine means to us both; we all share the glories of Italian and Spanish painting, while such music as Beethoven's belongs to the whole of Europe.

Some Americans, of course, have learnt from Europe as other people have. But what have they yet given in exchange which is in any way comparable? And what they begin to offer in contrast to our European heritage is something which the real Englishman and any other true European feels is very strange to him indeed. In the realm of great literature, America has so far produced only two major poets. They promptly identified themselves in diverse ways with Europe, and one of them was treated by Americans precisely as we would expect: he was condemned and worshipped consecutively in the manner Frazer makes familiar during his study of primitive peoples in *The Golden Bough*.

It is right that we should feel these things which rest on basic truths, but wrong that we should be driven into hostility to Americans just because they profoundly differ from us.

Let us recognise frankly the contrast between us and America, and the affinity between us and the rest of Europe, yet remain on friendly terms with America. The United States helped us most generously in our dark days after the war, and we should never turn our backs on men who have helped us, but rather be ready to help them in any hour of need. In practical terms between us and America, the more our economies divide, but our policies coincide, the better. By that I mean that we cannot and will not be an economic dependency of America, and to be mixed with it in the international trading system would be a disaster for reasons I have already described. We can have our own trading system in Europe, its African and other territories, and they can have theirs in their hemisphere, without any need to clash or even to be in economic contact.

But it is desirable that our policies should coincide in face of the common menace of Russian communism. We should be ready to support each other if either is attacked. For that purpose it is not necessary for America to occupy us, or for us to occupy America. Three hundred million Europeans in union can face Russia along the European frontier, and America can, if necessary, be in support from its own territory by long distance rockets with a range of over 9,000 miles. In return we will support America in defence of its own land; though not if it plunges into adventures in Asia, which is not its concern and is certainly not our interest. This is the sound basis for relations with America: friendship and mutual support, but no mixing of Europe with another system which has very different values and way of life.

Question 140. Does not your strong European policy divide us from Americans who are closely related to us, and is this not wrong?

Answer: Our policy brings us out from underneath America, and that is right. We are at present completely subject to American power. The only way to save Britain from this ignominious and ultimately fatal position is to enter Europe. We must become independent of America. We must stand on our own feet and become a great country again. The only way to do this is to enter Europe and to play the part already described.

You might almost as well argue from similar premises that we should attach ourselves to Russia, and become subject to communism. After all, Russians, too, are a fine European stock, and apart from their political system we no more have a quarrel with them than with the American people.

We must face the fact that America is now ruled by Wall Street, just as Russia is ruled by communism. We do not want to be subject to either system. We want in Europe to make a third system, without usury and capitalism and without tyranny and communism; a system which suits the European and his way of life. The only way to do this is to make a European system in independence both of America and Russia.

As most Americans and most Russians are European people, we hope and believe that one day the success of our new system will draw them again towards us. But we are not staying under alien systems in order just to stay near our relations; we do not want to live in the mud just to make a cosier family circle. If our ancestors had adopted that principle in place of the long effort of evolution, we should still be at the bottom of the pond with the other tadpoles. We insist on our independence and our own development - British and European.

Question 141. Are not British values nearer to American values than European?

Answer: Only if your knowledge of life is limited to two things: You know you can understand the American language and you know you cannot talk the European languages. If you know nothing and care less about the European way of life, European literature, art, music - in fact, everything which gives purpose and deeper happiness to individual life - you may feel more akin to an American than to a European just because you can understand what he says when he offers you a cigarette. But this is a very elementary stage of human existence from which all our people with present opportunities of education are capable of escaping. If you do not take advantage of these opportunities, it is your own fault. Do not on that account try to deny your more enterprising fellows and above all your own children their share of the joy and beauty of European life. It belongs to us Britons just as much as to any other European people. We have contributed at least our share to the thought and beauty of Europe. All this belongs to us. Do not try to rob us of it just because you prefer Coca-Cola and everything that goes with it. If you love your children you may hope that they at least will learn better.

Question 142. Are you aiming at a third system politically, economically and psychologically?

Answer: Yes, we stand firmly for a third system in all respects. Politically we will be subject neither to Russia nor to America. We stand for the freedom of all Europe. But as already stated, we will certainly remain in friendship and alliance with America for mutual defence against communism, because it is only the Soviet powers which in the present situation may possibly attack us with military force. Yet we warmly offer to Russia co-existence and friendship if it will let the argument between us be settled by proving which is the best system and not by force of arms.

Economically, we stand for the economic leadership of government by means of the wage-price mechanism, which has already been described. This is a free system depending on the leadership of government and not on compulsion. That is where it differs from communism. But it is not a system of laissez-faire like American capitalism which means, finally, government by finance. Our economic system differs fundamentally from Russian communism and from American capitalism. It is a third system which suits us.

Psychologically, our European system will be as different as our European civilisation is already from either American or Russian civilisations. These are both materialist systems, and their peoples at present worship different forms of material success. We recognise the necessity for material progress-this is why we always give the support of science an overriding priority-but Europe has deeper spiritual values and an immense cultural tradition which neither capitalist America nor Soviet Russia possesses. In this respect America may eventually learn from Europe or one day develop a culture of its own, and Russia may well return in the end to the true instincts of the Russian people whose culture has contributed much to European civilisation. Meantime we insist that we are Europeans, and we mean to live like Europeans without subjection to any alien, materialist civilisation.

Government and State

Structure and Method of Government, Question of Power

Question 143. What principles of government do you propose?
Answer: I think the following is a fair summary of the principles of government I propose, which we will study in more detail in the answers to subsequent questions. These proposals will:

(1) Effect more rapidly the policy for which the majority of the people voted.

(2) Give government more chance to deal with sudden crises.

(3) Prevent abuse of power and corruption, more effectively than any present system.

(4) Extend and guarantee personal liberty by enactments which make impossible under any circumstances either imprisonment without trial or retrospective legislation.

(5) Promote new ideas by new measures, which will be embodied in the whole system of the state and will enable men of ability to get their chance early in life.

(6) Encourage in the state an atmosphere of scientific discovery rather than sterile controversy, in which discussion will be free, informed and valuable.

Let us now see whether you will agree that these general principles are implemented by our more detailed proposals.

They are set out in the form applicable to British government, but in the main they are equally suitable to European government. In my view it would be essential for a European government to possess the powers here suggested as appropriate to the executive, in order to carry out the will of the people in an exacting, creative period. But some of the powers suggested for the British national parliament might be delegated from the European parliament to parliaments in the individual states which will unite to make Europe aNation. I regard it as important by such devolution to preserve to the utmost the national cultures and traditions of each people forming the new Nation. To that extent only I would suggest federal forms.

But for effective action in a period when it will be extremely necessary, my own bias is always towards centralised power in matters concerning Europe as a whole. I feel, as I wrote in The European Situation (1950) "We do not mean any miserable federal compromise which retains all the vices of the old system and achieves none of the virtues of the new. If you maintain national divisions, sovereignties - call them what you will - you are merely creating states within the State. Every question will be regarded not from the standpoint of Europe, but from the 'interests' of the old States. . . . There will be no peace in Europe until Europe becomes a nation."

But we should not at this stage be drawn into suggesting a detailed constitution for Europe. These are questions which the people of Europe will be asked to decide at subsequent elections, when Europe a Nation exists.

Question 144. What structure and method of government do you propose?

Answer: First of all we need a definition of function which is absolutely clear. This is the basis of all efficiency. Let everyone know with precision just what his job is. In government, this principle means a clear division of function between Government, Parliament and Judiciary.

We believe that government elected by the people should, for its period of office, have complete power of action in foreign affairs, defence, economic policy, finance and science. In this sphere parliament should have the power only to question and criticise, except in the case of gross abuse which could be subject to vote of censure. An adverse vote of censure should lead not to a fresh election but to a referendum, because this procedure would provide less incentive for parliament to play the party game. But I agree that parliament should have the means to prevent abuse of power even in the defined spheres where rapid action by government is essential, in addition to the other safeguards which will later be defined and which do not exist under the present system.

All social legislation should be the sphere of parliament, but parliament would, of course, be able to confer on government special powers of rapid action in urgent matters; e.g. housing; Government should have the power to initiate legislation, but the decision would rest with parliament. Government, by reason of its power of finance, would have power to veto legislation initiated and passed by parliament on account of excessive expenditure. The remedy of parliament would be to publicise the matter, and thereby to secure the defeat of the government at the next election if the veto of expenditure could not be justified to the satisfaction of the electorate. Alternatively, parliament could proceed by vote of censure, but in the event of an attempt to force expenditure on the government there would have to be safeguards; e.g. in this case more than a bare majority should be necessary to implement the will of parliament. A means designed to prevent the abuse of power should not itself be abused.

The judiciary would have the power as at present of interpreting laws passed by government and parliament. It would also have additional power to safeguard individual liberty, and certain new functions which I will describe.

Question 145. Will elections be free?

Answer: Yes, absolutely free. Any party could enter the elections

Government and State

and engage in any propaganda it liked. They should be held at regular intervals, and at least as frequently as at present. But once a government is elected it will have the power during the period of office to do the things for which the people have voted. That is why parliament would not be able to interfere in the decisive sphere of government described in the last question, except by vote of censure. In the modern world the government must have power of rapid action in such matters.

Question 146. Would Parliament have other rights?

Answer: Yes, parliament should be able to question every minister for at least one hour every week; a more severe test than ministers have today. If he could not stand up to it, he would not be fit for the job. And the power of questioning would lead to the discovery of new talent, which is one of the most important functions of parliament. A minister could, of course, refuse to answer a question which was dangerous to the nation. The people would quickly judge if he were just dodging, and in that event the government would have to sack him before the election or risk being sacked themselves.

Question 147. Will the judicial system guarantee individual liberty-Habeas Corpus for example?

Answer: Yes, more so than today. Habeas Corpus can now be suspended in time of crisis, as it was for example in the last war. Men were then detained for years without trial at the will of the government. This makes a mockery of liberty. The only time you really need Habeas Corpus is exactly when it is suspended.

There should be a constitutional enactment that Habeas Corpus can never be suspended. Consequently judges would always have the duty of ordering the immediate release of anyone detained without trial.

Judges should further have the constitutional duty of declaring invalid any retrospective legislation which penalises the individual. At present a man may do something which is perfectly legal today, and be hit for doing it by some subsequent law or regulation. Retrospective legislation can be a vicious instrument of tyranny; it must cease.

Then we can begin to talk seriously about liberty. At the moment it is a shady farce, only kept in being at all until the government really wants to get rid of it, which happens when they have landed us in a situation of popular panic. Let us have real liberty. These reforms will secure it.

I believe government elected by the people should have the full power of action, which at present it does not possess in normal times; that is the only way to get done what the people want done. But the liberty of the individual should be absolutely protected from any act of government, by a law which no government can ever set aside.

Question 148. What will be the new powers of the Judiciary you have just mentioned?

Answer: First of all the judiciary should take over some of the functions at present nominally exercised by parliament. As you saw already, we suggest the government should have complete power over finance instead of the present time-wasting procedure which consumes most of the year in detailed discussion. It really gives parliament no effective control at all, owing to the complexity of modern budgets. All this rigmarole of so many repetitive stages for a finance Bill just enables the Opposition to show off at the expense of wasting the time of ministers and exhausting their energies which should be given to their job. The old, detailed control of parliament, which checked corruption and abuse, has ceased to be effective. All such matters are in the hands of civil servants, such as the very able Treasury officials who really do the job which parliament is supposed to do.

But I think there should be a very clear authority in a power outside government or civil service to enquire into every suspected case of corruption or abuse. The judiciary seem to be the best fitted to perform this duty. Some judges should have the power at any time to enquire into the conduct of the government and civil service, and to reveal any case of corruption or abuse. The judiciary should then have the power to report to the nation. The government would then have to clear up the situation or be condemned by the electorate and defeated at the next election. We must stop corruption, and this seems the best, surest and cleanest way to do it.

Question 149. Have you not suggested the use of the Judiciary to protect and assist inventors, men with ideas?

Answer: I propose an entirely new function for the judiciary which may surprise many people. But I believe it to be a necessity in this age of science. We must keep abreast in science, invention and new ideas of every kind. We simply cannot afford the suppression of ideas by vested interests, or by lethargy in the government or civil service.

What I propose is new in principle, because at present the real purpose of the judiciary is broadly to preserve the status quo, the existing order or Establishment. In the system proposed, some judges would have the new function of assisting the steady, driving force of progress toward a higher form of living, which is now vital. We can no longer stand still. Life moves up or down: it always moves-now more than ever, and faster than ever.

I am always much concerned by the possibility of new Ideas being suppressed by all the lethargic institutions of the established system. We all know of inventions being bought up and suppressed. It is difficult for new men with new ideas to make themselves and their proposals known in present society. Yet it is quite essential that they should be heard, and their ideas tested.

Question 150. How will your system promote new ideas in practice?

Answer: I suggest the system which was first proposed in my book, *The Alternative*. In special courts, Proposers should advocate such ideas, Critics should submit them to a ruthless examination and an Assessor should sum up and make report on them for the action of government through the appropriate instrument of state. The Assessor would be one of the new judges, and he would have the power to publish his report if the government took no action. The system will work in the same way as the proposed method of exposing corruption. If the government were revealed to the electorate as lethargic and incompetent, inadequate to the modern age, it would be defeated at the next election. This method would keep the government up to the mark, and the country in the forefront. A new age of science impels new thinking, and the emergence of some new system.

Question 151. Do you accept the U.N. Charter of Human Rights?

Answer: Yes: in so far as these principles apply to the maintenance of human liberty, we should make freedom inviolable. Anyone who reads the principles set out in this book will see the importance we attach to the subject. The synthesis of national action and of individual liberty is the most important social problem of this period. In regard to some wider questions raised by the United Nations Organisation, I have something to say in other answers concerning the abuses to which it can be put.

Question 152. Do you advocate an occupational franchise?

Answer: I think it is the best method, but it is not essential to our system. So long as government has sufficient power of action in its defined sphere to carry out the mandate of the electors during its period of office, the essential is there. Government elected by the people will be able to do what the people want done, and they can sack it by their votes at the next election if it does not do the job to their satisfaction.

But as parliament still plays a very important part in our system, it is preferable that it should be elected in a modern instead of an obsolete way. I mean by this that in early days of the geographical franchise, when the main industry was agriculture, men exercised the very limited franchise of those days in the area where they both lived and worked. Residential and industrial interests were really identical. But now a man's occupation may be completely separated from his residence. Certainly his interests in these two spheres are no longer identical, and most men and women are more interested in their occupation than in the region where they happen to live.

In their occupation they are well informed concerning its problems and the people engaged in it. They are more likely to select the best people to represent them.

Further, the resulting parliament will be a serious one, more likely to approach problems in the spirit of the search for truth, rather than in the frivolous mood of party warfare. That is why I prefer an occupational franchise, but it is not essential to the success of our system. People may prefer not immediately to change so many of the traditional methods.

Question 153. Is power really necessary-as much power in government as you suggest?

Answer: It is too late to ask whether power is really necessary. The time to ask that question was before society became so complex. There was a strong argument against ever developing modern civilisation. But once this has happened, it is idiotic to deny the means to run it. There was much to be said for walking instead of using modern machines. But once you are in the bus which at present is running fast down-hill, it is just plain silly not to allow anyone to touch the brakes, steering-wheel or, when necessary, the accelerator. Those who desire these inhibitions are really in a condition of psychological trauma, induced by some unfortunate experiences, and also by a very acute propaganda from some powerful people who have a vested interest in the crash of the bus; "Bears" in more senses than one.

Modern society is much too complicated to run itself. Some men, somewhere and under some conditions, must have the power to run it. The real problem is to give the men chosen by the people for this task the means to do it, without giving them the means to abuse power. I believe a proper balance in this matter can be secured by combining a strong executive with the general control of the people's vote, the power of censure in parliament and the particular check of judicial enquiry and public report, which I have described. But no doubt more perfect methods could ultimately be evolved, when many good minds have been applied to the subject over a considerable period of time.

The trouble at present is that the problem of power is met with the negation of fear rather than with the positive of constructive thought. In fact, there has been little real thought on the subject since the days of Plato. He was concerned with the problem of making men fit for power, because he recognized the necessity for its use. And if the use of power was necessary in that simple society, how much more necessary is it today. But as our technical civilization has developed far more rapidly than man's moral nature, it remains more than ever true that none of us is completely fit for power. Yet the use of power by some men, somehow and under some conditions, is an absolute necessity. That is a problem; it will be settled not by the excited chatter of fear and inhibition but by clear thinking.

The best solution we can offer at present is to give men chosen by the people the power to act, but to give the people full information at all times about what is being done by means of expert and impartial enquiry, which will enable any men who abuse power to be quickly dismissed by the free vote of the people. If you can think of anything better, let us hear it. But do not just sit still in the runaway bus until it has gone over the precipice. It is not your children who will collect the insurance money, or any other benefit of the disaster. You need power exercised under conditions of a free society to defeat the power which seeks to destroy you under the conditions of a slave society. If you persist in refusing reasonable power with adequate safeguards to humane men in a civilised system, you will certainly end under the tyranny of communism, because the system will fail and the people will prefer even communism to economic collapse and anarchy.

You need power also in the hands of the people's government to prevent the exercise of money-power by men who are elected by none and responsible to none. For government by money power, in the absence of any effective power in elected government, at length produces the chaos which also ends in communism.

Question 154. Have you not, on the subject of power, written of three forms of will, in describing the psychology of power?

Answer: Yes. The first is the will to comfort. This is very frequently found among present statesmen. Such a man just wants to get there, stay there and keep things as they are. That is comfort for him, both physically and psychologically. His nightmare is change, because that necessity of the age requires an effort of mind and will from which he shrinks and for which his method of life soon renders him incapable.

The second is the will to power type, in the Adlerian rather than in the more complex Nietzschean sense. He is the man who wants power for power's sake without further objective. In the final analysis, the man who wants the trouble of power without achievement is surely just mentally defective. The simple reduction to absurdity of this type is a comparison of such crude ideals with the conduct of a keeper in a cage who continually cracks a whip to make monkeys go round in a circle without aim or end. The will to power for its own sake is just mad. No sane man can conceive a more tedious or repulsive occupation.

The third type is as rational as the first, but far more admirable. He is the will to achievement type, the man only interested in power as a means to an end. Only the end interests him, not the power necessary to its attainment, which is merely a necessary nuisance. Plato illustrated this attitude in his description of the philosopher king who disliked power, while recognising the necessity for its use.

The will to achievement man only uses his power as an artist employs brush and palette to paint a picture. It is the work, not the instruments, which interests him, though he must understand the instruments and will the means as well as the end. My own case I can express in much simpler terms. When I look at the present state of the nation I feel like a mechanic who sees a good machine lying broken on the side of the road because it requires a few obvious and quite simple repairs. I just want to have a go at putting it right.

Question 155. Are you loyal to the Crown? What would be the position of the Crown within the European system you suggest?

Answer: Yes, we are entirely loyal to the Crown. The position of the Crown within the European system we suggest would be unchanged. Each country making up the European union would naturally retain any such national institutions as it desired. Some would continue to have kings or queens, some presidents. The only difficulty that could arise would be in the cases where kings or presidents had executive functions to perform, and this does not arise in the case of the British Crown. Nor, so far as I am aware, does it do so in the case of other European royalty.

The Queen is a constitutional monarch who acts in affairs of state solely on the advice of her ministers. Such action at present is undertaken on the advice of British ministers. In the new system it would be on the advice of European ministers. The most that could happen would be a change of technical formalities. All other functions of the Crown today would be entirely unaffected.

It is in every way desirable that the great national institutions should be preserved within European union, provided of course, that they do not impair the structure of the new state of Europe and the effective action of its government. Within Europe the British Crown might in due course perform a greater rather than a lesser part.

The Leadership Principle

Question 156. Why is your party called Union Movement?

Answer: Because union is strength. The union of the British people is the first necessity, to end the present drift to disaster and to take the great decision to join Europe. The union of the European people is the second necessity, to end the divisions which can destroy us, and to make Europe a Nation. These are the two basic ideas: the union of Britain and the union of Europe. You cannot get the great decision necessary to great action until you unite the people. But within this political union we need, too, the union of generations and the union of classes. Union is strength for all great purposes. We need the strength of union for the decisive purposes of this great age, and we shall get it when the people see the necessity for a supreme effort. The strength of union can move mountains. That is why we aim at union. First must come the union of the spirit. It is for this we now strive. First always comes the Idea.

Question 157. What does your symbol, the Flash and Circle, mean?

Answer: It means the flash of action within the circle of union. We can only have action if we have union. Only a united nation can do the things the people want done, and the things which it will soon be vitally necessary to do. Union alone can save the nation in present dangers. We need action, and can only get it within union.

Question 158. What is the need for Union Movement?

Answer: The answer to nearly every question in this book shows the need for Union Movement. Can you imagine any of the old parties carrying out this complete alternative policy? Surely, if you agree with the policy, or with most of it, you must also agree that a new movement is necessary to put it through.

But that is by no means all. Far more important even than the practical results, is the Idea of Union Movement. Are you satisfied with the moral situation in Britain today? Do you agree that an awakening of the spirit is the first necessity of this age?– that spirit which took our people out of this little island in the northern mists to become a world leader in high achievement. More than ever is that spirit-which was born of England-needed in this age of great decisions. It is a spirit of heroism, yes, but of construction, not destruction. I described it some time ago in words I believe to be true:- "We need heroism not just for war, which is a mere stupidity, but heroism to sustain us through man's sublime attempt to wrestle with nature and to strive with destiny. To this high purpose we summon from the void of present circumstance the vast spirit of man's heroism. For this shall be the epic generation whose struggle and whose sacrifice shall decide whether man again shall know the dust or whether man at last shall grasp the stars."There is need for Union Movement.

Question 159. Why do you think Union Movement is bound to win?

Answer: Because our analysis is true, and is now being proved true; because our policy alone meets the consequent situation; because our character has been tested in our long effort, and the nation will soon require proved character which can be trusted in a serious situation; because our movement and our companions throughout the continent alone have the spirit to bring a European revival, and the faith which can move the mountains between us and the greater future.

Question 160. Do you believe in the leadership principle in the sense of team leadership?

Answer: Yes. All parties accept the principles of leadership in the sense that some person is always the leader. That is true of the Conservative, Labour, and Liberal parties in this country. But we have more of the team spirit. In all things we work and organise as a team, and a leader is necessary to the effective working of any team. We believe that the leadership principle is always necessary to get anything done. When the people want something done they want leadership, because they know that it is the only way to get what they want. The method of individual responsibility is the only basis of effective action. It always operates in all serious things. For instance, you run ships, airplanes and armies on the leadership principle. If you don't you are all soon dead. That is why the people in serious times turn to the leadership principle. Then they want men with character to take decisions and to act. They want men to do things they know have to be done.

Question 161. How would the leadership principle operate in the government of the country?

Answer: In our system of government the leadership principle would be confined to giving individuals a job to do and holding them personally responsible for it, rather than handing over the task to a talkative committee in which everyone "passed the buck" and dodged personal responsibility. "Give a man a job to do, give him the means to do it, and sack him if he does not do it"- is our principle of government. And that goes for the government itself. The people as a whole will give the government a job to do by their votes, give it the power to do the job, and sack it by their votes if it fails to do the job they want done.

The principle of individual responsibility has often been used in human affairs when it becomes really necessary to get things done. It is no more open to abuse than the committee system; in fact less so, because responsibility is clear if any thing goes wrong

Question 162. How does the leadership principle work our in Union Movement?

Answer: Our Movement, at every point, works like a team. The leader embodies the collective will of the team. He may be able to express their feeling a little more clearly, he may be able to see things a bit quicker than most, and he must have the courage of decision. But he has the job because he best represents what the team feels. And our team system does not require only one leader. The principle goes right through the Movement, and produces some natural leader in every activity we undertake. The result is to run things by means of individual responsibility and not by committee.

At the beginning of such a development, a man declares a policy and forms a movement. He raises a political standard which others can follow if they believe in the principles and in him. If they cease to believe in the principles or in him, they can leave any day they like and form a party of their own if they wish. It is a free country, and we are a free movement. No-one need join our movement unless he wishes, and we certainly have neither the power nor the desire to detain him if he wants to leave. But while they are members, our people are expected to follow the rules of the Movement just as they would follow the rules of any other club or institution to which they belonged. And our rule is the leadership principle, and not the committee method. This principle cannot be abused because it is entirely voluntary. In our movement no leader can become any sort of dictator.

Question 163. Does the leadership principle operate throughout the Movement, and, if so, what say have members in its policy and conduct?

Answer: Yes, it goes right through the Movement. As you will see in answers on our organisation, our members form teams and the team leader leads, or when they work as individual political workers in a ward, the ward leader then leads. This is the system of action which the people will want to replace the system of chatter directly they need something done. But that does not mean members have no voice in the shaping of policy, or power of criticism and suggestion. They have a far more effective part in these matters than in the old parties. Our consultation of members is more frequent and contact with members more complete than in the old parties. In our frequent conferences all are asked to speak out and take their part in forming the policy and strategy of the Movement, and they certainly do. But we have the spirit of a great team, not of a mob. We are not allowed by law to organise as an army, and we do not in any way so organise. But we have the spirit of a dedicated army, each one of us dedicated to a great cause.

Question 164. What is the difference between the method of running your Party, and the method you suggest for running the country?

Answer:. There is a very clear difference. The system we propose for running the country will make the life of the government completely dependent on the vote of the people. As stated already, elections will be held at regular intervals, and all parties will be free to enter them. This is a democratic system which is absolutely necessary to make sure that freedom is preserved. Everything is settled by vote.

The position inside a party is quite different, because any man or woman can leave the party any day they like. This preserves the freedom of the individual in relation to the party. It is therefore possible within a party to apply a higher degree of the leadership principle than is possible within the country as a whole. As liberty is clearly preserved, it is possible to use the most effective method for running the Movement which works under great difficulties. After all, any party or institution has the right to make its own rules within a free country, provided the rules do not conflict with the laws of the country. If you deny that right, you deny freedom. It is thus right and proper that a party or movement dedicated to a cause should be able to contain more of the leadership principle than is right within the community as a whole.

Question 165. Can you summarise the differences between the leadership principle and dictatorship?

Answer: There is all the difference in the world. The leadership principle is the voluntary acceptance of guidance you desire. Dictatorship implies compulsion to do something you do not want to do. For instance, I accept the leadership principle from someone else every time I ask a policeman the way and he tells me. He knows something I do not know, and I am very glad to accept his guidance. Every time my car breaks down I accept the leadership principle when I ask someone's help, because I am a complete mug about motors. I like to persuade myself that this is due not to natural stupidity, but to the fact that I have never given my mind to the subject. In any case, I have to face the fact that I know nothing about cars. So when I am in trouble, I ask for guidance and help from the first kind man that passes, or the next garage mechanic I can find. I am completely dependent on them.

These are simple examples of the leadership principle. In daily life I am often grateful for the help of people who can do something better than I can, or who are more experienced in some matters. And I do not stay awake all night because I am not so good at these things as they are. Nor do I develop an inferiority complex and want to murder them, because they can do the job and I can't. I have not yet even been talked into being a mental case on this account by some of the modern politicians and psychologists-I go on accepting the leadership principle from anyone who can do the job better than I can. But I console myself with the thought that there are some things I may be able to do better than he can, and I can hope to repay his kindness one day by doing for him something he cannot do. Getting someone to run the government for you, if you think him good at the job, is really just the same thing. And, of course, it means in practice getting a team of men to run the government. You are then accepting the leadership principle. This is really all there is to it once we can see through current nonsense to the clear reality beyond.

Question 166. Supposing someone tries to turn the leadership principle into dictatorship-how can the people prevent this?

Answer: There is a very simple remedy against dictatorship in any advanced country. Just stay away from work. If enough people do it, the country comes to a standstill and the government must fall. In other words, no government can carry on if the people really do not want it.

Technically, of course, any majority in parliament can now pass an Act to prolong its life indefinitely, and then remain in power for good. During time of war it has been done for a number of years. Or anyone backed by a few troops with modern weapons can seize the seat of power. But it is no good sitting in the seat of power if nothing works. Just stay away from work, and you can stop any nonsense of that kind in any modern country.

In a backward country it is another matter. Any brigand with a gun can rule a desert, particularly if no-one else wants it; or if you begin where people are used to an inefficient tyranny, as the communists began in Russia, the people continue in the habit of accepting a more up-to-date tyranny. But dictatorship cannot work in modern countries which have known freedom. No form of government can last without support of the people.

The method here described to get rid of a dictatorship which was governing against the will of the people-a government which had usurped power by force - would be altogether wrong if used against a government elected by the vote of the people. A government elected by the people should be obeyed by all, whether they agree with it or not, and any attempt to overthrow it by force or strike is utterly wrong. In such case the remedy of opponents is to persuade the people to vote against it.

Hitler and Mussolini

Question 167. Wasn't Hitler a dictator?

Answer: In the sense that he had almost absolute power, yes. In the sense that he ruled against the will of the majority of the people, no. The evidence on the latter point seems quite conclusive. At one time it was said German votes were faked. But then came the vote in the Saar in 1935 with the secrecy of the ballot protected by British troops. The issue was whether the Saar joined with Hitler Germany or not, and the Germans in that population knew very well what their brothers, sisters and cousins across the border were feeling and thinking. The German population in the Saar gave Hitler 90.8% of the votes recorded, which is very much the same proportion of votes that he was getting at that time in Germany. That result blew out of the water the story that German votes were faked.

Then again, how could one people fight the whole world in arms for six years if they really detested their government and wanted to be through with it? The Germans had only to slack their war effort for a weekend to be rid of their government, and were exhorted over every Allied radio to do so. But they kept up their struggle and their support of the government for six years in conditions of terrible hardship until they went down in complete defeat. It is true that like other peoples they often had not the faintest idea of many of the things being done in their name, but their peace time votes and war time loyalty showed that they supported Hitler's main policy which until the war disaster brought them great benefits. The story that Hitler was a dictator in the sense of compelling the people to support him against their will is absurd. Yet a lot of now middle-aged people were - brought up on it, and still swallow the silly tale.

Question 168. Did you meet Hitler?

Answer: I met him twice in my life, in April, 1935, and October, 1936, about three years before the war began. My object was to do then what everyone is trying to do now. I wanted to get a summit conference to prevent war. That is just what Eisenhower, Macmillan, Gaitskell, Kennedy and the rest have been trying to do lately. It is now supposed to be very praiseworthy. After we declared war it was subsequently supposed to have been very blameworthy. Lloyd George and others tried too, though in his old age he was less active in political opposition to war. Personally, I think it is always right to try and prevent war. I should always try, no matter who is on the other side.

Although I had no official position, I had had experience of government and understood the German viewpoint better than most Englishmen. It therefore seemed right to find out what the Germans wanted, and to try to bring the two sides together. After this meeting I published my views of the situation and did what I could to secure peace. It did not work, because very powerful interests wanted war. But it is still my opinion that we could have kept the peace with Germany without loss to Britain, indeed with great advantage to Britain as well as to the world.

Question 169. What did you discuss with Hitler at these two meetings?

Answer: How to keep the peace. In short, the outcome was this: he maintained that he wanted nothing from British Empire. In fact, he thought British Empire was a great influence for good in the world. In the event of trouble any where, he said he would always be on our side. Equally, he had no claims on France or any other country in the West. His reason for this attitude was that the western countries were all over-crowded, and he wanted adequate living space for Germany to develop in eastern Europe. He did not want to mix with other peoples. He wanted to bring all the German peoples together with room enough to develop their own civilisation.

He was, of course, strongly anti-communist and he thought a clash between Germany and Soviet Russia was, sooner or later, inevitable. In that event he wanted a friendly Britain which would keep the peace in the west. He naturally wanted to avoid his rear being attacked while he was fighting Russia. He said it was in the interests of British Empire as much as in the interests of Germany that communism should be defeated if a clash came. He saw no reason for a quarrel between Britain and Germany, whose interests were different. He did not use the illustration, but in effect saw Britain and Germany as a whale and an elephant, one paramount on the sea and the other on land. He thought the friendship of two such powers could maintain the final peace and stability of the world. Such were the views he expressed to me.

Question 170. What was your attitude to Hitler's proposals?

Answer: I replied that in my opinion Britain should certainly not intervene in a war between Germany and Russia. If I were responsible for British government I would not lose British lives in any war which did not directly affect the life of Britain. But I would certainly use any influence I possessed to persuade the British people to live in peace and friendship with Germany. It was no interest of Britain to save communism, which everywhere threatened the life of the British Empire. Friendship between Britain and Germany could ultimately maintain the peace of the western world, and this could be of the greatest benefit to mankind. With these views he appeared well satisfied, and it seemed to me quite possible to reach agreement with him.

In short, a clash between Germany and Russia appeared inevitable. It seemed to me best for Britain to keep out of it and to use her unimpaired influence at the first opportunity to secure a saner and safer economic and political arrangement in Europe.

I was fundamentally opposed to the sacrifice of British lives in quarrels which were nothing to do with Britain; and in this view I was in line with the main tradition of British statesmanship, which had always resisted emotional appeals to fight wars anywhere that anyone was having a bad time. I was on yet stronger ground in opposing a war to save communism and make it a world menace; for that was the practical effect of the war.

Question 171. Did you think it possible to reach agreement with Hitler?

Answer: I thought it was possible to reach agreement with Hitler for the fundamental reason that he wanted something different from us. The man you quarrel with is the man who wants the same thing as you do, not the man who wants something different. We wanted a worldwide empire maintained by sea and air power. He wanted German living space in the relatively empty region of eastern Europe maintained by their land power. The last thing Hitler wanted was a worldwide empire consisting of many races, for reasons he spent his whole political life in explaining. He wanted to bring all the German peoples together into one solid Volk with living space in Europe.

It seems to me clear from the whole history of Hitler and the Nazi party that this was his opinion. He thought that any mixing with very different peoples would be the ruin of the Germans. That is why he wanted us British-and not the Germans-to run overseas possessions like those of the British Empire. He thought it had to be done in the interests of world peace and order, but he would rather we did it. As he wanted something different we really had nothing to fight about. What we fought for was not a British interest.

Question 172. Supposing Hitler had double-crossed us by turning round and attacking us after he had defeated the Russians?

Answer: I do not think this would have happened for reasons I have given. But in this world you must always be ready for a surprise and double-cross. We have to take all possible precautions when the life of our country is at stake. We have always to be ready for anything. We must always be armed when others are armed.

That is why I agitated for national re-armament throughout the pre-war period, even before Churchill began his campaign for it. So if Hitler had double-crossed us, we should have been rearmed and ready for it under my policy. This was the exact opposite of the policy of the Labour Party, which refused to give us proper defences while they were agitating for war.

Question 173. Can you give details of your campaign for the armament of Britain before the war?

Answer: I have always stood for the armament of Britain against any attack, no matter from what quarter it might come. For instance, I wrote in 1932: "We will immediately raise the air strength of Britain to the level of the strongest power in Europe" *(The Greater Britain)*. In 1934 I demanded a national loan: "To give Britain immediate air strength. To modernise and mechanise our Army. To put the Fleet in proper condition to defend our trade routes."

In my book *Tomorrow We Live*, I wrote: "That Britain should be fully armed in a troubled world, to defend herself from any possible assault, has been a basic principle of British Union long before the National Government, which had criminally neglected our defences, consented to tardy and inefficient re-armament." In the same year I denounced the failure of the Tory Party to provide proper armament in the following terms: "The state of these defences is a national scandal and disgrace. The Tory Party is, therefore, right to be alarmed; and, having been in power for the last seven years, they should also be ashamed" (15/10/38). "The policy of British Union is to make peace with Germany, but not to accept a position in the air, or in any other sphere, inferior to her or any other country in the world" *(Action, 21/5/38)*. These are just a few of the quotations which prove my position.

Some members of the Labour Party suggested I desired the defeat of my country. Is this the record of such a man? Compare it with their record. What cheap nonsense from what cheap little men the wartime attack on me was.

Question 174. What precautions would you have taken if Hitler had defeated Russia without us interfering?

Answer: In practice, if Hitler had defeated the Soviets and expanded in eastern Europe, it would have taken him at least a generation to develop the results. It would have given us plenty of time. But I like always to act as if time is short, I should, therefore, have asked the other western powers, France, America, etc., to be ready armed to join with us in defending the West in case Hitler had attacked us. They would, undoubtedly, have been moved to this precaution if Hitler's European power had increased substantially as a result of the defeat of Russia.

But even if they had not so joined us, we could have maintained our position in the face of any continental power with the arms of that period. We did so in face of Napoleon's continental system, and we could have done so again in face of Hitler's, if the necessity had ever arisen. After all, he could not get across the Channel when the years of betrayal by successive British governments had virtually disarmed us. He would not have had a chance if we had been properly armed as I proposed. We were still paramount on the sea, and had a greater natural aptitude for air design and combat than any other people. It was miserable defeatism to suggest that Britain could not have defended itself. And it is always hysterical folly to want a war today because you are afraid of a war tomorrow, particularly when you have the time and means calmly to prepare for it to a point which would ensure success if it be forced upon you.

I do not believe Hitler would have attacked us, for reasons I have given. But I should have been prepared for a double-cross, while doing my utmost to establish a firm friendship with Germany. That is why I always so strongly advocated re-armament before the war. My policy was strength and peace; my opponents' policy was weakness and war.

Question 175. What do you think of Hitler?

Answer: It is often said that all contemporary judgment on such men is faulty, and that the real verdict must be left history. This is true to some extent of all controversial figures whose deeds have much affected their generation. But I do not think it is too difficult to discuss either the qualities of mind and will which led to his achievements, or the faults of character which caused his downfall and the destruction of his system.

His outstanding quality was will. He banished the hopeless mood of Germany after the first World War, he broke the chains of his people, restored their self-respect, confidence and hope in the future, and, in the material sphere, solved the unemployment problem and restored their economy. All this was done in an unnaturally confined space under conditions of extraordinary difficulty. It is not surprising at this point of great achievement that the Germans were grateful to him for his outstanding will and energy.

The basic reason for his downfall and the disaster to all his work was that he understood no kind of practical or moral limitations to the will. In the practical sphere he drove his own instinctive view of things to the point where he divided his friends and united his enemies; the exact opposite of the profound process of real policy in the hands of a true master. Such a phrase as "my patience is at an end" is a simple illustration of this point. Loss of patience should be an emotion as unknown to a man of action in politics or war as it is to an athlete in any contest which rests on judgment, nerve, endurance, will. You move when you see an opening to advance your purpose, not when your emotion indicates; emotions in great affairs are luxuries which such lives cannot afford. The contrast between the character of Hitler and that of Bismarck in this relation may provide some key to their respective results.

But it is in the moral sphere that we find the reason for Hitler's final disaster. He knew no moral limitation of the will. He suffered in extreme degree from what the classic Greeks called hubris; the belief that man can usurp the place of the gods in complete determination of his own fate. The supreme exponents of the art of action have known better. Julius Caesar exerted the utmost qualities of will and energy to a point where it could truly be said that everything possible had been done; but he then never for a moment lost the sense that after the ultimate effort of man the outcome must rest with the power which some call God, and others fate, or destiny. It was this restraining sense of the final realism which gave him his calm, sad resolution to achieve by the complete dedication and expenditure of himself everything humanly possible-more in the sphere of action than any other man has ever achieved-without a trace of self-deception and hysteria which some outstanding men in face of great events find as necessary as small men find alcohol in the minor excitements of every-day life. His great opponent, Cato, summarised the verdict of history on this extraordinary character with the succinct judgment: "Only one man came sober to the overthrow of the State, but on that occasion the State was overthrown."

In lesser degree the same quality is discernible in Napoleon's admirably balanced sense of destiny and realism, in Bismarck's subtle but massive purpose which secured the widest measure of union yet achieved during so short a period within the modern world; in the "cold, sad eyes" of Marlborough which moved Macaulay to such contradictory emotions in his portrait of the English genius who won so much with so little support. They all possessed will in extreme degree, but they none of them drove it too far, except Bonaparte during his one moment of fatality in Russia.

All these men, in their very different ways, and by the diverse standards of their various epochs, were, in the modern terminology, very tough. But it is impossible to conceive any of them in the modern age ordering or allowing what occurred during the war in the German concentration camps, even if only a fraction of the record be true. This inhibition may be ascribed to moral sense or merely to their realism, the sense of what is possible. But without a doubt it would have existed in all these supreme men of action.

Caesar in his vile treatment of Vercingetorix, who was perhaps the only man who managed really to annoy him, might for once forget a magnanimity which in general almost anticipated the Christian era. Bonaparte in a moment of almost petulant passion might shoot the Duc d'Enghien. These were grave errors, and were blots on their names, but you cannot conceive either of them being guilty of the twentieth century concentration camps. Such a thing might be inconceivable to the moral nature of the former, while the latter might merely sense it would not work; whatever the motive, it is certain that they could not have done it.

Hitler in the final period had no sense of moral law or of the limitations of the will. He tried to inflict on a whole people a cataclysm of nature; he usurped a higher function than that of man. Everything can be taken into account without excuse for this deed; the agony of defeat, his fixed belief that the Jews were responsible for the war, the fact that Germans were dying and starving and that Jews suspected of relentless enmity to the state had to be guarded and fed. None of these terrible things justify a breach of the supreme moral law which is reflected in the simple instinct of brave men, that you cannot kill helpless prisoners in your power who, as individuals, have committed no crime. Morality and the nature of manhood combine to forbid it.

The motive for such crime may be remote from the crude concept of current propaganda. But whether it be hubris, or in simpler modern language, a monstrous vanity, it is deeply wrong.

The same quality emerged at the end of the war in the sacrifice of young German lives when it was clear the war was lost. These children running out to meet a stream of irresistible fire erected an enduring monument to German heroism but not to the leadership which ordered or permitted it. This had neither immediate nor ultimate purpose. It was surely vanity again: the world ends with one man's will; "apres moi le deluge". The part of a true immortal was at that moment rather to prepare the future. Hitler's duty then was to lose himself but to save his idea. The only thing that then should have mattered to him was to preserve and to transmit whatever truth he possessed for the judgment of posterity. He should in his moral terms have committed suicide long before, directly it was clear the war was irretrievably lost; again, vanity, fantasy, the belief in miracles which accompanies this character in disaster as it did Wallenstein in Schiller's great drama, inhibited that calm, objective realism which never deserts the supreme man. As it was he prolonged his own life for a few weeks as a last exhibition of ineffective will, but tarnished his idea and jeopardised the future by the wanton deed of the concentration camps and the useless sacrifice of German youth. If he had gone a little sooner, leaving his idea and his fame inviolate, he might have been among those who in the German proverb must succumb in life in order to achieve an immortality in the minds and hearts of men.

It may indeed be preferable for the individual both to conceive and to achieve like Chatham in British Empire and Bismarck in the German Reich. But even in the sphere of action it must be conceded that noble failure on a colossal scale can sometimes lead to the greatest results. Caesar in the moment of his assassination left behind him a concept, a shape of Europe, and also the Caesarean attitude to life; it would be difficult to discover anything which in practical affairs has more influenced the world. But Hitler and all his work passed, despite his extraordinary qualities and achievements, because he did not understand any moral limitation to the will. Inscrutable is the working of nature and of destiny which so often in disaster prepares the way for a higher idea; a concept not beyond understanding in the very German terms of the contrasted characters of Siegfried and Parsifal in Wagner's music drama, which unites high art with profound reflection on the fate of men.

Question 176. What did you think of Mussolini?

Answer: I knew him better than I did Hitler as I saw him several times between 1932 and 1936. The last time was about three years before the war. After that I became so busy in England that

I could hardly travel at all. Mussolini's notable characteristics were the speed, range and penetration of his intelligence. He had the quickest and clearest mind of any statesman I have met except, possibly, Lloyd George. They were very similar in their capacity to go directly to the heart of a subject. He had depth rather than width of erudition, as he had concentrated strongly on the subjects which interested and concerned him. His early training as a schoolmaster, however, gave him a considerable knowledge, including a command of languages. He spoke French excellently. We used that language until, unfortunately, one day at the beginning of our interview he proudly announced he had learnt English. After that I scarcely understood a word he said.

No-one who knew him could deny his charm or his sense of humour. His fun was as straightforward as his manner; he was certainly gay. In private, after the first encounter he was entirely devoid of pose, a direct and natural being. The posture was reserved for public occasions. He must have thought it went well with his people, and the receptions accorded him certainly indicated he was right.

He was ruined by a world war he did not desire, because he was not a man who would risk much for small gain. His actual entry into the war, I believe, was a miscalculation inspired by the narrow concept of national interests prevalent in those days. He left behind him something of his work for Italy, which ranged from such practical tasks as the reclaiming of the Pontine Marshes into prosperous farm lands to a certain resistance to decadence which still endures among the elite of that nation. In the larger sphere his concept of corporate action has influenced, and will influence, the thinking of the world. Some of these ideas are in no way incompatible with a democratic system.

The roughness of the young fascists to their red opponents (the castor oil, etc.) can only be excused at all by the incredible savagery and brutality of the reds, which were proved among other things by an exhibition held in Rome in 1932. When they found the dead bodies of comrades who had been killed by having their heads held in furnaces, etc., some of them lost their tempers when they next met the party of the assassins. We now live in a world where everything is permitted to communists of any race, and nothing - not even one per cent, of such deeds - to their opponents. History will one day correct some of these remarkable errors; unless their consequences prevent any truthful history ever being written, owing to the victory of communism.

Attack and Counter-Attack

The Last War

Question 177. Why did you oppose the war when it came?

Answer: For three reasons, all of which were published at the time and have since been proved right:

(1) That the war would lead to the loss of a large part of British Empire.

(2) That it would make Russia the strongest power in Europe, and would create a world danger of communism.

(3) That it would divide and weaken Europe in fratricidal strife, with the result that world influence would pass from the European continent to the outside powers of Russia and America. Who can deny these things have happened?

Question 178. But is not a man a traitor who opposes a war in which his country is engaged?

Answer: All British history makes plain nonsense of this suggestion. If it were correct Lord Chatham must have been a traitor. He opposed the war with America. Yet it is an odd thing to call a traitor the man to whom we owe the British Empire. For this elder Pitt, judged by his constructive achievement for Britain, was by far the greatest statesman in British history. We should also have to call Charles James Fox a traitor. For the founder of the Liberal Party opposed the war with Napoleon. And during the brief Peace of Amiens all the Whig opposition went to Paris to see Napoleon and try to arrange a permanent peace. Lloyd George also was called a traitor in his early life, for opposing the Boer War.

The fact is we have a tradition in Britain for statesmen to have not only the right of free speech to say what they think, but also a duty to say it fearlessly. I should have failed in my duty if I had kept silent when I thought the war would lead to disaster for Britain. That would have been a cowardly and unworthy thing to do. For this war could only lead to disaster. To lose the war would have been complete disaster. But even winning it involved the loss of British Empire and promoted the rise of communism.

Question 179. Did not your campaign against the last war adversely affect civilian morale?

Answer: No. The people are not children, and should not be treated as if they were. They are perfectly capable of hearing the argument in favour of peace and of making up their minds for or against the policy. If they then decide to go on with a war, their morale for that purpose will be all the better if they first thoroughly consider the matter.

In fact, we stated our case for peace during the "phoney war" period at the end of 1939 and beginning of 1940, when there was no serious fighting. Remember it was our government who declared war, and we could at that time have stopped whenever we liked. Throughout we said to all our members in the forces that they should do their duty, and to all civilian members that under no circumstances should they do anything which could possibly assist an enemy of their country. Thus I issued the following message to members on 1st September, 1939: "Our country is involved in war. Therefore I ask you to do nothing to injure our country, or to help any other Power. Our members should do what the law requires of them, and if they are members of any of the Forces or Services of the Crown, they should obey their orders, and, in particular, obey the rules of their Service. We have said a hundred times that if the life of Britain were threatened we would fight again."

We also said that we would all fight as we did before if our country were attacked. On 9th May, 1940, I published the following: "In such an event [invasion] every member of British Union would be at the disposal of the Nation. Every one of us would resist the foreign invader with all that is in us. However rotten the existing Government, and however much we detested its policies, we would throw ourselves into the effort of a united nation until the foreigner was driven from our soil."

But in the lull before real hostilities occurred we asked the country to give a considered judgment against a war which we thought was unnecessary. The judgment was never given, because there was no election between 1935 and 1945, and we were arrested and imprisoned without charge or trial before the real war began.

Anyone who suggests that we had no right to ask our countrymen to consider the matter, should reflect on the result of his argument. First, a government could at any time take the country into war, not only without the people being consulted at a general election, but without anyone being permitted to express a contrary opinion. All this when the government had been elected years before on quite different issues; in fact, on Mr. Baldwin's pledge - "Peace in our time." For this argument to be valid the country must be given no chance to consider the matter at all in the new circumstances which arise. Where then is freedom of speech? Where then is democracy? Where then is the people's will?

Second, if this principle had been applied throughout our history, several famous statesmen (as already noted) would have been condemned and unjustly imprisoned for opposing war. They were not so treated because alien values did not then rule in England. Your suggestion tears up both our liberty and our history, as well as the facts of our particular case.

Question 180. If you had taken a similar line about the war in Germany or Italy, would you not have suffered a fate worse than imprisonment?

Answer: Not only in Germany and Italy, but also in France and many other continental countries, a man who opposed the war would have been shot. Their system is entirely different. In effect, all are called to the colours at the outbreak of war, and a soldier who disobeys orders is shot. In my view this is better in one important respect: everyone knows where he is. It is much better than pretending that we really have democracy, free speech for all even in time of war, and then suspending Habeas Corpus and putting in jail without trial everyone who dares to use the boasted freedom, on the lying suggestion that they are a danger to the state they want to save. This procedure combines hypocrisy with falsehood. A clear and clean position of government is preferable. I am a regular soldier by original profession, and I would certainly have obeyed orders if called to the colours. But if I am told as a politician that I am free to express my opinion, I am a coward if I fail to express it just because it is unpopular.

Question 181. Did not Labour leaders oppose the first World War in 1914 and the campaign in Suez in 1956?

Answer: Yes. Mr. Douglas Jay, Economic Secretary to the Treasury in the Labour Government of 1945-50 summed up the matter when Labour was opposing war at Suez in the following words: "Don't let's forget that Chatham, Charles James Fox, Gladstone and Lloyd George all carried out full-blooded political campaigns against what they judged to be unjust wars .... " (Forward, 14/9/56).

This true statement, however, did not prevent some other Labour leaders covering me with vile abuse because I had opposed a war which I thought not only wrong but ultimately disastrous to my country; despite the fact that I had fought in the previous war in which so many of them were conscientious objectors or column dodgers.

Question 182. Is your opposition to the war a handicap to you now?

Answer: It was for a number of years. Now it is becoming an advantage to our Movement for two reasons:

(1) More and more people see it is true that the war lost us the Empire and created the power of communism.

(2) More and more people, whether they agree with us or not about the war, like men with the courage of their convictions.

The war began over twenty years ago. Plenty of people who disagreed with me then agree with me now on other issues. And they feel as I do, that we should need our heads seeing to if we allowed a twenty year old quarrel to divide us when we agree on the vital issues of today. Whether you agreed or disagreed with my opinion, you will agree that I had the right to express it. If not, what is free speech? What humbug to talk of free speech and democracy, if men may only express opinions which are popular. It is the right and duty of statesmen to express opinions on great issues, even opinions which are unpopular. Otherwise the truth of tomorrow would never be heard.

Question 183. In summary, what do you think is the right attitude for a statesman who is opposed to a war in which his country is engaged?

Answer: He should stay in his country and do his utmost to persuade his fellow countrymen to make peace. That is exactly what was done by the long list of British statesmen already mentioned. That is the true tradition of British statesmanship.

Of course, it is the most difficult position in which any man can be placed, to be opposed to a war which the majority of his countrymen support. Nothing could be more painful or difficult.

In such a situation, we must hold simply and firmly to first principles, and they are the following: A man must never do anything against his country. But it is his duty to tell his countrymen the truth as he sees it.

I summarised our attitude in My Answer (1946) as follows: "Supposing a man's old mother expresses her firm intention to go down in fighting mood to the 'local', where a number of tough characters are wont to assemble. He may, in fact, foresee a packet of trouble; and his disquietude will be in no way lessened by the fact that his old mother has seen fit to arm herself for the occasion with nothing more formidable than an umbrella and a shrill tongue. But his course of conduct is perfectly clear. He will do his utmost to dissuade her from an undertaking which he feels can bring no good to her or the family as a whole; if he fails he will not absent himself, but will accompany her. When the inevitable row begins he will do his utmost (1) to protect her, and (2) to extricate her as soon as possible with the minimum possible hurt. Any other course would be contrary to nature and every normal feeling of man . ... It matters not, in this simple analogy, whether the son's view of his mother's behaviour was in any way valid. All that matters is the acceptance of the principle that, rightly or wrongly, he may profoundly disapprove of her conduct, and yet be inhibited by every law of nature, and every normal feeling, from raising a hand against her, or doing anything except succour and protect her in her difficulty, whatever its origin. He will seek to dissuade her-Yes-but he will never seek to injure her. Such was our attitude to our country in the last war."

Question 184. Were you arrested under Regulation 18b?

Answer: Yes, under a special part of that Regulation which enabled anyone to be detained without trial or even charge as a member of a political party whose Leader had had any association with leaders of the countries with which Britain was at war. The last time I saw Hitler or Mussolini was in 1936, three years before the war. Mr. Chamberlain had associated with them at Munich two years later. I had in the course of my political life associated with-in the sense of meeting-nearly every foreign statesman of any note. For instance I associated with President Roosevelt some years before he became President, by accompanying him on a fishing trip as a guest in his boat.

As for the facts of our case, they were stated by Mr. Stokes, M.P., who became a minister in the post-war Labour government.

He said we had only been "detained because of our campaign in favour of a negotiated peace"(Hansard 10/12/40). This statement was accepted by the government. The Lord Chancellor added in the House of Lords (11/12/46): "They have never been accused of any crime; not only have they not been convicted of a crime but they have not been accused of a crime."

Question 185. Was the Habeas Corpus Act suspended?

Answer: This imprisonment without trial was made possible by a suspension of the Habeas Corpus Act which is supposed to be the cornerstone of British liberty. This safeguard of liberty was entirely suspended, and a dictatorship was established which imprisoned political opponents as easily as the negro dictators do today. The business came easily to Tories used to the suspension of the Act in colonies and Northern Ireland, and also to Labour leaders who followed Conservative policies when in office. We were imprisoned in 1940 for much the same reasons that the black dictators imprison their opponents today. Our speeches were proving too effective. As it turned out, my public meetings during the "phoney war" period, 1939-40, drew large crowds and enthusiastic support. It was subsequently admitted that the government feared I would persuade the people to make peace. So Habeas Corpus Act was suspended in order to suppress the freedom for which the government pretended to be fighting.

Question 186. Who attacked you most over the war?

Answer: I was most attacked by those who never fought in a war in their lives, and some of them took darned good care never to do so. Can you beat the impudence of this? For some Labour leaders refused to fight in the first World War; on the other hand I was flying over our lines within a month of my eighteenth birthday as one of the first sixty airmen who ever flew in combat against the Germans, and also fought them in the trenches with my regiment. During the second World War some of the present Labour leaders just rang up Whitehall and got soft seats in office chairs, although they were well within military age. Of course many members of the Labour Party fought honourably and bravely, but some who did nothing of the kind were those who attacked me most viciously.

Should an ex-serviceman of one war be thus treated for saying that the next one is a mistake? And thus abused by whom? By some of the men who were conscientious objectors when young enough to fight, but who agitated to send younger men to die in their political quarrels when they were too old to fight.

I said before the war: "All wars are good to some Labour leaders, provided three conditions are fulfilled: 1. That the war serves the interests of Soviet Russia and not the interests of Great Britain. 2. That British troops have no arms with which to fight. 3. That the Labour leaders are not included among the troops."

I leave this subject by repeating that I am proud to have suffered these things for warning my countrymen of the now proved truth-that this war would lead to the loss of British Empire and the rise of Soviet Russia.

Unpopularity in Wartime

Question 187. Do you think that any man of character, who stands for real principles, is bound to be unpopular at some time in his career?

Answer: Yes. It is almost invariably the case. In fact, one of the lessons of British history is that any great popularity of an individual is usually comparable to his previous unpopularity. The British seem to test the men they ultimately trust by the rough times they give them previously. Look at Lloyd George's unpopularity in the Boer War. And Churchill was for years far and away the most unpopular man in British public life, particularly among the Tories who have now made him the tribal deity in his old age.

Question 188. Did some of your pre-war supporters disagree with you about the war, and cease to support you?

Answer: Some did, as, of course, they were quite entitled to do. But most of them now agree with me on present issues, and consequently again support me if they are in a position to be active in politics. It would be very foolish not to work together now because we disagreed about something which happened over twenty years ago.

Question 189. Did anyone who agreed with your stand about the war cease to support you afterwards, because they thought your war stand had made you unpopular?

Answer: Very few. I was fortunate in my friends. Those who agreed with my stand about the war did not desert me because I incurred unpopularity in doing what they thought right. Our people are not the type who say: "Things are getting tough. The enemy is trying to shoot the general. So let us desert at once. Then anyone can slip by in safety who is too small for the enemy to notice." Armies with that morale do not get far. We were much better without the handful like that, and their places were soon taken many times over by new and abler men of firmer character.

Question 190. What are the general principles which in your view should govern relationships between Leader and Party in periods of stress and unpopularity?

Answer: As I said, this issue does not affect me, because I have been exceptionally fortunate in my friends. But the principles involved are clear, and they provide a lesson for the future when I and this generation are gone.

When a man takes the lead in doing something you agree with, it is clearly ignoble and absurd to desert him because he is attacked on that account. It means a party should always desert a leader it believes to be right, directly he is attacked by their enemies because he gives a strong lead. That puts a premium on cowardice in leadership. It would mean that only the hedgers and trimmers could survive. People who feel like that should join the old parties, where they will get the leadership they deserve.

The healthy instinct of manhood is, of course, exactly the opposite. When a leader is attacked for doing something you think right, you rally to him all the more. You reckon that any man who takes a strong stand against a corrupt system is bound to be attacked and made temporarily unpopular. The strength of the attack is the measure of his value to you. If he were not a good man for you, the enemy would not attack him. You may know the leaders you can trust by the power of the enemy's fire. They shoot at the eagle but not at the sparrow, who slips through unnoticed, a happy little fellow gaily chirruping his futility on any street corner to an audience of two kids and a cat. If you want a big change, follow the man who is attacked by the defenders of the present system - attacked by your enemies - not the man who is either praised by them or ignored because he counts for nothing. These principles will always be true, whenever a big change is needed in this world.

War Atrocities, Fascism

The Past and The New Age

Question 191. What about war atrocities, gas chambers, etc., do you condemn them?

Answer: Yes, I do. I have always condemned atrocities, whoever commits them. Some of my opponents condemn atrocities only when they dislike the politics of those who commit them; they never say a word about those committed by their friends. The Russian communists have been guilty in peacetime of at least as many atrocities as the Germans were alleged to have committed in time of war. They scarcely trouble to deny it. But the Left in this country have hardly a word to say about that. You do not hear them saying much about Red atrocities in the Spanish Civil War or black atrocities in the Congo, or the Stern Gang in Palestine, or the cold-blooded shooting of opponents by their friends in Cuba. But they have raised hell when some South African policemen fired at Sharpeville to save themselves from the same fate as nine of their comrades, who had been cut to pieces by a mob at Cato Manor a few weeks before.

The Left do not seem to care a rap about the atrocities of their friends. They do not care about the atrocities, only about the politics. A tyrant on their side can slaughter people by the million. But a police chief who has to deal with one of their organized riots may not order a baton charge. This is humbug-dishonest, lying humbug.

The final reduction of their position to squalid clarity is the red complaint - "Can't we yet forget that old story" - when reminded of the communist massacre of thousands of defenceless men, women and children in Hungary only five years ago. Yet they use everything that happened in the heat of war nearly twenty years ago, for the

172

purpose of defaming an opponent, even if he were so remote from responsibility for German concentration camps, as himself to be imprisoned, without trial in a British concentration camp.

The fact is that most countries at times have committed atrocities in various ways and in different degrees. I have fought those guilty of such things all my political life-whoever they were-and this is on public record.

The most satisfactory way to deal with these matters would be to have them all examined by a neutral tribunal. You would find some very startling changes in facts which are now believed. Let it examine Soviet atrocities in peace as well as in war, German atrocities in the last war or at any other time, the American use of the atom bomb after the Japanese were suing for peace, the performance of some unusual forces employed by British government and plenty more that other peoples have no reason to be proud of. Then -when the full truth is known-let us shut up about the past, and bring to an end this bitter argument which is poisoning and dividing Europe. Let us resolve together to build a better and cleaner future. Let us resolve to do what we can to improve man's moral nature, including our own. Let us determine to behave in moments of passion like honourable men, more like true and tested soldiers with discipline, dignity and restraint in triumph and disaster, and less like spiteful, hysterical, vicious animals. For this is the character necessary to all great achievement, the character of honour and of manhood.

Question 192. Have you not always believed in Anglo-German friendship? - Do you still?

Answer: Yes, more than ever. The division of the British and the German people has been a world tragedy. In union they can become one of the most beneficent influences the earth has yet seen. Their great qualities are essentially complementary. They need each other. Together they can become an irresistible force for good. That is precisely why so many of the forces of evil have long been concerned to keep them apart. Neither usury nor anarchy, neither corruption nor communism can conquer when the English and the Germans come together. Their creative and constructive potential is unlimited.

Further, if nature is allowed to take its course, it is inevitable that they should come together. The mass of the English and the mass of Germans have a similarity closer than that between most peoples in Europe. Nothing but language and a sinister, vicious propaganda divides them. They are natural friends and companions.

Possibly not all Englishmen get on quite so well with the French for example. I happen to be one of those who do. In fact, as an Englishman I feel equally in Germany or France, that I am in another home. Friendship with the one should never exclude friendship with the other. The fact is we are all of the same, closely related family of Europe. Even when we sometimes feel that we are getting on better with Cousin This than with Cousin That, it should never be forgotten that we belong to the same family. And when we fight each other it is fratricide, a brothers' war.

Question 193. Do you much prefer some of the European peoples to others?

Answer: No, I think that close experience of the European peoples soon takes us beyond all that. Within the family of Europe, we like individuals with similar feelings, beliefs and tastes to ourselves, and do not like so much others whose feelings, beliefs and tastes are very different from our own. It is impossible to generalise about a whole European people, because the individuals within each people vary so greatly. I know men in most of the great European countries whom I love like a brother. I know other men in most of those countries for whom I have a very different sentiment. Among such closely related peoples, the division of the soul eventually becomes more important than the division of the soil; we all really have the same roots, and our differences are divergences of mind and spirit. We understand this when we become Europeans, as I have done since the war.

When you reach a certain degree of understanding, there is no more question of liking Frenchmen better than Germans, or vice versa, than in England of liking Yorkshiremen better than Lancastrians, or vice versa. If you ever feel this you know very well you are being parochial, and you know, too, so many exceptions that it breaks up your rule.

To become a European you must extend your patriotism and also your understanding. Both are now necessary. It is a very natural process. Not long ago in terms of history our ancestors were hating any man in the next village, even taking the opportunity any dark night to cut his throat. It is just a matter of growing up, a process which continues all the time in the advance of humanity.

Question 194. What was Fascism? Was it right or wrong?

Answer: What was right in Fascism was the urge to act. What was wrong was action at any price. In a period of bad housing, vast unemployment, low wages, etc.-when modern science could remedy all these things-it was right to feel the drive to action. That is why we were fascists, and our view of fascism was right at the time. I do not withdraw a word of that, nor retreat an inch. All of us at that time who could both think and feel wanted action. Only the dead in mind and spirit were against it. They were responsible for keeping much of the world in misery that was quite unnecessary. It was right to want to get rid of the old Conservative, Liberal and Socialist parties who had failed and were sunk in complacency. It was right to organise movements of action. What was wrong was that some people were driven by the desire for action and by the sense of national humiliation to the point of overriding human liberty and ignoring the basic decencies of life. Even action to remedy unnecessary suffering can be too dearly bought at the expense of the things which are essential.

Fascist drive to action was in some cases too ruthless, and thus damaged the cause and rallied the opposition. We have learned from this experience that the first necessities are to preserve individual liberty and the basic decencies of life. That is why

I so much stress these things in our present policy as you can see. By these mistakes the pre-war conduct of fascism in some countries divided friends and united enemies. Wise action in life and politics divides our enemies and unites our friends.

Question 195. What are the main differences between your post-war policy and pre-war Fascism?

Answer: The basic difference is that fascism faced the facts of the pre-war world, and we face the facts of the modern world which science has brought. Fascism was essentially a national movement, in the sense of belonging to each of the individual nations which then existed. That is why it naturally took different forms and had such different policies in various countries, e.g., the difference between our policy and German policy already described. Now the old individual nations of Europe are too small to survive separately between the giants of America and Russia. That is mainly why we have passed beyond nationalism, and have become a European movement with the aim of Europe a Nation. The main differences between our policy today and the fascism of the past are the movement beyond the old nationalism to a patriotism which seeks the union of all the European countries, and our belief in the prime importance of maintaining personal liberty, which is a key point of our present policy. There are, of course, other differences which I have described in other answers. For instance, the idea of the totalitarian state was not really contained in our pre-war policy for Britain, because we always advocated a free vote of the people which could change the government; but we have moved far beyond even suspicion of such a concept in our policy today.

I believe we have really managed to synthesize, to combine the principle of freedom with action to secure continuous progress. As I wrote in 1950: "We reconcile the old conflicts and begin to achieve, today in thought and tomorrow in deed, the union of authority with liberty, action with thought, decision with discussion, power with responsibility, vigour with duty, strength with kindness, and service of the people with the attainment of ever higher forms of life."

Question 196. Is there, then, any relationship between your post-war Movement and pre-war Fascism?

Answer: The immediate answer is another question which clearly illustrates this point. What was the relationship of the Reform Bill and of Lord Grey to the French Revolution and the wars of Bonaparte? The liberalism of the nineteenth century was made in England. Yet no historian would deny that it had some relationship to the revolution made in France. This impulse of liberalism began there. It ended temporarily in the defeat at Waterloo, after beginning in the savagery of the guillotine. Later in Britain it assumed an entirely different, more enlightened and humane form, which succeeded and became the dominant creed of the nineteenth century.

It is a commonplace for anyone who has read history to know that the new impulses of mankind usually begin in violence, but later develop stable systems where order, tolerance and kindness can prevail. As Macaulay puts it: the planets move violently to their places, but serenely in them. He was writing of great men, but the same thought applies to great creeds.

Fascism and National Socialism in origin contained nothing like so much violence or brutality as the French Revolution, and could not be compared with the horrors of the Russian Revolution. Our post-war movement of the vital forces of Europe is as remote from fascism's early errors of violence as English liberalism was from the bloody beginnings of the French Revolution. All tendency to violence belong to the adolescent and not to the adult stage of human progress. We retain the vitality, the urge to action, the will that Europe shall endure and achieve fresh heights. These qualities we shall develop in ever higher forms. The error of English liberalism was to discard the dynamism of the French Revolution as well as the initial brutality. What we discard is the sacrifice of human liberty which is not justified even by the urgent need of action. The basic decencies must be preserved at all cost of political expediency.

Differences from Communism

Question 197. What are the main differences between your Movement and Communism?

Answer: The differences are fundamental. The fact that we believe in change, and the communists believe in change, does not mean that we are in any way the same. For the changes we want are entirely different. Some Conservative opponents who appear incapable of any movement at all think that any two men who do move must be the same. But we and the communists are moving in completely different directions.

We believe in leadership, they believe in compulsion. We believe in freedom, they believe in tyranny. If we want a man to go overseas to open up virgin country we raise the reward until we persuade him to go. But if communists want a man to go to Siberia, they put him and his family into a train at the point of a machine gun and pack him off. We achieve our results by free enterprise and the economic leadership of government. We thus encourage the maximum efficiency of every individual. They achieve their results by universal bureaucracy which controls everything, is wasteful, inefficient and only reaches its end through great suffering and loss. We have the freedom system of the west, which leads but does not drive. They have the mandarin system of the east, which controls and compels.

Question 198. In what main principles does the spirit of your Movement differ from Communism?

Answer: Their creed is purely material while our creed reaches beyond material things. Suppose Soviet civilisation had achieved complete material success, and everyone were living in the same comfortable circumstances as the average suburban family in America or even in England. It is an achievement which modern science makes easily possible. Even the inefficiency of the Soviet bureaucracy will reach that state before long. What will then be left as the aim of Soviet civilisation? They have yet to give us any answer to that question. "Sputnik races round the stars to relieve the tedium of being a Communist" was the answer I suggested. At least they will at that stage be able to get their scientific results in a more humane way than the present method, which is to make the population go short of the first necessities of life like decent housing in order to concentrate everything on spectacular scientific results.

To make a row of suburban villas each with a television set on which the people can watch a few men landing on Mars should not be the final objective of a civilisation. Yet, in fact, such things are the ultimate aim of the Soviets, the be-all and end-all of communism. They have no idea beyond material things. In the last resort mankind will find that the communist is a bore, as well as a brute.

Question 199. When you say your final aim as well as your present policy and method is fundamentally different from Communism, are you referring to the idea of higher forms?

Answer: Yes. I believe the idea of higher forms is derived from the main European tradition. My part has been chiefly to simplify and synthesize some of the most far reaching concepts of a very long trend in European thought which has endured and developed during at least two thousand five hundred years. I hope that I have added some effective, practical thinking because I have always said that our thinking should combine original thought with a synthesis of what already existed. The creative minds of each generation should add to what has gone before, but it is against the organic process of nature to depart entirely from it. As Bernard Shaw first pointed out, we can sometimes see further, and more clearly, than our predecessors in thought, because we are standing on their shoulders.

The idea of higher forms in political aspect contrasts completely with communist ideology for the following reasons. We believe that the life principle is a continuous movement from lower to higher forms. We and the communists approach the question of life's purpose from completely different positions. The communists began in envy, hatred and malice. They had some good reasons for their attitude, because the mass of the people were very badly treated at that time. Their first principle was to tear down what was on top, and replace it with what was underneath. The object of their hatred was anyone who had anything they had not got, and their ideal was the most oppressed section of the community early in the nineteenth century. Their values are consequently all upside down. Their drive is down, not up.

Their cult of the proletariat almost defines a type which no longer exists in advanced countries, but in the last century was denied not only education and culture but even the food, warmth, housing and clothing necessary to develop a full man. This was consequently not a type to be idealised but to be surpassed, as he has been already by modern life. It was right at that time to feel compassion, and to strive to remedy these things. But it was wrong to feel envy, hatred and malice, which inhibit men from moving to any higher form of life.

We, on the contrary, believe that the main purpose of life is a movement from lower to higher forms. We have advanced beyond our fathers largely by reason of their exertion and sacrifice on our behalf. And we hope our children, by reason of our exertions, will advance beyond us. So we shall continue until humanity rests on heights which today we can scarcely conceive. And we do not mean by this merely material achievement. We mean that mankind should strive to achieve an ever higher moral nature. In fact we believe that this must happen, if humanity is to survive, because it is quite clear that the material achievement of man outstrips the corresponding improvement in his moral nature which is now necessary. This limitation threatens the very life of the world with destruction.

We aim at the emergence of a higher form of man. When we find a high form of life in past or present we believe we should build upon it. We believe this is the discernible purpose of the world; despite all the flux of civilisations, men have moved, on the whole, from a very lowly beginning to the relative height of the present. Therefore in placing ourselves in the service of a movement from lower to higher forms we serve the revealed purpose of the world.

This is a belief which you can hold whether you have any religious faith, or none. It rests on a study of the facts of this world as revealed in history and biology, and conflicts with no faith or religious belief concerned with matters other than this world. Yet our belief is in essence a spiritual creed, because it seeks to move beyond material things to ever higher forms of life. It is this idea which, above all, divides us entirely in final aim from communism.

Question 200. When you have thus defined your profound difference from Communism, is it necessary to detest Communists?

Answer: We differ from communism completely, both in final aim and immediate method. But it is not necessary to detest communists, or come into conflict with them nationally or internationally, provided they leave us alone. We propose three main spheres of influence in the world for three different systems. There is no reason why three very different experiments should not be conducted peacefully in them, which may settle the ultimate development of mankind. There we could find a practical answer to the vital question: who is right?

We are certain that our system will triumph; the communists feel sure about theirs. Well, let us see. If one system is clearly the best, the other two will have to approximate to it or go under. We believe that this will be the fate both of American capitalism and of Russian communism, which will both be obliged by pressure of facts and by our example in the end to approach our system. We are strong believers in the principle, "Live and learn," and we shall not close our minds on occasion to learning something from either of them. This is the way peacefully to settle the affairs of mankind.

But as realists-always-we have to face facts. And the first fact is that the Russians are not yet ready for the issue to be settled by peaceful competition between rival systems. It is probably true that they have ruled out their old method of imposing communism by war in the present period, because the power of modern weapons makes it too dangerous. But they are actively engaged in the attempt to overthrow other states by a mixture of internal politics and street violence, in order to establish the world dominion of communism. When this attempt has been decisively defeated, they may be ready to see sense.

Question 201. Will you suppress the Communist Party?

Answer: Any conspiracy against the state will be dealt with under the existing law; it will be a matter of evidence and law. We would introduce no special law to deal with communism. The present law gives ample power to deal with any conspiracy to overthrow the state by force, and that law would be rigorously enforced by our government. The Communist Party would, therefore, be dealt with effectively if it pursued the usual practices of communism. If communists in Britain or Europe confined themselves to the expression of their opinions and the attempt to win power constitutionally by the vote, they would have the same liberty as anyone else. It would be up to us to defeat them with a higher and stronger idea, and with the effectiveness of our action as a government.

Question 202. What are Communist methods, and how can they be defeated?

Answer: Communist strategy is to take countries from within, not without. Of course, if the rest of the world disarmed they would impose communism on us by force. That has always been in the programme, if opportunity offered. But they know now that world war will mean universal destruction, so the method of war is off. They now rely entirely upon their communist parties in other countries to secure the aim of world domination when crisis offers an opportunity.

The coming paralysis of the military machines for fear of mutual destruction, and the strategy communism would then develop, I described eleven years ago in The European Situation. Tactics, based on that strategy of which I also gave warning, have been extensively employed very recently. The result has been notable communist successes. They have succeeded in preventing the President of the United States from visiting Tokyo, the capital of an allied power. They promoted the overthrow of the governments of Turkey and South Korea. They have produced disorder in Italy which led to the resignation of the government. They achieved widespread disorder in the Congo which shook the whole white position in Africa. There is no doubt that a method which has been so successful will continue, until we can meet it with something like the technique which I described eleven years ago.

The communists use different occasions and different excuses to employ their tactic. But the strategy remains. It is to exploit any grievance, real or imaginary, and then to infiltrate the mass of the people with highly trained communist groups. The object is to promote disorder by using masses of people against the state under communist leadership. If police or military are compelled to fire to protect themselves, or to save the state, a very skilful propaganda represents it as the massacre of innocent people. It is increasingly difficult for them to maintain order in such situations.

The only effective answer is for other groups - teams as we call them - to mingle with the mass of the people, and to persuade them not to act under the communist leadership.

The communist object is the overthrow of the state. Our object is to prevent the overthrow of the state, and to persuade the people to secure necessary changes by constitutional means. The task of our teams is to capture the leadership of the people from the communists. And in these early stages we have been very successful: for instance in persuading the people not to follow communist leadership to make disturbances at our meetings.

All this is at an elementary stage in most European countries. In fact, the communists know they cannot do much in this respect until a real economic crisis develops. Not only are they certain this will occur, but the Soviet government is doing its utmost to expedite crisis by the method described elsewhere. Meantime the communists are engaged in Britain in infiltrating the trade unions with considerable success. Here, too, it is the task of our "Trade Union Action" to combat them within the trade unions.

In general, and in all countries, the communists seek to exploit any grievance or minor crisis to promote disorder; then they try out their method in what is now a tactical exercise but will later become the real thing. Their final object is to establish street mastery, and to make government impossible until communism can achieve power.

In Britain it is the duty of the police to maintain order in the streets, difficult as that duty can be made by the developing communist method. We are forbidden by law to do anything of the kind (Public Order Act, 1936) and we scrupulously obey the law. But we can persuade the people not to act under communist leadership. We can thus capture the leadership of the mass of the people from communism by gaining their trust and support as crisis develops. This can be a great service to our country. For it can prevent the communists producing in Britain the situation familiar elsewhere, by methods the old parties do not begin to understand.

We on our side seek to become a government only in the British way, by vote of the people at a general election. A suggestion to the contrary once cost a national newspaper £5,000 in damages when I brought a libel action and the whole matter was thrashed out in court.

All these things can be reduced to a great simplicity in the final analysis. Apart from the fact that every patriot must wish to support the constitution and way of life of his own country, we have the sense to know that advanced peoples like the British can only be governed by consent. And what is more, to do the great things we want to do we have to win their enthusiasm as well. That time will come when they see in the approaching situation that a sweeping change is necessary.

The Blackshirt Movement

Question 203. Why do you think your Union Movement is the most effective party to defeat Communism in the coming situation? - Has this anything to do with the Blackshirt tradition.

Answer: Our Blackshirt Movement brought red violence to an end in this country before the war. For years previously the communists and fellow-travellers in the Labour Party had broken up the meetings of any party they did not like. It was necessary to act, and we defeated the reds. The chief reason that you are comparatively free from violence in British politics today is that the communists know that we can always see them off. They know they will lose any clash in the end, and it will certainly do them no good.

Fortunately, also, British politics have become more and more adult. English people are interested in serious argument, and do not want rowdyism. You do not get trouble at meetings unless the communists organise it, and they have learnt enough from their past experience not to do so in recent years. But, of course, if a really serious situation comes, the communists will again make a great effort here, as they already have elsewhere.

The law still permits us to defend ourselves, and if they attack us we shall defeat them again. But nothing will be settled by events of this kind. The future will be saved by men with brave hearts but clear heads, who can mingle with the people, persuade them and lead them. The strong-arm boy without a thinking head is right out of date; in fact he was never our type. He belongs to the childish period of British politics, not to the deadly seriousness of the coming situation. We need new men who can both think and act, real leaders of the people. They will lead because they will be their friends, helping them every day in affairs of their everyday life. And they will lead because they have the finest idea, which they will be able to explain to the people. The battle of ideas will now decide the future, because in all things the settlement by pure force belongs to the past.

We still have the dedicated spirit of the Blackshirts which inspires us with the strength of men ready to give all for their cause. But in the development of our Movement to full manhood, we add mind to will, restraint to strength, and kindness for all our fellows to the honour which binds us to each other and to our cause.

Question 204. Why did you organise the Blackshirts? Who were they?

Answer: This is what happened. For several years before I left the Labour Party and resigned from their government, I had addressed many of the largest meetings in the country, Which were always very enthusiastic, with scarcely an interruption. When I resigned and launched the new movement, the same people came to listen to me at very large meetings.British people always give a fair hearing whether they agree with you or not, and they came because they knew me and had been interested to hear me before. But among them came the organised communist opposition, assisted by some members of the Labour Party.

For example, I held a meeting in the Rag Market, Birmingham, where I had spoken before for Labour during an election fight when, for the first time, we captured the city from Conservatism. This time the place was packed with an audience of twelve thousand. Among them were about five hundred reds, determined that the audience should not hear a word. I was then new to this experience and had with me only sixty young men in plain clothes for the purpose of showing people to their seats, taking the collection, etc. When I appeared the reds rose in a body and began a steady chant of abuse and violent threats. After warning, I went down among them with my sixty stewards. They attacked me at once. The consequent fight lasted nearly an hour, but we put the whole lot of them out. Most of the audience had gone too, and so had the furniture which was smashed to pieces. We remained, alone, on top of a heap of rubble.

This was the beginning, and so it went on. That is why I organised the Blackshirts to prevent the organised violence of the reds stopping our free speech. And we succeeded. That meeting in Birmingham was in 1931. Eight years later we held the indoor meeting which was stated to be the largest ever seen in the world (Earls Court Exhibition Hall) in July 1939, and there was not the slightest disorder. In fact for several years before the war there was no disorder of any kind at any of our indoor meetings.

If I had not organised and led the Blackshirts our Movement would never have existed under these conditions. We had neither press, nor big money, comparable with the immense sums of Conservatism fed by big business and of Labour Party fed by the Trade Unions and some large business interests as well. The only way to make known our case was in public meetings, and these were the largest in Britain. If we had allowed them to be broken up, we should never have existed.

Question 205. Why did you wear the blackshirt uniform?

Answer: The origins of the blackshirt and the uniform were very simple. When fights like those described in the last question are forced upon you, it is a serious business. You do not win unless you have organisation and method. The first thing is to be able to identify each other in the fight. That was the simple reason why we wore first the blackshirt which was then a distinctive colour, and then the uniform. For the same reason police, soldiers, etc., who are obliged to fight, wear uniform in order to recognise their own side. It is as simple as that. Then like many other things of simple beginning, it developed in hard experience. Our men suffered in the blackshirt when they fought for free speech. It became a symbol of freedom, then a symbol of our whole cause. It became, in its way, a sacred symbol. Young men were proud to wear it, and others wanted to wear it. It attracted men and women to our Movement, because it came to represent an ideal. It became part of our strength and success.

In this way something of very simple origin developed into a powerful inspiration in British political life. That is why our opponents took it away from us by a special law. But the spirit it had created lives on. Our men have a loyalty, a companionship, a dedication to the cause which you do not find in other parties. We are not allowed by law to organise as an army, and have no wish to do so. We are very careful never to organise in this way. But we have the spirit of an army dedicated to a great cause.

Question 206. Is it true that your members were responsible for introducing violence into politics?

Answer: This is one of the most absurd lies ever circulated in British politics. We have proved repeatedly, and it has been admitted by left-wing writers, that the reds organised violence against us as they had against others. Our men acted in self-defence at our own meetings. Men who had come to break up our meetings then complained of our violence. And these communists were sometimes supported in this ridiculous charge by Conservative newspapers, which would stoop to use any method in order to attack us, because they feared our victory and did not believe the communists had a chance in Britain. They used the communists against us by encouraging their violence at our meetings.

Our members are forbidden to use violence, or force of any kind, except in self-defence. We have suspended, or even expelled, good members if in moments of excitement they have broken this rule. Violence existed in British politics long before our Movement was organised, and years before I was born. The truth is that it was our Movement which brought violence to an end in politics over large areas of Britain; and ended it everywhere, in the old serious form.

Question 207. What is your evidence for saying you have prevented violence?-What about Notting Hill?

Answer: Notting Hill was the scene of some of the most serious riots in British history in September, 1958. We had not a branch in that constituency at that time. Our members had strong feelings on the colour question, yet not one of them was involved in the rioting. Not one was even charged, let alone convicted. Not one had a complaint made against him.

I was subsequently invited to stand as candidate in the constituency, and agreed to do so in April, 1959, on our complete policy, including a constructive, peaceful and humane solution of the colour question.

Before my arrival the press and most other people said the rioting was bound to break out again in the following summer, which is the period of maximum tension in such districts. My vilifiers said I went with the intention of making it worse. Even such a responsible and honest opponent as Sir Patrick Spens, M.P. for the neighbouring constituency, said: "It is absolutely certain that there will be more trouble in the area," if I persisted in expressing my views on the colour question. Times, 27/4/59.

What happened? I at once issued an appeal to settle the question "by votes not violence", and used my utmost influence to prevent disorder of any kind. We also then began to organise for the first time within the constituency. The result was the end of violence. Not only did we have an orderly election campaign, but two summers have gone by and there has been no return of rioting in Notting Hill. We did not begin violence. We brought it to an end.

And we have done this everywhere. When young men are given our idea and enter our organization, they are inspired by our spirit and learn our method. They become responsible people, resolute but calm, who develop self-control in the service of a great cause. That is why our Movement brings violence to an end.

Question 208. What about pre-war violence? What about Olympia?

Answer: Well, let us have a look at this old example from way back in 1934. It is a good example to take, because more lies and general nonsense have been turned out about this meeting than almost any other subject connected with our Movement. And that is saying a good deal. What are the facts?

For weeks before the meeting the reds publicly organised to break it up. Anyone who is interested can see the quotations from the *Daily Worker,* etc., or check for himself in the files of the British Museum. The main quotations are published in a book written about me, Mosley: The Facts.

It will be noted that not only the communists but members of the Labour Party and I.L.P. were involved. Official Labour Party organisations decided beforehand to take part, and did so. The result was the most systematic attempt ever made in Britain to break up a meeting by force. A march was organised from East London to Olympia, carrying banners expressing the intention to smash the meeting. Our members were assaulted in the streets on the way to the meeting. Several, including women, were slashed with razors before it began.

Several hundred well trained red fighters were then dispersed inside the hall at strategic points. Many of them were armed with a variety of weapons, such as razors, knuckle-dusters, coshes, etc. The moment I began to speak an organised pandemonium broke loose. Not one word of the speech could be heard by an audience of fifteen thousand who had come peacefully to listen, and had even paid for their seats.

After the usual three warnings, I gave instructions to our stewards to eject the interrupters. The Blackshirts then, with their bare hands, put out all those armed men. They were forbidden to carry weapons of any kind, and were even searched if they were suspected of doing so.

Question 209. Were many people injured at Olympia?

Answer: Some sixty-three Blackshirts were treated at one dressing station alone "for injuries, mostly abdominal, and injuries caused by blunt and sharp instruments". Despite repeated challenges the reds failed to produce comparable evidence on their side. Such are the facts on record at the time, which anyone can verify for himself.

Yet it is this occasion which is made the basis of the charge that we introduced violence into politics. It is the case of a lie continually repeated being accepted by the ignorant. Lloyd George, the famous Prime Minister of the first World War, with his long practical experience, summed up the controversy about the Olympia meeting in the following words: "It is difficult to explain why the fury of the champions of free speech should be concentrated so exclusively, not on those who deliberately and resolutely attempted to prevent the public expression of opinions of which they disapproved, but against those who fought, however roughly, for freedom of speech. Personally, I have suffered as much as anyone in public life today from hostile interruptions by opponents determined to make it impossible for me to put my case before audiences. Naturally, therefore, I have an antipathy to that class of interruption, and I feel that men who enter meetings with the deliberate intention of suppressing free speech have no right to complain if an exasperated audience handles them rudely". (The Right Hon. David Lloyd George, M.P. *Sunday Pictorial* 24/6/34).

Question 210. But they say that the Blackshirts began the disorders in British politics?

Answer: Think a minute. They say I organised disorder at my own meetings, do they? Let me ask them, why? what for? why should I do this? I had for years drawn to my meetings the biggest audiences in the country. I had proved my power to convert audiences by speech. That is why for years the Labour Party used me at eve of poll meetings in so many by elections. Also it is claimed by my supporters with facts and figures in the book: Mosley: The Fact, that I had at that time the best election winning record in British politics. Do you then believe that after leaving the Labour Party I drew great audiences to meetings not for the purpose of converting them, but of beating them up? Did you ever hear such nonsense? This is the kind of puerile stuff to which our opponents are reduced when they cannot answer our serious arguments. Any man who spent time and money on advertising meetings and attracting big audiences, just to set about them with a lot of toughs, would certainly be certified as insane. Yet this is the sort of rubbish which passes for argument among opponents who cannot answer a single point of our serious case. But it need not worry us, and certainly will not stop us. Similar lies of one kind or another have always been told at some time or another about anyone who ever counted for anything real in politics.

The Question of Violence in Politics

Question 211. What, then, is the truth about violence in British politics?

Answer: The truth is that violence in British politics began long before I was born. Why, the very first meeting I ever attended was a Liberal meeting broken up by the Conservatives. I was nine years old at the time, and went along to see the fun because I heard it was going to happen. That was in a country district which was a Tory stronghold.

Then for years before our Movement began or the Blackshirts were organised, Conservative meetings were broken up in all the great cities by Labour Party supporters, generally led by trained communists. So bad did it become that no Conservative leaders ever dreamed of addressing open meetings. They were all carefully ticketed meetings of their own supporters, who came from all over the place by train and charabanc. The general public could not get in at all. It still continues like that, and if anyone gets in on a fake ticket the Tories are much rougher to the odd interrupter than our Blackshirts were in handling a mass of armed roughs. Just see what happened at Blackpool when one or two freaks interrupted Macmillan (Tory Conference, 11/10/58).

The fact is that this sort of thing has always gone on in British politics, but it went beyond a joke when organised red violence brought to an end every meeting of which they disapproved. This happened in the thirties, and if anyone who grew up later doubts the facts, he can easily verify them for himself from contemporary records. Endless instances were quoted in the press during that period of lesser Conservative meetings being smashed all over the place by the extremes of red violence. It was just impossible to hold a meeting unless you were approved by the red tyranny.

What we did was to bring violence to an end. When we have a chance we always bring violence to an end.

Question 212. Why cannot the police keep order at meetings?

Answer: That is a difficult question I have often asked myself. I think the answer is twofold (a) it is not really the business of the police to keep order for a political party, so they do not like it, (b) also it makes the political party look foolish to appear to be protected by the police, so they do not like it. There is something unnatural about it. We have never asked for police protection since our Movement began. On the other hand, if the police turn up we give them every facility to do their duty. And, so far as possible, we always let them know what we are doing, in order to avoid any complaint that we are doing anything in an underhand way.

In short, anyone who knows anything of the psychology of the British workers knows that in practice it is impossible for the police to steward meetings, though it is difficult to explain why. It is a job which political parties have to do for themselves. Otherwise, there is the feeling that we are being turned into a police state.

In fact I only know of one city in Britain where the municipality used to insist, during the thirties, on the police stewarding meetings as a condition of the hall being let. As it happened, the reds always seemed to be in far worse state when they were put out by the police than when they were put out by the Blackshirts. The police, no doubt, had the intention of being gentle as lambs. But they just had not had so much experience of an affair which was not their business. Police stewarding of meetings does not work, in practice. That is why, even under the Public Order Act, political parties are still allowed to steward their own indoor meetings.

Question 213. Was not a special Act of Parliament, the Public Order Act, passed in 1936 to suppress or control your Movement?

Answer: Yes, Parliament has passed two special measures to suppress our Movement, the Public Order Act of 1936 and the Special Regulation 18b(la) in 1940. They were undoubtedly designed to finish us off, but we emerged from both these tests stronger in the end.

The Public Order Act helped to clarify the law relating to indoor and outdoor meetings. The expressed purpose of suppressing my "private army" was not achieved, because I had not got one. We had stewards to keep order at meetings, for reasons already described; at indoor meetings they are still permitted. Since the Act the police alone are responsible for keeping order at outdoor meetings. Our members can sell literature at outdoor meetings, and can persuade people to take an interest in the proceedings, but they may in no way act as stewards.

Any form of uniform for political purposes is now illegal. But we no longer needed it by the time the Act was passed. The Movement had then been going long enough at least for leading members to recognise each other when acting as stewards at indoor meetings. And the period in uniform had given our Movement an outlook and psychology, by removing such impediments as any remaining sense of class and by creating a sense of companionship and a team spirit, which happily it has never lost.

Question 214. What were the practical results of the Public Order Act?

Answer: At first, much more disorder. I was the first victim, and was in hospital at Liverpool for over a week. This is what happened. I went to Liverpool for an open air meeting (10/10/37). Pursuant to the Public Order Act, the police alone were in charge of order. Our members were told by the police to stand around the platform, and the police then encircled them. Then from behind the circle of police the reds-at their ease and with complete impunity-put over a barrage of missiles on to the platform. The two previous speakers were laid out before

I arrived. A hail of bricks and iron fragments greeted me, and before I had spoken for five minutes I was knocked unconscious by a piece of iron which would have killed me if it had struck an inch further up the head. I in no way blame the police for this. They did not mean it. They were just new to the job. They arrested a young man whom they stated they saw throw the piece of iron in question. The magistrate said he was not satisfied this was the man who had done it, and acquitted him.

Question 215. What effect did the Public Order Act have on your own supporters?

Answer: At the other end - in East London - the situation was very different. The uniform which maintained discipline had been removed from our members. We were by then very strong in East London; practically all the young people were with us. Even in the L.C.C. Election in 1937 when the franchise was confined to the older generation of householders, we polled in Bethnal Green 23% of the votes recorded.

Our members, of course, remembered well the time when they were under attack by the red razor gangs who marched to Olympia from East London to "smash Fascism", before we had become so strong in that area. When discipline was removed, it must be admitted that nature to some extent took its course. Then opponents' meetings were, for the first time, broken up. Previously they never had been. Clement Attlee and Herbert Morrison, who both sat for East London constituencies, then left for seats in quieter localities. I did what I could to bring this situation to an end, and eventually succeeded in creating the calm but resolute spirit which animates our Movement today.

Question 216. Did you not suggest in the chapter on the Party in *Europe: Faith and Plan* that what began as the Blackshirt Movement should, in the end, be turned into a great social service to the people?

Answer: Yes, this is so. The first and greatest service to the people of Britain and of Europe is, of course, to defeat communism. We have met and defeated its violence before, and our members will always be ready when called upon by the state if that party tries to overturn it by force. But communism can best be defeated in advance of any such situation by winning the friendship and trust of the people. They will then turn to our Movement and not to communism for leadership in the coming crisis. Our members are expected to help the people in their daily lives in every possible way, and to become in every true sense their friends. And friendship rests not on words but on deeds, in doing things every day which prove they are the friends of the people.

Question 217. Have you still got the old tough character of your Movement, its ability to save the country from the reds?

Answer: Yes, certainly. Our men are expected to keep as fit as ever, and anyone who attacks them will find they are as tough as ever. But it is the fitness and toughness of men and of athletes, not the petulant violence of hysterical boys. That is why sports like boxing, wrestling and fencing are so valuable and why we encourage them. You soon go out feet first if you lose your temper or become hysterical in a boxing match. Men learn in these sports that the real champions are cool and calm, as well as quick, resolute and courageous. You do not find them throwing their weight about in pubs or streets, like some of the boastful boobies who are not really tough at all. We build the character which makes both a man and a friend; a man and a friend whom the people can respect and trust.

Question 218. What is your attitude to violence today?

Answer: Our members are absolutely forbidden to use force of any kind except in self-defence, and then only the minimum of force necessary for this purpose. And they may only defend themselves in the absence of the police, because if the police are present they must look to them to maintain order. These rules are absolutely clear, and even under intense provocation are followed by our members. There may of course be occasions when young men, particularly new members, get excited and break the rules. Such things happen occasionally in all human affairs. But the rules are rigorously enforced, even by the expulsion of good members.

We expect members to behave like serious men whose lives are dedicated to a great cause. They must have the calm of athletes, not the hysteria of mobs, the dignity of dedicated men, not the nervous excitability of the Red rabble without roots or faith, without past or future. We hold this attitude not only because we obey the law but because victory belongs to the cause which can so inspire men.

Miscellaneous Abuse – Or So Intended

Question 219. Are you a power maniac?

Answer: Obviously not, otherwise I should have gone for power at any price. I would never have spent all these years in the political wilderness. After all, many newspapers and distinguished people prophesied that I should be Prime Minister; they thought me mad to throw away this prospect. You cannot be denounced both as a power maniac and as being mad because you renounce power for principles. The fact provides clear proof that I preferred ideas to power. A power maniac wants power for its own sake. I want power only in order to turn ideas into reality. We believe we have ideas, a policy which can save Europe and can even save the world. Naturally we want to make that policy effective. That is why we ask the people to vote for it. We cannot get power unless they agree with our ideas; it is up to them. Where is the power mania in this? Is it not elementary sense to want the means to do something you believe in?

Question 220. But did you not go into the wilderness because you wanted more power than the present system could, or would, give you?

Answer: I went into the wilderness rather than acquiesce in the immediate betrayal of our people and the ultimate collapse of our civilisation. I thought it a betrayal to tolerate an unemployment problem which could easily be solved. That is why I resigned from the government on that issue. I thought also that our civilisation would ultimately collapse unless the system was changed. That is why I thought the creation of a new movement was necessary to challenge the system which all the other parties in different ways and degrees supported. It also seemed to me clear that before long it would be necessary for government to have more power both to meet the economic problem and to secure the necessary changes in the system. The necessary power and the method of built-in safeguards and checks to preserve liberty more fully and securely than before, have already been described.

A man who takes on a job without the means to do it is a charlatan. Such conduct means that he wants power for power's sake, for personal aggrandisement and the wielding of patronage. On the other hand a man who only takes on the job if you give him the means to do it shows that he is interested in serving the people, rather than in his personal position. I went into the wilderness to get the means to do the necessary work. For this task we need the support of the mass of the people, not only their vote, but their enthusiasm to get the work done.

Question 221. Are you the tool of big business?

Answer: What contradictory charges are aimed at us. At one moment we are charged with wanting to set up a dictatorship, and the next with being so feeble as to be somebody's tool. We are supposed to be too strong and too weak at the same time, too tough and too pliant. Our opponents cancel each other out.

The simple fact is that we are a movement formed by the people, and we shall be a government elected by the people to do what they want done. We shall have just as much power as they give us - no more and no less - for their own purposes. But I would never take office unless they gave us power enough to be dependent on no one. This means, of course, we must wait until they see the necessity for such action. We should have had money, press, radio andtelevision long ago, if we had been the tool of big business, and many of these things too if-like the communists-we had been the tool of the Soviets. Instead we have chosen slowly, laboriously, painfully to build a movement of the British people in challenge to all vested interests, and to communism, which will be ready when the mass of the people sees the need for change. Then we shall form a government above all interests, which can therefore serve the interest of the nation as a whole.

Question 222. Are you hoping for a crisis, as the only means of coming to power?

Answer: No-I hope very much that the people will wake up and vote for our ideas before we come to crisis. That is why I am so busy trying to persuade them to do it. The best hope is that they will see what is coming in the early stages of crisis, and take action in time.

As for the suggestion we want crisis, you might as well tell a doctor that he wants a patient to have a cancer in order to do an operation. No one would make so vile a suggestion in private life. Why then make it in public life? We remain the same people, whatever our political differences: we are mostly by nature decent and humane people, and we prove it if we work long and hard for what we believe to be right.

Let us look at the matter sensibly, in terms of everyday. A doctor may say to a patient: "I believe you have a tumour and should have an operation; it is wrong to tell you that a little gentle massage will cure it, and such advice is endangering your life." You would not say such a doctor was glad that the patient was ill and wanted a chance to cut him up. So do not think this of us; for in relation to the nation we are in much the same position as the doctor in relation to his patient when he thinks it his duty to give such advice.

Question 223. What happened to your sister-in-law Unity Mitford?

Answer: My sister-in-law shot herself when war broke out. She was a young woman, twenty-five years old, who had many friends in both Britain and Germany. She was in no sense a political person, just a beautiful and charming girl, full of life, affection and friendship. When war came between her own country, which she loved, and Germany, where she had so many friends and happy associations, she felt an intolerable strain. She resolved the situation by shooting herself, and died a few years later from the effects. This is one individual example of the grave tragedy which occurs when similar peoples fight each other. She and others felt it was like a civil war.

You remember that old and moving story during our own civil war, when a notable man lowered his weapon at the battle of Edge Hill and rode into the ranks of the other side to be killed. Some people will always prefer suicide to life on such a scene. Anyone who knows well both the British and the German peoples must feel that war between two peoples so related has something of the character of a civil war.

Question 224. What was the origin of the untrue rumour that Hitler was best man at your wedding?

Answer: The truth is that I was married in Berlin, but Hitler was not my best man.

My visits to Germany were very rare, and I took advantage of this occasion to have with him one of the two political discussions which I have already described.

I was married in Berlin because I wanted for the time being to keep it secret. The reason was that my wife then went to live in my Staffordshire homeland which was a good centre for my northern meetings, and I did not want her to be visited in the depths of the country when I was away by some of the genial opponents who were then continually threatening my life.

Question 225. Has your controversial life led to the loss of personal friends, and to social ostracism?

Answer: No. You do not lose real friends on account of political controversy. In fact you do not quarrel in private life with any intelligent people on account of political differences, because if they are intelligent they are capable of reasonable, objective discussion. At a certain level of character and brains they are even capable of replacing controversy by what I describe as the "search for truth."

People who are silly enough to want to shoot someone because they differ from him politically have never been the types I found interesting as friends. There are, of course, always such people to be found in all places and periods. I remember an old lady recounting that she and other children were having tea in some drawing-room when Mrs. Gladstone was announced. The children promptly disappeared under the table. They were pulled out and asked what was the matter. The ingenuous reply was: "We know Mr. Gladstone is a murderer, so we thought Mrs. Gladstone might be one too." These have always been the amenities of political life in the duller circles of our native land. But who would choose as friends those quaint specimens who are so distorted by hatred that they impute to opponents all kinds of villainies? The underlying psychological reason for these turgid emotions is really that they desire to answer a political argument but feel themselves incapable.

The love engendered by political struggle finds us very fine companions and hatred deprives us only of the company of very uninteresting people. It is rather time which has deprived me of friendship; I simply have not had the time which should be given to it. This has been particularly true in recent years in my own country. When I have been in England I have had to work so very hard. In the process of becoming a European, the little leisure I had was mostly spent abroad. As a result I probably have more intimate friends in most of the main capitals of Europe than in London. But it was time rather than bitterness which separated me from English friends. We English are not a bitter people.

Question 226. Was pre-war Fascism derived from a German or Italian inspiration?

Answer: So far as we are concerned-neither. It is quite clear to anyone who studies our policy of that time that it was derived from a purely British inspiration. The Germans did not copy the Italians, and we certainly did not copy either. In each country fascism meant a love of the homeland, a national expression of a European people's will to revive and to live greatly. Fascism was in essence a national creed. That was both its strength and its ultimate weakness. We have now overcome that weakness by becoming Europeans. We have extended our patriotism to the whole homeland of Europe.

Any Briton in the pre-war world who relied upon Italian or German inspiration would have lacked the necessary creative capacity. He would have been a sterile specimen, a mere imitator without place in our ranks. You will see from another answer that I was thinking on these lines at my first election. As for today, whether you agree with my ideas or not, no-one can deny that they are in the forefront of present European thinking. The only effective charge against them is that they are too far ahead. But fast moving events will soon remedy that.

Question 227. Was not the blackshirt a foreign import?

Answer: We put on the blackshirt as already explained for one simple reason. We wanted to recognise each other in the fights forced upon us, and black was the most distinctive colour. It was the answer everywhere to red violence which was the first foreign import. Political uniform was worn sooner in other countries because red violence developed earlier in those countries; first Italy, then Germany, and later in Britain and other lands.

The desire and the will to win, if you have to fight is an old fashioned British habit. To recognise your own side helps you to win. It is as simple as that. The need was the same everywhere. You might as well say drinking was a foreign import because both an Englishman and a German drink a glass of beer when they feel thirsty. Which of us invented beer? I don't know and I don't care. Probably the man who felt thirsty first.

Question 228. Was your party ever accused of accepting' foreign funds?

Answer: This was a nonsense story - again and again denied - which in this case would not have caused us the least embarrassment if it had been true. Our opponents suggested that our party had received funds from Italy during the years 1934 and 1935. They were challenged to produce any serious evidence, and failed. This showed in them an unexpected sense of propriety, since after the war all the forgery factories of Europe were available to them if they had so desired.

They were also themselves in an embarrassing position. For Lord Snowden in his autobiography stated that the respected leader of the Parliamentary Labour Party, Mr. George Lansbury, had been connected with a question of funds from Russia when he was editor of the Daily Herald. The vulnerable absurdity of the Labour Party's position was nearly matched by the situation of the Conservative Party, whose rule for years depended on American subsidy, while the connections of some of its prominent figures with American finance and market provided a comfortable personal affluence.

For my own part no such allegations would embarrass me at all. I have been accused too often of the atrocious crime of being a rich man to feel any difficulty in this controversy, and even after sacrificing much of my original fortune to assist the Party (as did other members and supporters) I have always had the sense to keep enough to render me entirely independent. I am barred by our constitution from any responsibility for party finances.

As for the Movement, if our opponents had succeeded in proving that we had been assisted from Italian sources in the early years of 1934 and 1935, the reply would be in the elegant terminology of modern controversy - So what? At that time there was no question of a European war. Our policy was to arm our country far more strongly than it was then armed, so that no-one could conceivably have wanted to help our party with the object of weakening Britain. No war time atrocities had then occurred, and no one else in the world had ever been accused of even a fraction of the crimes committed by the Russian communist who, according to Lord Snowden, were busy shovelling roubles through to the Labour Party with one hand while they shovelled the corpses of their victims into mass graves with the other. Some of the most honoured figures of Conservatism shortly before this period had both denounced the Russian leaders in the strongest terms and eulogised Mussolini and his work.

Yet perhaps it is too much to expect our opponents to be consistent in their guides to statesmanship, or even to suggest that they should be careful about throwing stones from palace of glass.

There was, in short, no reason at that time why one group of Europeans should not have helped another group of Europeans if, in fact, our party had desired to accept such assistance. It would be in no way embarrassing now to admit it. And I freely give notice to all the busy little men who occupy themselves with such questions, that in the future I would certainly help any other Europeans who were working for the union of Europe if I had the means and facilities to do so, and I should certainly expect them to do the same for us if they had money and we had not. The only difficulty is that all the best people in Europe at present seem sadly short of cash.

If anyone objects to these principles, will he inform me why Sir Stafford Cripps when Chancellor gave permission for the British Labour Party and individual trade unions to send money to the French Socialist Party and the Confederation General du Travail Force Ouvriere, and why the Conservative government in recent months allowed the T.U.C. to transfer money to the Belgian Federation of Labour to "relieve distress" during a strike, which to many appeared as a direct subvention to a strike designed to overthrow the government of a friendly power?

Briefly, this old nonsense (1) would not have caused us the slightest embarrassment, even if it had been proved, (2) was entirely unsubstantiated by our opponents who were themselves not above suspicion, but (3) was always denied as a lie by our party. So enough of this humbug; silly humbug at that.

Question 229. Was not William Joyce once a member of your Movement?

Answer: Yes. He was also once a member of the Conservative Party. The difference was that we expelled him and the Conservative Party didn't. We expelled him in March, 1937; two and a half years before the outbreak of war. I have always condemned and still strongly condemn the very few men who left Britain in order to aid the enemy.

Question 230. Some people say your movement has an aura of evil-what is your answer?

Answer: This is the effect of novelty on conventional minds. Galileo no doubt had an aura of evil in the eyes of contemporary churchmen. All proposals to change existing ways are evil to the smug, the satisfied and the complacent members of an existing establishment. This mood vanishes quickly enough when events shatter the context and the content. When we then put things right, our souls will be much more in danger from the halo such people may then accord us than from the aura of evil with which they previously decorated us. For then we too could risk becoming smug, saddled, contented, and that would be a disaster. But I think memories of our hard times will always save us from that.

Question 231. But is not the alleged aura of evil really due to some people's belief that you and other pre-war fascists delight in violence?

Answer: I myself have never delighted in violence; still less now when I have seen so much of it. In fact I detest it. The use of force can never be anything but a sad necessity. Nothing in the world is sadder than the all too frequent experience of violence succeeding where reason has failed. The history of recent British politics has been a long record of conceding to successful violence what was previously refused to reason. Governments will never act until too late. Then they wake up in a panic and simply abdicate.

I suppose I was charged with delighting in force because I would never surrender to force. For instance, I would not just close down our meetings and go home, when attacked with violence in the manner already discussed. Then also, to be what is called an executive type, a dynamic kind of person, has long been very unfavourably regarded. Anyone who wanted to get anything done was made out to be just a brute. Bernard Shaw put his finger on this during one of the occasions when he was good enough to defend me; this time against critics in the Labour Party when I resigned from the government. He wrote: "You will hear some more of Sir Oswald before you are through with him. I know you dislike him, because he looks like a man who has some physical courage and is going to do something; and that is a terrible thing. You instinctively hate him, because you do not know where he will land you; and he evidently means to uproot some of you."

People who give the impression G.B.S. described are, of course, unpopular until you are "landed" in the mud and want to be "landed" somewhere else. Many people do not like anyone who looks like doing something until something has to be done. Then the popular view of such qualities changes. They want a bit of "uprooting" and want to be "landed" somewhere else than their very unpleasant position. But I can assure you I am very averse to uprooting anything if it can possibly be avoided. Leave everything alone which is working, growing and developing: only uproot a tree which is so rotten that it has become a public danger.

When all is said and done, I suppose many of us, in our youth, did give the impression of being a little too gay in combats forced upon us. We may have been too ready to accept a challenge. We did not try as long and as patiently to get things through without a row as I do now. It is only in later life that I developed the fixed principle: always be much more patient than most people in trying to do things gently and quietly, and only get tough - tough enough to do what has to be done - in the very last resort when it is quite clear that patience and gentleness will not work. Any real man in his maturity should feel nothing but sadness when it is necessary to be tough, because nothing is sadder than force and nothing is more wasteful. This feeling comes when we move from the adolescence to the manhood of the mind; when we grow up.

Question 232. What do you say to the suggestion that there is a cult of violence or even gangsterism in your movement?

Answer: Men who behave like gangsters in our movement are thrown out. We expel them. We are as determined to stamp out gangsterism in our movement today as we shall be to stamp it out in the whole nation when elected to government. We succeed now, and we shall succeed then.

It is perfectly true that at various times some people who like violence have come into our movement. The main reason, perhaps, is the untrue suggestion which has so often been published that we like violence. We get rid of them. We free our movement from such elements and make it what it should be: a movement which any decent man or woman may enter to serve their country. We want to make it a model of such patriotic service.

The original legend of violence arose from the fact that we defended ourselves at our meetings when attacked by red violence as described in other answers. I hope that need is now behind us for good. Obviously our men will always defend themselves if attacked, in the manner which is every man's right under the law. At the same time we do anything to avoid violence except to abandon our country and our cause.

Question 233. Has "Fascist" now become a term of abuse?

Answer: Yes. "Fascist" is now a term of abuse for any patriot who tries to do his duty. We who have thus been abused for so long can take it as a compliment. For we think that the words-"patriots who tried to do their duty"-are not a bad description of us. The word "fascist" is now applied indiscriminately to anyone the communists and fellow travellers do not like, from policemen who have to deal with their riots to any of the voluntary workers in various social services whom the red rabble dislike. Those who use the word "fascists" in this way have usually not the slightest idea what the term really means. But knowing nothing of a subject has never yet prevented them from bawling their opinions. So the long and the short of it is that we who have been denounced as "fascists," today find ourselves in a large and good company.

No-one with any historic sense will believe for a moment that making a word a term of abuse, and throwing it at us, will eventually impede our progress. "Fascism" in origin was a word with a good and honourable meaning. But the term, "Tory", for example, had a most disreputable meaning. Consult an early dictionary and you will find it defined as follows: "a bog trotting bandit, a robber of other people's lands." But any Conservative prime minister today will say that he is proud to be a Tory.

Abuse of a crude and silly kind which imputes to the guiltless the crimes of the guilty never stopped any real movement. In the early days of the Labour Party "Bolshevik" was shouted at their speakers wherever they appeared. Their opponents tried to fasten on them every crime committed by the communists in the early days of the Revolution in Russia. I sometimes recall something which appeared far from amusing at the time: the indignation of that eminent Nonconformist lay-preacher, who was then the Secretary of the Labour Party, Mr. Arthur Henderson, when some low Tory circulated a story that the Labour Party intended to "nationalise every woman in the country." A shrewd blow at all this nonsense was struck by Mr. Jack Lawson, who later became Minister of War in a Labour government. His Conservative opponent placarded his Durham constituency with the words: "Lawson is a Socialist, so is Lenin." Lawson replied with the following poster: "The Tory candidate is a doctor, so was Crippen." The attempt to saddle us with other people's crimes will be defended in the end by the same factor -

which our opponents are still far from understanding - the good sense of the British people.

Question 234. Does not your record-first in the old parties, then fascist, now European - show political opportunism?

Answer: On the contrary, it might be nearer the mark to ask whether I have shown opportunism enough. I have suffered from an almost exaggerated consistency. It is not a virtue of which I am particularly proud. The most consistent man is obviously he who lives a lifetime without ever changing or even developing an opinion. And to live so long without developing is to live without learning anything. So my apprehension is rather that I may have been too rigid in my consistency rather than too opportunist.

It is quite true that I have pursued the same ideas through different parties. But is it not always right first to try to do things by existing means, and only to go to the extreme of creating new means when you have proved there is no other way?

I always stood for two main principles: patriotism and progress. This idea is in essence a synthesis, because patriotism has been regarded as belonging to the right and progress to the left. I first expressed in very crude form an idea combining these two principles at my first election in 1918 when I was twenty-two. The phrase was "Socialistic Imperialism", and I deal with its application to modern thinking in another answer.

When as youngest M.P. I got back from the war and found we were given the Versailles Treaty instead of peace, and slums and unemployment instead of "the land fit for heroes to live in", I realised that my generation could not get what we wanted through the Conservative Party. I then stood twice as an Independent in a Conservative stronghold and was returned by a large majority. But it was, of course, soon clear that I could do nothing effective by remaining in isolation as an independent. I joined the Labour Party, and worked very hard during seven years for what we were told and believed was the people's cause. But, as a minister, I was prevented from dealing with the easily soluble unemployment problem of that time, and the promises of the party to deal with other great social questions were equally broken. I should have shared in that betrayal if I had stayed. I therefore left, and formed the new movement: with what principles?-patriotism and progress.

The patriotism now extends to embrace all Europe. Progress will be achieved through the economic leadership of government by means of the wage-price mechanism. These are ideas which are immensely developed-yes, I have lived and learnt in some forty-years-but they are the same basic ideas, living and organic ideas, which are always growing but never changing. The beginning of the European idea I first expressed in cruder form in 1936, before any of the present protagonists had first embraced and then renounced Europe. I have followed the idea of Europe consistently. But do not fear that I am claiming credit for the whole patent; we will allow their share to many others from Charlemagne onwards. I wish that I had no worse troubles than a charge of inconsistency.

Question 235. Do you agree with some newspapers that you are unpopular?

Answer: I am in the best position to find out whether I am unpopular or not, because I am so often among the people. I see much more of them than any politician, and more than most journalists. I not only hold meetings in halls but continually in the streets, and afterwards move among the people, talking to friend and opponent alike. They are not backward in stating their opinion, I can assure you. And I am still looking for this much advertised unpopularity. I do not find it among the people. In fact I regularly receive messages of greeting and support from all over the country, sent by my friends and often by old opponents. In reality I believe the hostility to be confined mostly to the square mile which comprises Westminster, Fleet Street and some of the lower reaches of what was Mayfair. My alleged unpopularity was always a rather artificial, press boosted business.

I never find any hatred among the people except from the extremes of right and left, who are both pathological in their dislike of anyone with whom they disagree. My natural relationship with the British people was always one of warmth and friendship. I always got on exceptionally well with them. Otherwise I could never have had the election winning record, which my friends have claimed without contradiction was the best in the inter-war period, when I was still with the old parties.

My present position, that a fundamental change of system is necessary, naturally impedes me during elections until people become convinced by events as well as by our arguments that so great a change is really necessary. Then I am quite sure that my old close relationship with the British people will be reflected in election results. Meantime, I find them much the same when I talk to them in the streets or on the doorstep, ready to listen to any opinion or to have any reasonable argument, tolerant, cheerful, friendly - just as they always were - and, I am sure, ready to act again in the great fashion that is worthy of them, when they see the need.

Housing and Transport

Question 236. How would you deal with the housing problem?

Answer: Housing must be treated as a national problem. To leave it in the hands of the local authorities is another case of stage-coach politics. You do not fight wars by farming out the job to local authorities. Why will present government never take anything seriously except fighting a war? It is only then that we have a national effort.

The housing of the people should be taken seriously, and treated like a problem of war. Many of the same slums disgrace us today as when I entered politics. We have got to clean up the British housing problem in double quick time.

I would go about it in this way. Produce the materials exactly as you do munitions in time of war. Mass produce them, giving one part to one firm and another part to another firm; use mass production methods throughout.

This would bring down the cost of house building as the cost of producing shells was reduced in the first World War, When Lloyd George got going in the Ministry of Munitions he not only gave us enough shells and airplanes which we sadly lacked before, but he greatly reduced the price. And he did it with this method I want applied to housing. Lord Beaverbrook with a similar dynamism broke the bottle necks of supply in the last war. Remember that the surest way to bring down rents is to bring down the cost of building. This policy will not only mean enough houses, but houses at rents which people can afford

Question 237. What about rents and rent control?

Answer: They will fiddle about for ever with rent control under the present system. And they will never solve the problem. There is only one solution - build enough houses. And I have just suggested in the last answer how to do it. When there is no longer a shortage of houses, the rent control problem is solved. Then you can do away with rent controls without the people being exploited. By our method of national effort and mass production, we shall build houses at rents the people can afford to pay. Rents can further be reduced by the system of differential interest already described. Enough new houses at rents the people can afford will hold down to a reasonable level the rents of existing houses. You can get rid of rent control when there is no shortage. We have all learnt this already in experience of other things. To give a fair deal to all, we must build enough new houses.

Question 238. What about slum clearance?

Answer: We mean to deal with this problem more drastically and on a greater scale than any plan yet proposed, for two reasons: (1) it is an absolute duty to house our people properly; (2) this form of public works is one of the most effective to lift the country out of any tendency towards depression. For slum clearance let us have temporary dwellings just outside the cities which we rebuild, and national transport to take the workers to and from their work; let us go about the job section by section. Move the people from the first section to be cleared to the temporary accommodation. When their old houses or tenement buildings have been pulled down and the new houses or flats have been built, they will all go home. Their places in the temporary accommodation will then be taken by the people living in the second section scheduled for demolition and rebuilding. And so on until the job is done with all the drive of an operation of war.

We should, of course, give guaranteed long-term employment to those engaged in the building industry in order to introduce more labour. This we can easily do. When we have dealt with the rehousing of the people those in the building trade can move on to other works of national importance which can occupy them for years ahead. Nothing must stand in the way of the prime duty of rehousing the people. It is quite a time since our generation in the first World War were promised "homes fit for heroes to live in". We are going to do what the others promised to do, and we tell you how it will be done.

Question 239. What will you do about traffic jams in cities?

Answer: Here again we have to enter the future in a hurry. Otherwise we shall soon find traffic completely jammed in the main cities. I would not commit myself to a final answer until in government we have the advice of some of the best engineers and experts in several countries. But I am thinking along lines which people might think fantastic today but will be obvious tomorrow. This has already happened to me several times in my lifetime. So take a deep breath and have a look.

All ordinary motor traffic stops at the outskirts of main cities at large parking places. Further movement by escalators to moving platforms at various levels and varying speeds, within cities covered in by sections and air-conditioned. It is probably best in the long run to take a jump into the city of the future, directly the cost of the enterprise is made possible by the revolution in production which science will secure within the new system of Europe-Africa.

Question 240. Could anything be done about traffic jams short of this complete change?

Answer: There are plenty of intermediate possibilities, e.g., stopping all cars in large parking places at the outskirts of cities in the same way. Thereafter public transport and small taxis, all run by electricity obtained from coin slot machines in every street. Traffic jams would be reduced and petrol fumes eliminated at the same time. The underground system, of course, would still be used and greatly extended. Much could be done even within the limits of existing resources by using tunnel systems in cities as the French are now doing.

Question 241. Does not the present cost of the city of the future put such a city out of the question?

Answer: today, yes. But when automation industries really get into full swing in Europe-Africa it will be another matter. If people do not wish to spend all the extra purchasing power, as Professor Galbraith and others suggest, public works on a very large scale will be necessary to keep industry going.

There is no real limit to consumption power if we regard the private and public sectors together. Economic depression through lack of demand in an economy large enough to be viable is, in real terms, ridiculous. It is simply a breakdown in organisation. Cities of the future will be one of the public works which create demand in an ordered fashion when it is required.

Looking ahead? Yes, but it is time we started looking ahead instead of looking behind. Simply messing about with the traffic problem will get us nowhere in a few years' time.

Question 242. What will you do for motorists in their present troubles?

Answer: Build national roads. I have been trying to do this for thirty years, but the British people all that time have been voting for governments which would not have it. When I resigned from the government in 1930, I suggested among other plans for curing unemployment a national road scheme.

The roads were still in the hands of local authorities as they were in the days of the stage-coaches. At that time there were thirty different road surfaces between London and Birmingham. Now, after a time lag of thirty years you have got one short motorway. If you allow this time lag between idea and execution to continue in every sphere of life as we enter the modern world, we shall run into a national disaster. And still you have the same old road system over nearly all the country. Build the new roads and let a toll system pay for them; they need be no charge on the Exchequer. Do you want this country to become the "museum of Europe"?

Question 243. Did you foresee the present breakdown on the roads?

Answer: Thirty years ago I said that if we increased motor output without improving roads, the only view that the Englishman would eventually have of his beautiful countryside would be the backside of the big car in front as he sat immobile in his own super-luxury model on the goat tracks which have been called roads in Britain since Roman times. This is now beginning to prove true in practice. Other warnings on even more serious matters will prove true too if we do not wake up in time. The remedy for motorists is still simple. It is to elect a government capable of action and to accompany it into the modern world, where it has been proved again and again that it is possible to build a national road system. And others among our fellow-countrymen should be warned while there is time by the present fate of motorists.

Question 244. Are you in favour of a Channel tunnel or bridge?

Answer: Yes, certainly, I am in favour of a Channel bridge. This will provide a physical link with the continent which is in every way desirable. A bridge is better than a tunnel because cars will cross it under their own power, while in the case of a tunnel trains would have to take the cars through and this would mean advance bookings and delays. We should have communication with the continent which is as free and quick as the M1 or any other modern road. The bridge will cost rather more than the tunnel but the extra cost is a very small charge to the nation. Of course the bridge should be a national undertaking, and again a toll system can finance it. We do not leave the roads, or even any longer the railways, in private hands.

Question 245. What do you think of the objections to a Channel bridge or tunnel?

Answer: Very odd objections to the bridge are heard which are all too characteristic of the old-world mind which still rules in much of Britain.

We are told that ships will run into the well lit pylons, even with radar to help them. Surely if they are as incapably managed as this they will run into anything. Is incompetence always to be the excuse for inaction? We are told, also, the force of the wind will sometimes be too great for cars crossing the bridge. Why should it be any stronger than the wind on the bridge of the Firth of Forth which is further north in a stormier region? And in any case it is said to be quite easy to add wind protection to the bridge.

We are still solemnly told that it will increase the risk of invasion, by insular people who still think of an enemy paddling a canoe across the Channel, when the real dangers to Britain are H-bombs and rockets. The short answer to all that is surely this: If the British Army cannot see an enemy crossing a bridge twenty-one miles long in time to blow it up, we shall have reached the point where Britain is dead anyhow. After all, it is a good many years ago since bridges were first blown up in time of war. Men have learnt how for a long time past. Such arguments just serve to illustrate the kind of fossilized nonsense which any man is up against who tries to bring the government of Britain up to date.

Customs, Crime, Youth and Class

Question 246. Should customs be abolished within Europe?

Answer: Yes, certainly. In the modern world, with a properly organised Europe it would help a lot more if some of the men employed in opening the luggage gave a hand in carrying it. The whole silly business is yet another unnecessary waste of time in a continent still organised on a 19th century basis. We shall not need customs because trade within Europe will be absolutely free, without fear of undercutting competition. It is this fear which leads to the tariffs between countries which, in turn, lead to all the tedious business in the customs when travelling.

The customs can go with the passports, once Europe is united under European government with real economic policy. Then you will be able to take a ticket at Victoria or London Airport and travel all over Europe as you do through Britain today or drive your own car over the Channel bridge from London to Paris in a journey which has no more check or delay than a drive from London to Birmingham. It is measures like this which will really set the people free, once the basic economic problem is solved.

Question 247. Should passports be abolished within Europe?

Answer: Yes, certainly. We must be ready for the day when all our people can afford to travel. It will soon arrive when we have the new system. This is one of the many ways in which we have moved backward instead of forward. Before the first World War the only European country where you needed a passport was Russia. Then it was the only police state. Now many countries are police states. And they are mostly very inefficient police states, because the one thing certain is that no criminal who knows his job is ever prevented from travelling by the absence of a passport. Criminals are the only people who are quite certain to have their papers in order, and most efficient underground organisations exist to provide passports and other simple requirements necessary to walk past a frontier policeman. The travelling public is pushed around and harried in order to make life difficult for criminals who are the only people who find it all easy. We are determined to get rid of all the silly bumbledom which frustrates our own people's desire to travel, prevents the Europeans getting to know one another, and denies to many the beauty and charm of the Europe which belongs to us all.

Question 248. What is your answer to the travelling criminal?

Answer: The answer is to throw open the frontiers of Europe, and to organise an efficient European police force which has the criminals of all countries well taped. At present they find it all too easy to slip into another country when one country becomes too hot for them. Meantime our security officials waste their time bumbling through the papers and luggage of respectable citizens who are made to queue up even to enter their own country. Open the frontiers, and let the officials read Magna Carta which enacted some time back that Englishmen might enter and leave England as they wished without hindrance.

Question 249. What about the present crime wave, particularly crimes of violence? What will you do to stop it?

Answer: There are two ways to stop the crime wave particularly crimes of violence. One is positive and the other negative; both should be used at the same time. The first is to give youth an ideal to live for. The second is to get very tough indeed with those of all ages who are insensitive to any appeal to honour. And when I say tough, few will doubt my intention. For I have spent some years trying to live down a reputation for being too tough; a reputation which, for reasons given in other answers, was not entirely just. But at any rate it is clear that I have had an almost lifelong experience of dealing with tough situations. Yet I believe more than ever in being gentler and more patient than other people are prepared to be during the early stages of any action, till it is clearly proved that method will not work. Then

I believe in being equally ready to be tougher than most people are prepared to be when, and only when, this should prove to be absolutely necessary. And in the matter of the crime wave, that point is very near. My practical proposals are:

(1) Give young men a cause and an idea which makes them feel it is worthwhile to go straight. This we have been able to do in some measure already. As a government we could, of course, do far more.

(2) Secure at all cost efficiency in the police force, on the simple principle that the best deterrent to crime is the certainty of detection.

(3) To this end have enough policemen, and pay them so well that the best are attracted to the force in sufficient number. The most foolish of all economies is a police force too small and underpaid.

(4) For purposes of efficiency let us have a national police force. Local police forces belong to the days of highwaymen riding horses, not the days of cars, airplanes and scientific robbery.

(5) Let the national police force always be equipped with more effective means of force than criminals are using in any given situation. If necessary, a special force within the police must be highly trained to meet and to overcome the violent criminal. We must never shrink from the appropriate force against those who use it. But again we should never use more force than is necessary, and in such a situation this restraint depends on the discipline and training which only a national police force can provide.

Criminals guilty of crimes of violence should be held liable to compensate their victims. They should be paid full rates for the harder and more disagreeable tasks which have to be performed in the service of the community, and the payment should go to the victims. Such measures in combination will stamp out the crime wave in quick time, and national energies will then be free from this unhealthy preoccupation to face the constructive future.

Question 250. What about preventing sex crimes?

Answer: Here our first concern is for the victim rather than the perpetrator of the crime. The first duty of the state is to save the innocent victims of crime rather than to reclaim criminals. This principle seems sometimes to be reversed by the old parties. But it will be the primary principle of the laws we shall propose and enforce.

Apart from crime it will by now be clear that I am strongly in favour of individual freedom. The less interference with private life, the better. But in some things we must take a much stronger line. First of all our power for dealing with offences against young people must be greatly strengthened. We must have such severe penalties that offenders against young people are really deterred. Beyond that we must stop the present exhibition of vice, because it is another factor in the corruption of others. The law would be strengthened and the police instructed to close down all establishments, clubs, etc., where vice is flaunted and spread. The present public sale of pornographic literature would also have to be stopped. I do not for a moment want to return to the bumbling philistinism of earlier days, where literary works of art were suppressed in the name of puritanism. But the present commercialism of silly filth must stop.

Apart from more severe measures to stop the corruption of the young and the propaganda and flaunting of vice, I would within any reasonable limit leave adults alone to do what they wish in private, provided always that they in no way intrude their habits on other people. I share the view of a great majority of Britons that we will not have the young corrupted or vice propagated. This must stop.

Question 251. What is your attitude to youth? Have you a youth organisation?

Answer: We do not believe in making men into boys, but rather in making boys into men. That is why in our team organisation we do not discriminate between adults and youths. If a boy can form a team and do the work of the movement, he is treated on exactly equal terms with an older man who forms a team and does similar work. The same goes for girls. Boys and girls have equal rights, and are just as much a part of our organisation, and just as much taken into consultation as older people. I am always as ready to listen to their views, and to take ideas from them as from others. And that goes for all our officials and organisers. We want the young to enter into the full life of the movement, and to do the full work of the organisation. It is not a question of age but of capacity.

Of course, we have older people ready to give their advice and guidance when the young require it. And such men or women get asked for advice, because our young people admire those who have done much for the movement, and are glad to learn from their experience. Among us the usual modern slogan - "I'm as good as him" - is answered quite simply: "Yes, when you have done as much". With us youth has its chance. But because our young people love the movement and wish to serve it well, they are willing - like the rest of us - always to learn.

Question 252. What is your view of social class?

Answer: For me this question simply does not exist. I just do not know what is meant by social class in the modem age. In our movement it never has meant anything. Men and women among us are judged by their character and intelligence, and nothing else. We neither know nor care how they begin, whether in castle or cottage, palace or slum.

For some time it was possible for professional snobs to keep up these distinctions because people of different origin talked in different ways. But with the spread of education and of radio listening, similar ways of speaking are developing in all sections. In fact, as such differences are disappearing from notice, a vested interest in old-fashioned snobbery has to invent them.

The only thing worth being a snob about is human intelligence and character. Let us by all means admire brilliant men and women whatever their origin, and love their company. To be a snob about people just because once their ancestors were clever enough to found family fortunes, without any regard for their own personal qualities, is really a sign of mental deficiency. We have seen too many people who resemble the potato - the best part of them is underground.

Question 253. What is your attitude to ex-servicemen?

Answer: I am naturally on the side of ex-servicemen, because I am one myself. After the first World War I was an official of their local organisation in my first constituency. I feel just the same about those of the second World War, although I was politically opposed to that war itself, because I thought it a mistake.

My feeling is that the ex-servicemen of both wars were led up the garden path by the politicians. We were told in the first one that we were "fighting the war to end wars", "fighting to make the world safe for democracy" and would come back to "a land fit for heroes to live in." It certainly was not a war to end wars; so far from making the world safe for democracy, it brought all chance of democracy to an end in a large part of Europe; and many of our comrades came back from the trenches to the slums which have lasted ever since despite all government promises. Our sons in the second World War were made similar promises with much the same result. "Lend to defend the right to be free" was the slogan I remember best just inside the gate of Brixton Prison. That slogan was a winner, because the big moneylenders have run the world ever since. But they live in Wall Street, New York, not in London.

Does this mean that all the sacrifice of ex-servicemen in two wars was in vain? Not a bit of it. Because in these two wars we made our character, and it is that character which is going to save our country, save Europe and save the world. We may have been tricked and betrayed, but in our struggle and sacrifice we acquired that finely tempered steel of resolution which will be needed for the coming task. We were sent to the work of destruction, but we there developed the qualities necessary for great construction.

This is what I meant when I wrote after the first World War: "Through and beyond the failure of men and of parties, we of the war generation are marching on; and we shall march on until our end is achieved and our sacrifice atoned."

It has been a longer march than I then conceived, but on that journey we have found our younger companions of the second World War and also the new generation. And with them we shall win.

Question 254. Do you believe in complete religious toleration?

Answer: Yes, I believe in complete religious toleration. All shall be free either to worship as they wish, or to keep their religion to themselves. And I have no great respect for anyone who tries to introduce such questions into politics in order to advertise his part in them. It is nearly always the sign of a humbug and a charlatan.

Question 255. How can national dictatorship in Spain and Portugal join a free Europe?

Answer: Do not assume that systems propaganda portrays exist in either of these countries. It certainly does not do so to the extent prevailing in some of the coloured countries of the Commonwealth which are greatly favoured in Westminster and Whitehall. But we will let that pass for the moment and get on with the answer to the question.

Each European country must decide how and when to join Europe in its own way. When the British people decide to enter Europe, it is safe to say that Europe will be created so far as most of the countries now engaged in the Common Market and free trade area are concerned. Now let us consider the attitudes of the remarkable men who rule in Spain and Portugal in a manner which is remote from my policy but is very different from the allegations of their opponents. They would almost certainly be glad to see their countries enter a European system which guaranteed stability, order, freedom from communism and a rapidly increasing standard of life. These regimes represented a last, desperate attempt to save their countries from anarchy and communism, which Spain so terribly experienced. What happened then gives more than enough explanation for anything which has happened since. As patriots I believe they would eventually welcome the entry of their countries into a wider and freer system once they were certain it would be strong enough to save European civilisation from communism. And in any case the growth of European sentiment among all the vital peoples of Europe will certainly in the end sweep these very European countries into this great civilisation.

But if any particular country decides for the time being to stay out, we can afford to continue with our plan until it is ready to enter. We shall have enough to prove overwhelming success. No country can then afford to stay out. Success now depends on one factor: A great decision by the British people.

Question 256. You have described a comprehensive policy which would stop present pressure on Europeans in South Africa and Algeria, but what is your attitude if trouble occurs in these countries at present or in the near future?

Answer: Absolute loyalty to our fellow Europeans. It does not matter whether we agree or disagree with some particular policy in these countries. We must always stand by our fellow Europeans. That is what loyalty means, and without loyalty between Europeans our continent will be lost.

In fact I believe that the vicious attempt of some of the sinister forces in this world to bring South Africa down has failed, and that the future of this potentially great country will become ever brighter. In any case we stood by South Africa in the darkest hours, and will always do so again.

We have always stood by the French in Algeria, too, and always will. We will not sacrifice a million of our fellow Europeans. Whether we agree or disagree with French policy at any particular time, we will stand by France. That is what loyalty means, and we must be loyal to Europe. But the great policy of European Union, for reasons given in many other answers, will bring all these temporary troubles and problems to an end in a manner which can be just to all.

Psychology and How to Live

Question 257. What is your view on psycho-analysis or analytical psychology?

Answer: While in prison under Regulation 18b I read much of what was written on the subject in English and German. I could not speak a word of German, by the way, before the war. But as I was shut up with a number of Germans I took the chance to learn the language, and emerged speaking it almost as easily as English, though often incorrectly.

In prison I was able to read and to learn a great deal. It was a very rough and not very ready way of fulfilling Plato's requirement that statesmen should retire in middle life for a period of reading, reflection and intensive preparation for the final phase of action.

But to return to the subject of psychology, which I can only deal with here in very crude summary. I was more impressed with Jung than with Freud or Adler, whose works seemed to be both synthesized and surpassed by the remarkable Swiss. But the trouble with this infant science is that it has fallen into the hands of many charlatans, and has been exploited to the point of the ridiculous by the sob-sisters of the popular press. The result is that any bad boy can get away with anything by saying Mummy once held him upside down.

Worse still, it has become a method by which the Establishment, the existing system, can reduce its opponents in popular opinion. All challengers and reformers are accused of having complexes. Otherwise, of course, they would be in on the racket. The psychologists of the Establishment invent and ascribe complexes to the opponents of the system. Like the witch-doctors of a primitive tribe they smell out the sins of any suspected enemies of the chief. So what began as a science has in this respect become a racket for the perpetuation of the existing system.

Any challenger in history of an established order could have been dealt with in this way, from Caesar and Mohammed to Gladstone and Shaftesbury. The latter in this analysis must obviously have been full of complexes, when he spent his life stopping children being sweated in the early factories instead of pursuing the usual social rounds of his class and period.

So today the psychologists of the Establishment say in effect to their challengers, the modern reformers: "If you do not like the smell of our cesspool, then you need an operation on your nose". What a game, what a racket! But when all the crooks large and small have been cleared out of the business, it will remain a science with a considerable contribution for the future.

Question 258. What in your view is wrong with family life, why is there trouble between parents and children?

Answer: It is part of the modern disease, which comes from an abrupt transition to a new way of living. In earlier times, boys went out with their fathers to the work and sport of the fields and forest. The things they did together were difficult, and to some extent dangerous. The father, being older, was at first much stronger and more experienced than the son. He was therefore naturally the leader and became both the friend and protector of the boy. The perfect relationship was thus founded, which was continued when the son became adult in a business like agriculture, particularly when it had been conducted by the same family in the same place for generations with sons succeeding fathers. The father then saw in his son a successor whose prowess could carry on further the thing he loved. The son saw in his father a predecessor on whose work he could build further. There was no question of rivalry between them in this natural succession of nature, and little occasion for anything but superficial friction.

Now this natural order of life is replaced by an existence in which father and son often have little or nothing in common, neither work nor interests, nothing together except the place they live in which is often miserable. The order of nature is broken. To the youth the father often seems a jailor rather than a friend or leader. To the father the son often seems a noise, a nuisance and an irritant in the confined space of present-day congested living. We really need not look for deep complexes in a situation which arises from the break-up of an old and natural order of life, because we have not yet found anything to replace its natural harmony. Rather we should seek by community centres in cities, and opportunities for recreation in more natural conditions, to restore something of the old healthy relationship. This will not impair family life, but will help to restore it.

Question 259. Has not father-son trouble always occurred?

Answer: I believe it is along these lines just mentioned that we shall find the practical solution, although I am fully conscious of the Oedipus complex and believe it to be one of the strongest forces in modern society. It is the root of the present resistance to all authority which tends ever more towards anarchy. It arises in the late stages of a society which feels itself absolutely secure, and consequently demands freedom to the point of licence because it no longer feels any need for the protection and cohesion which authority gives. That feeling of exaggerated security is, of course, at present very much an illusion, but it underlies a very prevalent trend.

The Oedipus complex was never very obvious in the earlier, more natural societies. When it became one of the main themes of Greek tragedy the seeds of dissolution were already there. (Forgive my apparent dogmatism on complicated subjects, but I have here to summarise and simplify.) It diminishes to vanishing point, even in modern societies, when they are faced with dangers which make men desire leadership and admire the stronger human qualities. The Oedipus complex is always at its most virulent in societies which both believe themselves to be absolutely secure, and are divorced from all healthy conditions of nature. At that point the complex becomes a disease. If we can understand both its existence and something of its cause we are on the way to curing it. We can never return to nature. But we can to a large extent recover the health of nature in the more conscious society of the future.

Question 260. Do you think that the gulf between generations can be bridged?

Answer: Yes, certainly. This gulf only exists because of the present limitations of our humanity. It will disappear when we have progressed far enough. Already it does not exist in the case of remarkable men, those who are gifted enough. For instance, during my youth, talking to Lloyd George when he was an old man always gave me the impression of conversation with a complete contemporary. At my present age, talking to some men in their twenties, gives equally the impression of conversation with a contemporary, if they are gifted. Of course, an older man of any sense does not feel a contemporary of some lout who can only shuffle his feet, blow a saxophone, twitch his shoulders and roll his head to get the sawdust out of it. But an older man of any capacity feels the contemporary of any young man who can think, feel, and talk about things of immediate or eternal interest. It is just a question of the degree of talent. Eventually, in the course of evolution, everyone should reach this point. Directly men become capable of real thinking and of acquiring true culture, this so-called gulf of generation is bridged by common interests. It is an absurd limitation to be imposed by the brief period of a few years.

When in any sphere of the mind or culture you feel divided from older or younger men by the gulf of generations, you are not really leading in thought or culture but in ephemeral fashions. People so often think that a passing fad is a great discovery, because they have not read enough or lived enough to know that something of the kind has happened a dozen times before. It is a fashion - often continuously recurrent - not a thought. Two men who were capable of "taking all knowledge for their province"

- something which is no longer possible since the range of knowledge has become too great - could not conceive of any gulf of generations, not even if one of them were twenty and the other were one hundred. Of course, a gulf occurs if one party has lost possession of his faculties, and the other has not had time or occasion to acquire them; quite a common occurrence. But between educated men of good, active minds there should be no gulf of generations; or of anything else. And should one man be educated and the other not, he should always be able to reach to things of interest and human sympathy in the other if his own mind and character are good enough. To feel these so-called gulfs is not a thing to brag about, because it is just an admission of a sad limitation.

In a society of failure much of this "generation" nonsense arises from the search for men who have not yet had time to make asses of themselves; particularly in politics because all men within this system work under impossible conditions and must in the end be blamed for their willingness so to work for its rewards. If our present politicians continue much further in discredit, the Establishment will soon have to lift their cabinets out of the cradle. But if you look at the classic periods of creation and stable success, you will find a very different story. So until the next great age, do not let good men be divided by trivial fashions which prove not a difference of mind but rather the absence of mind.

Question 261. What is your view of recreation - is it necessary for men who work hard?

Answer: I know nobody with more capacity for enjoying life than I have. And I am often amused when my present way of life is regarded as austere by people who in my view do not even know how to begin really enjoying life. But if you serve a cause in which you believe-or if you are serving your country in high office-your work must come first. Everything you do should have this end in view. At this point in life what is called recreation must merely be a means to make you more fit to serve. And I do not believe that in the final phase of a man's life he is made any fitter to be President of the U.S.A. by chasing a little white ball round a golf links -strong advocate though I am of manly sports in an earlier and less exacting phase of a man's life-nor do I believe a man is made any fitter to be Prime Minister of Britain by the "recreation" of playing bridge, reading a trashy crime story or even getting lost in the trivia of the last century by reading Victorian novels. If a statesman can find time to read seriously, he would be better employed in reading the history and literature of periods even two to three thousand years away from us. He would find some such epochs a good deal nearer in mind and spirit to the present period than the nineteenth century. The peaks of history are nearer to each other than to the valleys in between.

Worth reading in the literature of the nineteenth century are the philosophers, poets, seers and prophets whose works sensed in advance this decisive age of action. To read nonsense or irrelevant trivialities is not recreation but escapism. To paraphrase in everyday language the words of a famous philosopher: Filling the mind with silliness is like filling the stomach with bad food. I speak always, of course, in this context only about men who have reached the final and decisive stage of a man's life. This usually lasts only a few years, and if a man cannot even be serious for that brief span he is a poor fish.

Question 262. How should a statesman live?

Answer: A man who has reached a serious, decisive period of his life should long since have trained himself to exercise and think at the same time. I think the ideal method is to walk in a wood, preferably on a hill. If these surroundings are not available, then a London park can be excellent. The creation of these great gardens is one of our outstanding national talents. They are nearly ideal for the combination of exercise and thought.

The rest which some seek in trivial games or books should be real rest. By this stage in his life a man of action should have trained himself to go to sleep at any time of the day or night for a short or a long period. If you put something over your eyes and sleep for ten minutes, you will find the increase of your capacity very remarkable.

Of course, the man should try hard to find some time for reading apart from his work, but he should read things of interest or of beauty which elevate and stimulate and do not drug the mind. Listening to great music or looking at beautiful pictures bring us nearer to the creative impulses, while the trivia are an escape from them which can end in being permanent. He should try also as far as his means allow to surround himself with things of beauty, or to see them as often as possible in the galleries, museums and exhibitions of Europe's capitals. I was lucky in my earlier life to acquire a few of the beautiful things of Europe before the prices became prohibitive, and I have adhered to them through all vicissitudes. In short, live strenuously, live hard, but also live with great thoughts and things of beauty.

Does all this sound strangely priggish from someone who detests puritanism? I think not, because it is the way of living appropriate to the final phase of life. In a previous phase I found recreation in boxing, fencing and some gay things; before that in earlier youth I had delight in the company of horses and dogs and in the sports of the field. These things are all good at the right time, but you should grow out of them by the time you are ready for your main task. There is a moment when even the most vital among us must become adult.

Brilliant talk of friends and the stimulation of beauty in all its aspects should never leave us. Nothing but the harshness of time pressure should ever divide us from these things. In any case it was good, in preparation for the life of action, to have had some blessed periods when life was greatly enjoyed. I once wrote in a very different context: "Life is a better training than denial, but, in the moment of destiny, of fulfilment, all creative impulses of life must be fused in one decisive purpose."

Question 263. Did you keep fit by athletics, as you once represented Britain in international sport? What do you feel about such things as eating, drinking, smoking and general way of living?

Answer: The last time I fenced for Britain was in the world championship of 1937 in Paris, when I was forty. Athletics certainly keep you fit, provided you do not overdo them, and have other interests. There are few things sadder than the old champion, if he has overtrained himself and if he has no other interests when his prowess leaves him.

More important than keeping fit by athletics is the general way you live. Not to eat, drink or smoke too much, especially the latter. I do not smoke, because I found it did me a lot more harm than good. When my mind is engaged and I am really concentrated, I tend to forget whether I am smoking or not and become quite oblivious of all physical things. Therefore I smoke too much if I do not stop altogether. I am quite ready to believe that other people are differently affected by smoking, though I sometimes wonder if the cigarette which is supposed to soothe or stimulate is not really an escape mechanism for putting off the task. Everyone dislikes beginning something difficult, but it is surely the will and not the pipe which really makes a start.

Question 264. What do you drink, and what is your attitude to the subject in general?

Answer: I do not drink much, and then only wine or beer, very seldom spirits. And I believe in drinking water much of the time; during most of my life, most of the time. I never touch anything before I speak or do any difficult work.

The great thing to remember about drink is that it relaxes, and does not stimulate. It makes some people feel brilliant, but it does not make them brilliant. People who are brilliant usually find that alcohol takes the edge off their mind and slows them down. In fact, wisely used, wine or beer can be helpful in assisting men to relax when given a chance; this is their real use. But to employ these endowments of civilisation wisely and moderately is, of course, much harder than cutting them out altogether. "Moderation in all things, especially in moderation" said the classic Greeks. By that they meant a lifetime of careful living, interrupted by occasional feasts. And it is not a bad principle.

Question 265. Can you summarise your attitude to "having a good time"?

Answer: Have a good time, but do not lose time in having a good time. That sounds a paradox, but it is really quite a good principle. I mean, take what pleasure you can in life, but always give absolute priority to your serious purpose. When there is a choice between purpose and pleasure, always choose purpose without a moment's hesitation, quite automatically as a fixed habit. Without that clear principle, people who have great capacity both for work and pleasure are divided and distracted. They become unhappy.

Concentrate on whatever you are doing. Take pleasure when opportunity offers and concentrate on that as well while it is there. Pleasure must leave you, of course, at the moment of that final striving which leads to any supreme achievement. Then concentration on purpose must be complete, and another kind of happiness can come through the fulfillment of purpose. Until then, enjoy anything which does neither you nor other people any harm and does not divert you from your main purpose.

Question 266. What do you mean by your phrase: "Live like athletes"?

Answer: In practical terms, when I advise our young men to "live like athletes" I mean: Live in general like an athlete in light training; have a good time occasionally but not too often; be a man with the full vitality of nature, but also with self-control; neither a fool nor a prig; neither profligate nor puritan; never do anything which can impair your mind or body, for you owe this to yourself and the cause you serve.

Link a moderate way of living to the balance between mind and body, that harmony with original nature which the classic Greeks so deliberately achieved in their "Gymnasium", and you can reach the blessed state which the Romans later described as "mens sana in corpore sano". Some of those great lessons from the classic world might restore balance to our present civilisation.

Question 267. What about the drink trade?

Answer: I do not believe in treating the British people like children. It is nonsense to talk of freedom when in their daily life - which matters most to the people - you have a fussy old grandmother sitting on top of you telling you what you may or may not do every moment in the day. People should be able to get a drink when they want. The trade should be able to organise a shift system to do it, and should be freed from many of the present oppressive regulations. Set everyone free in private life.

I do not believe for one moment it would lead to more drunkenness directly we settle down to the system, and that would be very quickly. I notice in my travels that it is quite possible for people to be entirely free to get a drink when they like, and yet to be quite sober. Shortage often creates an abnormal demand for things, and restriction sometimes creates a desire for drink. Look at America under prohibition. I sometimes think that some Englishmen feel that they must take any chance to get a drink, while the foreigner who knows he can get one at any time does not bother. There is just a little contrariness in all of us. You want to beat a veto. It is quite possible there would be less drinking without restrictions.

When Britain is set free in this and in other spheres, the result will much depend on what social conscience and attitude to life can be given by those most respected among the people. Regulations cannot prevent sozzling in private, but a healthy atmosphere can. The atmosphere of the new state will do more than all the laws in the world. Let us begin by treating men like men and not like children. And that goes for everything-freedom for men and women to lead their own lives in every way. We have confidence that the inspiration of the new state, the new outlook, the new way of living will make them good lives.

Question 268. What is your attitude to gambling?

Answer: Gambling is a strong human instinct. You cannot suppress it, but you can use it. That is why I have always been in favour of state lotteries, the profits of which can be used to benefit the people as a whole. Those who disapprove of gambling are of course at liberty to abstain from it, and they will have the pleasure of profiting from the folly of those who do.

Question 269. What is your attitude to the small shopkeeper?

Answer: Help them to maintain their position, help them in every way possible. We believe they give service to the people which the chainstores and co-operatives cannot give. People like variety and individual attention, and they should be able to get these things. I am well aware of the argument that big stores and co-operatives have a pull in price, efficiency, etc., and from their bulk buying organisation. But something of this efficiency could be given to the small shopkeepers by placing a bulk-buying organisation behind them. We could then put them on more equal terms with the big concerns.

Efficiency is not the only thing in life. There is also the way of life. And if it is a desirable way of life, it is worth sacrificing a little efficiency to it.

A family-run concern ought not to be subject to the same rules and controls as the big combines. They ought to be able to give their individual service to the people in their own time and way. By giving them this freedom, you can give the small shopkeepers a pull in service, which will enable them to keep their end up and do very well.

Question 270. What about pensions?

Answer, As I have said again and again in these answers, the way to increase pensions as well as wages and the general standard of life, is to enter Europe with a common government as well as a common market. Then the economic leadership of government can raise pensions, wages and the standard of life as we organise mass production for a larger market which will give increased wealth for all to enjoy. The pensioners like everyone else will find their standard becomes reduced if we cling to the obsolete island system. All those people with fixed incomes are becoming the hardest hit in the collapse of the system. They are always the first to be sacrificed in the fight to live on world export markets. It will be the duty of the new state, with greater resources, in a saner system, to look after them.

Socialism and Syndicalism

Question 271. What are your views on education?

Answer: The first thing to recognise is that education is not something which ends in early life, when you leave school or even the university. Real education is a continuing process throughout life. People should be persuaded to understand this far more, and to take advantage of many more opportunities for adult education which the new state must provide.

From this standpoint it seems to me quite wrong to take any decision as to whether a child is clever or not at the early age of eleven. A boy may seem stupid at that age, and be brilliant later on. In fact, most outstanding men are apt to develop slowly, like many of nature's more remarkable phenomena. So all examinations and tests of that kind should be provisional. A child judged not very bright at an early age should always have the chance of full opportunity in education at a later stage. And the tests should certainly not be exams alone. More and more, in the future, skilled observers of the young with the aid of modern knowledge will be able to apply other tests.

The general aim of education should be to give to everyone the highest level of knowledge from which they can benefit, but not to waste their time in an attempt to teach them things which are no use to them, and which they do not desire. The way should be open to all remarkable children from the cradle to the university. We cannot afford to lose a single talent in any one of them. The system should be concentrated on their discovery and promotion. Above all we must find the scientists and technicians, educate them, pay them as much as or more than they can get elsewhere, and afford them opportunity equal to any in the world for giving those services which can lift our country and all Europe to fresh heights. Money spent on real education is never wasted.

We should try to give a good physique by every means which modern science makes available. And to each child we should try to give not only knowledge, but also some sense of the great beauty which nature gives to the world, and which the genius of man has given to the art which adorns it and inspires us.

Question 272. How will the union of Europe assist education?

Answer: The economic benefits of European union will rapidly increase the money available for the provision and improvement of educational facilities of all kinds. More can be spent on building well-designed schools, and on textbooks and equipment. Education is a vitally important duty, and it is time that its priorities were reflected in government action.

In particular, we intend to improve the position of teachers. It is a gross scandal in Britain, where so much can be wasted on unproductive investments, ranging from expense accounts to obsolete weapons, that teachers have long been deprived of adequate reward, and have had to threaten strikes before there has been much hope of better pay. Training and incentives for their honourable service must be improved. We also want better relations between parents and teachers, especially as both of them contribute to the training of character (as well as ability) in children.

European union will promote the sharing of diverse experience and techniques in educational methods. We shall take no final decision about the merits of relative expenditure on different types of secondary schooling (private, grammar, technical, comprehensive, etc.) until we have thoroughly examined the whole subject in relation to the general European educational system. We shall meanwhile encourage interest in the great museums, libraries and laboratories of Europe, and strengthen the long-established community of learning which exists between all our famous universities.

Our policy for each child is that of wise parents: only the best is good enough. But we have no wish to imitate old party rhetoric in this serious matter, especially as we shall provide funds for education beyond their imagination. Together we Europeans can achieve in education a greatness and radiance which more than befits a continent which has for millennia been a world leader.

Question 273. Do you think that the present insistence of those teaching philosophy in our leading universities on a closer definition of terms, can be of assistance to politics?

Answer: Anything which checks loose thinking and makes thought and expression clearer is an advantage; particularly in present politics where thought and speech are usually so woolly. But teaching in our universities is now so preoccupied with words that it begins to remind of the sterility evident in the schoolmen of the Middle Ages. This has all the symptoms of the end of a culture. I hope and believe that it may only mean an old culture is dying, because the time has come for a renaissance of thought.

Yet the only thing really wrong with these eminent professors is that they call themselves philosophers. If they faced facts, and called themselves lexicographers, they would play a useful part in the better definition of words in some distinguished back room. They only become a menace when they persuade the young that the processes which interest them can be described as thought.

One of the brightest products of one of our leading universities was asked what had occupied his latest studies, and gave the usual reply to the effect that it was a closer definition of terms. Asked to give examples, he replied: "Well, for instance, can a man say I am trying to become an egg? Is not the use of the word 'try' wrong in this context, because, of course, it is impossible to become an egg, and you should only use the word 'try' in relation to the possible". Well, it may indeed be preferable to use the word "attempt" on such an occasion, and this matter might well be subject of earnest study by learned lexicographers, provided it is not called philosophy. The short, practical answer to the whole business seemed to me that in the age of nuclear fission few things can be regarded as impossible, and, anyhow, a man who addressed his intellect seriously over a long period to such a subject, had plainly already become an egg. These are the latter day schoolmen with vengeance; the end of a culture. But renaissance begins.

Question 274. What should be the government's attitude to sport?

Answer: Friendly and encouraging, but not interfering. The management of sport should be left to those who take part in it. But the government should, of course, provide far more facilities for sport than exist today, particularly in and near large towns. That needs money, but it should be regarded as part of the health service. The government's part should be limited to provide this assistance; we do not want sport controlled from Whitehall, but by the institutions sportsmen have created themselves.

The distinction between amateur and professional has become a bit of a farce, and handicaps the country in international sport. Many of the people we have to compete against are really professionals. Some always were pros, in reality, and I understand some still are. So it seems to me far better to do away with the amateur and professional distinctions in international sport, and to look after our men and women as the other countries do, in order to give them a fair chance. But many can give a more valuable opinion on this subject than I can.

Question 275. What about minority problems in Europe; for example the partition of Ireland?

Answer: Yes, partition should certainly end. It is an unnatural division and unjust in the way it was done. Yet we cannot just ignore the minority problem. I long ago proved my friendship for the Irish by my parliamentary opposition to the use of the Black and Tans, but also as a loyal Briton I fully recognise the position of the British minority in Northern Ireland. In fact the only way to end partition without violence is through the union of Europe. If both Eire and Northern Ireland enter United Europe, the frontier will disappear like every other frontier within Europe. But the fear of being a minority under the rule of a very different majority will also disappear.

The same consideration applies to every other minority problem in Europe. For example, the question of the Tyrol will cease to exist when both Italy and Austria enter Europe. It is only the maintenance of present European frontiers containing minorities within them, which causes the trouble. When all are Europeans, every minority will have the protection of the larger community.

Question 276. What is "European Socialism"?

Answer: Any man has a right to call himself a socialist if he works for motives of public service rather than for private gain. That is why we used this phrase. Because our people have certainly proved that they work selflessly for the public good, and it is this spirit which is needed for the building of a new European system. But I am not going to use it in future because it has led to misunderstanding. British people in general think that socialism means the nationalisation or bureaucratic control of industry, that it means the Labour Party policy which was a concept of the last century. But Union Movement has never stood for anything of this kind. In practice, it has proved a mistake to use a phrase which can be misrepresented, and that is why I ceased to use it. I now use instead the term "European Service."

Question 277. What is your policy regarding Workers Ownership or Syndicalism?

Answer: I believe our new thinking concerning the economic leadership of government through the wage-price mechanism will surpass and render unnecessary our old thinking about syndicalism or workers' ownership.

As our policy stands, we shall transfer the nationalised industries from Whitehall control to workers' ownership. Only the industries now nationalised will be so treated. If the change fails to secure improved efficiency by awakening the workers' interest in their own business, these industries will be handed back to private enterprise. If, in proved practice, the workers make a great success of the business, they will have established a strong case for extension of the method to other long-established monopoly industries which are today called "ripe" for nationalisation. But I believe, long before then, the successful economic leadership of government by means of the wage-price mechanism will have rendered quite obsolete the old arguments about the ownership of industry. What is always necessary in my view, and will become increasingly necessary, is the close association of the workers with the practical management of industry. Wise management will try to consult them at every decisive turn, just as a wise political leader consults his members. And above all, they must profit from improvements in efficiency. Look after your own people-that is a first principle.

Question 278. Why does the Wage-Price mechanism make questions concerning the ownership of industry irrelevant?

Answer: The economic leadership of government which the whole people will elect, will operate through the wage-price mechanism at the two points which matter. These two decisive points are wages and prices. For reasons already given in detail, this system will release the vast productive power of modern science, and will soon secure such a much higher standard of life that the worker will lose all interest in controversies belonging to the past battle between employers and employees. As usual, the smaller material interests will cease when material wants are satisfied. We do not spend all the time thinking about food when we cease to be hungry. That is why discussion about nineteenth century ideas of socialism or syndicalism are really a waste of time in the twentieth century. Modern science within the new system will soon take us far beyond all that. Meanwhile our "dynamic pragmatism" will always be ready to try out new ideas and methods, and will be equally ready to revise them in the light of experience, fresh thinking and new scientific discovery.

Question 279. Why do you think the workers will eventually lose interest in the ownership of industry?

Answer: I believe the workers will lose all interest in the ownership of industry for reasons given in my book: *Europe: Faith and Plan*. The argument in favour of syndicalising industries now nationalised, and my reasons for believing the method would soon be as obsolete as nationalisation itself were summarised in the following passages:

I stated: "... a preference for the conduct and development of industries already nationalised by syndicalist method rather than by the present state bureaucracy. It is far healthier for industries which have already lost the principle of private enterprise to be owned and conducted by the workers in them than by the mandarins of state socialism.... the workers in them should be told they would get the benefit of any increased efficiency, which kept the prices they charged stable but enabled their own wages to be raised. Such direct incentive to efficiency and workers' co-operation in new methods would bring far better results than leaving the matter to the present functionaries." But I added: "This attempt in new thinking was right and necessary, but it may well be surpassed by further thinking and by greater possibilities. The plain fact, which must be recognised by all realists, is that the workers have very little interest in questions of the ownership of industry, or any other theoretical matters, when things are going really well. Small blame to them, for they find better things to do with their spare time and money than attending committee meetings; and as opportunity occurs for real leisure, holidays, travel and general culture arising from protracted facilities of education, the use of spare time and money will find ever more desirable outlets. In short, if we resolve the main economic problem through the wage-price mechanism, syndicalism may look as irrelevant as nationalisation begins to look today."

I believe these past controversies really belong to the last century, and will be made quite irrelevant by the new system which will arise from our twentieth century ideas.

Progress and Patriotism

Question 280. What is your attitude to the TradeUnions?

Answer: We are in favour of trade unions, and all our members who are qualified are asked to join them. But the trade unions like everyone else must obey the law of the land. And the law under the new system will prevent all the restrictive practices and manifold abuses of today. We shall ask the people to vote for the end of these relics of the past. In return, our system will secure steady employment at wages which will continually and surely increase as science increases production. Restrictive practices and other abuses are, of course, born of the fear of unemployment. The fear and the abuses will end together in a state which serves the whole and not the faction. In the meantime, nothing will be gained by middle-class organisations seeking to impose the handcuffs of small reforms on trade unions which are fighting for their members' interests in an anarchic society. The rule of present society is: "Each for himself and devil take the hindmost." The present attitude of the trade unions draws the consequence of that society, and will be altered only by a change of system.

We believe that under the present system the trade unions can be reformed only from within, not without. It is not possible for a small section of the population like some of the middle-class organisations already mentioned-to try to reform the unions by petty interference from outside. That will get them nowhere. Great reforms can only be carried through by a national government elected by vote of the whole people which includes the vote of trade unionists. Our members are asked to prepare for that day in the following way. All those qualified to join are asked to become trade union members. They can fight the communist influence within the unions. They have a stronger and more natural appeal, because our members are asking that the unions be used for the purposes the workers originally intended, which is to look after the workers' industrial interests. The communists and fellow travellers are always trying to pervert the unions and exploit them for their own political purposes; they must be exposed from within till the workers see through them. That is what our members are trying to do in their "Trade Union Action." This is how a new leadership can emerge by vote of trade union members, if the old bosses cannot clear up the abuses and do the real job of the trade unions.

Question 281. What will be the part of the Trade Unions in the system you suggest?

Answer: We want the trade unions to play not a lesser but a greater part in the new system, and we hope and believe that many existing leaders will be glad to co-operate with the principles of our government. We want them in every way to be free to play the part of another "Estate of the Realm." For instance, they can take on the job of doing many of the things done today by a wasteful state bureaucracy, such as questions affecting conditions of work, unemployment pay, welfare, sick-pay, holidays, compensation claims, legal representation. The administration of these matters should be entirely taken over by the trade unions. A larger life awaits trade unions in our new system, as it does everyone else who works, produces and creates.

Question 282. Do you agree with equal pay for equal work?

Answer: Of course, if a woman can do the same job as well as a man she should have the same pay. And if she can do a better job she should get better money. We should never have discrimination on account of sex. The only differential should be for skill, and if a woman has the skill she should get the rate for the job.

Question 283. What is your view of hereditary industry and hereditary wealth?

Answer: What is good in the hereditary system is the continuity in the conduct of life and industry. What is bad is the distortion and disruption of the economy by large accumulations of misused wealth in idle hands.

First, our policy means in practice that hereditary businesses should be relieved from the destructive effects of present day death duties. Whether they be small or large, farms or industries, it is desirable that they should not be broken up when one man dies. There is too little continuity and sense of inherited responsibility and duty in modern life, not too much. As long as a family can successfully conduct a business which a member has founded, it should be encouraged to do so even when the founder is dead. This should be a hereditary, organic element in national life of which we need more, not less.

Secondly, our policy means that large accumulations of hereditary wealth and its uneconomic, anti-social use will be prevented by the wage-price mechanism. The undue accumulation of profit at the expense of wage will be automatically prevented.

In short, we wish to support a hereditary system which is productive rather than parasitic. The question of public service, engagement in science and art or in their support should be taken into account as well as technical production.

In times of crisis we should always prevent too much being consumed by too few. We have long had the principle that "none shall stuff while others starve." When all such problems are resolved, and there is plenty for all, we must still prevent the upset of our economy by the means the wage-price mechanism will always provide.

Question 284. Do you believe in promotion by merit, and the end of privilege?

Answer: I believe in promotion by merit, and by merit alone. I believe that privilege is one of the great dangers of this old society. You see it all around you. Men are in positions simply because they were born into them, irrespective of their abilities.

And better men are held down because they were not born in the right place. Nepotism is rampant in Britain today. This must stop. No system which rests on privilege can survive in competition with systems which rest on promotion by merit. We are probably saved today only because comparable privilege exists in the Soviet bureaucracy, which is rapidly becoming a hereditary caste. Nepotism is rampant too in Russia, and the difference in standard of life between the privileged and the mass of the people is even greater. It is even harder for talent to rise through a communist bureaucracy than through a capitalist society.

We shall establish a system in which not only the way is open to talent-to ability alone-but the whole influence of the state is thrown behind the men of ability. Our system is designed to discover them and to bring them rapidly to the top.

We are not against the conduct of a business by members of the same family as the founders, so long as they are men of ability. In fact we will do much to free them from the burdens and penalties which break up family businesses today, but we are determined that no remnants of hereditary privilege shall keep new, good men down. We shall find them-or give them a chance to find themselves-and bring them rapidly to the front. It was said of Bonaparte's armies that every private soldier had a marshal's baton in his knapsack. And whatever the purpose be, this is the way to success, the method of achievement. Our system must have the same spirit in bringing new men of first-rate ability to the top without long, wasted years of waiting. We need them all, and quickly.

Question 285. Do you consider yourself to be of the Right or the Left in politics?

Answer: Neither. If any such description could be applied to us it would rather be the "hard centre," the opposite to the present soft core. But I never use these terms in relation to our thinking, because they mean nothing to us. Our policy cuts clean across the "right" and "left" of the old world. These expressions are nonsensical when applied to us. In thought, we are no more Conservative than we are Socialist or Liberal. Our thinking is a creation of the modern age, though it has deeper roots in the European past than that of the old parties. I do not speak of our people as "right" or "left" but give them their true name; the vital forces of Europe.

Question 286. Have you not often stated that you want to combine the principles of progress and patriotism which are today opposed - what do you mean by this?

Answer: Yes, this idea has always been basic in my thinking. In my first election I stated the principles of socialistic imperialism. It was a crude and clumsy phrase which belonged to that period, but it contained the idea to develop our home and overseas territory for the welfare of all. Progress was then regarded as belonging to the left and patriotism to the right. This was my first attempted synthesis of progress and patriotism. Later I developed the idea considerably.

In brief, patriotism is a vital principle not only because it is a fine emotion without which anyone is less than a man, but also because it embodies the essential principles of stability and order without which no state or community can endure. Progress is also a vital principle, it is at one with the nature principle that every organism must grow and develop or decline and perish, and it embodies the essential principle of using science, the energy and invention of man's mind, to elevate his condition, without which stability and order-even life itself-cannot be preserved.

Progress is frustrated without conditions of order and stability. That is why the anarchic character of the left ends not with progress but in chaos. Also order and stability cannot be maintained without progress, particularly in modern conditions. Because life does not stand still, and any policy which tries to conserve what exists without recognising the urgent need for progress ends equally in chaos.

Rightly regarded, progress and patriotism are not antithetical but complementary principles. You cannot have progress without the stability and order which patriotism includes, and you cannot have patriotism, the preservation of the state, without the progress which alone enables the state to live, prosper and advance. Yet those two great principles of progress and patriotism have been divided by the war of the parties. Our thought once again cuts right across the division of the parties. We achieve a synthesis at a higher level, by uniting the principles of patriotism and progress.

Press and Television

Question 287. Do you believe in freedom of the Press?

Answer. Yes, certainly. But I believe in freedom of other people as well. By this I mean the freedom of anyone to reply who is attacked in the Press. It is wrong that any of us can at present be blackguarded without any right of reply. That is not freedom but its reverse. It gives some freedom to abuse other people, but it does not give the people abused the freedom to answer back. It is true that if you are grossly libelled you can bring a libel action. But that is too expensive for most people, and a very uncertain procedure. And in any case skilled journalists know how to damage you without incurring libel risk. The only real remedy is to give any man attacked in the press equal space to reply. Let him have equal right to attack the editor, or press lord who owns the paper, subject, of course, to the ordinary libel laws. That would check all the present intrusion into privacy, and misrepresentation in many different ways to which the individual is subject. And government, or any other institution should have the same right of reply. No bumbling controls, just the right of anyone to answer back and have his say. That is surely the fair way of dealing with a free press.

Question 288. Has a Press boycott ever been organised against you and your Movement?

Answer. Yes, intermittently ever since I left the old parties. Apart from our private knowledge of the boycott, it is obvious that it is organised, because a man who can draw such large audiences is always news, particularly in recent times when most of the old party leaders could not get a meeting at all. Most of the national press alternated between boycott and abuse. Generally we are attacked, but all reply suppressed. Yet if a man is interesting enough to be attacked, he is surely interesting enough to be heard in his own defence. The danger of this suppression of the truth is that most of the people do not know it is occurring. Truth is smothered in the dark. This had nothing to do with the working journalist with whom I usually get on very well and there are honourable exceptions among proprietors who make their papers interesting by giving all news a fair deal. But more and more proprietors represent the big money interests. It is natural they should want to keep things as they are so long as they can. From their point of view, I do not blame them for preferring conservatism to us, though they need not have employed all the methods they used in an attempt to stop us.

When conservatism fails and the danger of communism is clear, things change very quickly. At that point we had support in the national press before, and we shall have it again. They may not like us, but they must know we are patriotic British people, and, in the last resort, they will prefer us to the gang whom Moscow hopes to put in power in this country when economic collapse gives world communism its chance. Until that crisis of the system, we shall have most of the national press usually against us. When that situation becomes clear they will change quickly. Meantime we nearly always get a fair deal from journalists in the provincial press, for two reasons. First, they have the old tradition of British journalism and usually report fairly. Second, if we have a big meeting in their neighbourhood and they report it unfairly, too many of their readers know they are not speaking the truth.

Question 289. Why do press, radio and television report so many trivial people with nothing to say, instead of reporting you and other serious people?

Answer. As a sense of crisis develops, press, radio and television are impelled to report serious things. Today they deal in triviality because the gravity and urgency of the situation are not apparent to very many. But when a sense of reality returns, they will give space and time to reality, or people will lose interest in the papers. Then there will be an overwhelming popular demand to hear us, as well as more and more devoted men and women to serve our cause. Today we get the biggest public meetings in the country. Tomorrow it will be difficult to exclude us from press, radio or television without that obvious prejudice and unfairness which will more than ever swing the people to our side. Already they say in effect: this voice is silenced, because it is feared. That is an uncomfortable position for the Establishment today, and will be a dangerous position tomorrow. Perhaps they realise the truth of something I say to our own people. Give us even a fraction of the press and television available to our opponents, and this would not be a match because it would become a walk over; so easy that it would hardly be interesting. When the people can really hear our case, the contest will be over. But then will begin the greater task of doing what the people want done.

Question 290. How can you meet the power of press, radio and television?

Answer. By the devoted work of our members, men and women in the streets, on the doorsteps or in the homes of the people. You can always defeat press, radio and television in the end, if you get enough such men and women who are really devoted to a new idea and a great cause. We have only to increase the number we have already. Adverse press publicity was even defeated in the past by the Labour and Liberal parties, in parts of the country where they had the press against them, in the days when they still had such men and women.

It is true that the modern power of the money machine, and the instruments of propaganda which it controls, is now greater. But so is the number of people who are educated and capable of leading others in the street and in the home. Many people are politically asleep today because they so far have no sense of crisis, and find no need to give their lives to a political cause. But the moment the situation changes this mood will change. Then we shall get more such people. Today we only get those who can see a little further ahead. It is simply a question of getting enough men and women who are the natural leaders of the people. We have the only cause in Britain which in the coming crisis can attract the educated, the energetic, the determined and the idealistic.

Past and Future

The Parties and Union Movement

Question 291. Do you feel you are getting old?

Answer. No, as I finish this book in August, 1961, I am exactly nine years younger than Dr. Adenauer when he formed a government for the first time in 1949. His prospects at my age must have looked a lot bleaker than mine do today. At 85 this remarkable man is still in office after twelve years of government, during which Germany rose from the depths to the heights of prosperity. Even his opponents must admit that judged by practical results this is by far the most remarkable achievement of any government in the post-war world.

Clemenceau, when he formed his war-winning government in 1917, was twelve years older than I am now. Churchill, de Gaulle and many others were older when in various ways they began their periods of success. For, on the whole, in the modern age, it has so far been the older men who succeeded in government and the younger men who failed.

This question of age, as Bernard Shaw pointed out long ago, is largely a question of what you want to do, what your line is. He observed in his whimsical fashion that a man was getting on at twenty if he wanted to be a ping-pong champion, but was on the young side at eighty for jobs which needed maturity like statesmanship.

To succeed late you must, of course, have staying power. You must have lived always with moderation, you must have a strong constitution and keep fit. In respect of health I have so far been fortunate.

Before leaving the subject may I draw your attention to something which may be a slight guide in the future. You will observe that the very dullest people in our native land always tell a man in the first half of his life that he is too young to do anything, and in the second half that he is too old to do anything; what they really mean is they are consistently against anyone in any circumstances ever doing anything. Every older man who is jealous of a young man says to him: you are too young. Every young man who is jealous of an older man says: you are too old. Age is the only card the dunce has to play. It means nothing; what really matter are ability, character and stamina.

Question 292. Briefly, what do you think of the Conservative Party?

Answer. The virtue of Conservatism is that it is the party of patriotism. It means well. Unfortunately, the leaders it selects always arrive at results precisely the opposite to its intentions. So the party which existed to preserve the Empire has ended by liquidating the Empire. The party which believes in Great Britain has been the main architect of Small Britain. The party which believes in stability is bringing our country to the verge of chaos. But we need not traverse again the ground I covered in another answer. It is enough to state the undeniable fact that the Conservative Party has been chiefly responsible for the policies of Britain during the last fifty years.

What is the character which has produced this lamentable conclusion to a chapter in British history? This is the party of the smug, the satisfied, in an age which demands dynamism; the party of privilege when survival depends on promotion by merit; the party which exploits talent but never trusts it; the party of the tired, which calls a yawn a policy; the party of snobbery about the wrong things, which rejects intellect but reveres rank; the party of the climber, without aim to climb beyond a perch on a rotten bough; the party without purpose or great design; the party of small expedients to face the need of great decisions; the party which is always late, and now exists only as an ineffective brake on socialist policies; the party which wills the end of greatness but always rejects the means; the party which excluded Churchill in all his years as a creative spirit, and used him only for the fatal process which finally destroyed the values in which it professed to believe; the party which detests brilliance and loves dullness; the party which idealizes the small, the grey, the mediocre, and will achieve its ideal in the state to which it is reducing Britain, if that condition be not the final lethargy of death.

Question 293. Briefly, what do you think of the Labour Party?

Answer. The virtue of Labour is that it is the party of progress. It is a virtue which it lost in youth. And the reason - you cannot achieve progress through chaos. For the Labour Party in whole character, structure and method remains a rabble, and rule of rabble ends in chaos. It wills the end of progress but always rejects the means, which are union, leadership, decision and action. That is why Labour always breaks under any test of reality. It broke during its last hard test in government, and now it breaks even in opposition when faced with decision on real issues. Only for a brief period Labour lived as a great party with a functioning government, because things were then so easy. They climbed on the shoulders of Churchill's victory, when the country was tired of effort. Then for a number of years they benefited from a sellers' market, which was caused by the destruction of war and the temporary absence of their competitors. Even then they could only carry on by the devaluation of the pound, which gave an artificial bounty to British exports during a considerable period until the unchecked rise of internal prices wiped out this advantage. It remains one of the paradoxes of history that British capitalism, and the successive Conservative governments which followed the proved ineptitude of Labour on all fronts, only survived for several years by reason of Sir Stafford Cripps' exaggerated devaluation of the pound. Now that prop is removed by the further inflation which occurred under conservatism, the system crumbles. But Conservative hats should be raised in honoured memory of the Labour Chancellor, if any of the heads beneath them had the faintest idea what really happened. Yet Conservatism can no longer be rescued in this way by skilled Treasury advisers, because the same trick cannot be played effectively twice. Other countries have now observed what occurred, and a British devaluation would almost certainly be followed by other devaluations with everyone back in the same relative positions.

So we return to normal with a Conservative government heading for crisis, and the Labour Party running away from the very thought of government in such a situation, by at once ceasing to be a party which anyone can take seriously. For, again, it is an extraordinary paradox of politics that the party founded on the expectation of capitalist crisis is always thrown into panic and surrender by its arrival. From the outset they have prophesied that capitalism will break down and have stated that the system must then be changed. But directly prophecy is fulfilled in the breakdown of the system-albeit for reasons very different to those they gave- a Labour government resigns as it did in 1931. My comment at the time was surely not unjust: "What are we to think of a Salvation Army which takes to its heels on the Day of Judgment?"

What is the reason for this paradox? The answer is the still greater paradox of a policy which seeks to create a socialist State in a small island which is dependent on the markets of the capitalist world. And it is a policy which aggravates every destructive force operating on those markets by promoting the exploitation of the backward in competition against us under the banner of brotherhood, and by favouring the extension of Soviet power within the international system which puts our national trade at the mercy of the dumped production of Russian slave labour. Thus Labour like Conservatism achieves the opposite result to its intention-the acceleration of the capitalist system's progress to disaster until the resultant chaos ends in communism. In reality the Labour Party has only one serious role- pacemaker for communism.

Question 294. Have not good judges expressed the view that you should have stayed in the Labour Party and used your influence to make it effective?

Answer. Yes. Bernard Shaw expressed to view to me with great force that I should stay in the Labour Party on the grounds that I was bound to succeed Ramsay MacDonald and could then carry through the real policy. The leading Labour Party journalist of that period, John Scanlon, expressed the reasons for that view in the following passage of his book The Decline and Fall of the Labour Party:

"By the time Sir Oswald rose to make his speech the Conference had returned to normality, and the volume of cheering which greeted his rising showed the amazing hold he had acquired on the mind of delegates [at the Labour Party Conference, October, 1930.] Next to the Prime Minister, he was the most popular man at the Conference ... Sir Oswald's vote was the biggest challenge ever delivered to the governing machine ... In the Press and the Labour Movement itself the discussions now centred round the question of how long it would be before Sir Oswald became the party leader ... No other leader was in sight ... every prophet fixed on Sir Oswald as the next party leader. Even Socialists, who had no particular love for Sir Oswald, were saying nothing could stop it. All the prophets, however, had overlooked the one man who could stop it - Sir Oswald himself."

Many other men urged upon me the same opinion and course of action. I am still reproached on the subject sometimes by old colleagues in the Labour Party.

They all seem to me to overlook two facts:

(1) The Labour Party in whole structure, method, character and psychology is wrongly conceived, because it is completely inadequate to a great age which requires decisive action. Labour may quite possibly come into office once more, but this will only make quite certain the dissolution and destruction of the Party in the conditions it will then have to meet.

The Labour Party was created in another epoch for quite

different purposes. It lacks all the qualities which are now necessary. Believe me I did not lightly come to this decision to leave old comrades, and many splendid people in the rank and file, without good reason. Nothing great could ever be done with the Labour Party, and something great has to be done. That is the long and the short of it.

The inadequacy of the Labour Party to this period has already been proved, and the necessity for great policies in face of coming events will soon be proved. I am more than ever convinced by subsequent developments that it was necessary for me to leave the Labour Party and to undergo the immense effort and protracted ordeal of creating a new movement from our people which is capable of doing what has to be done.

(2) Just as the character of the Labour Party is liberal to the point of the anarchic, so the policy of the party is in essence liberal to the point of laissez faire. The fatal paradox lies in the attempt to combine socialism in this island with the extreme free trade doctrine of the Manchester school in world markets. Nationalised industries have to compete in the world markets of capitalism when capitalist industries have failed to do so. State industries have to be more competitive in terms of world capitalism; the idea is almost a contradiction in terms. Further, the life of this island depends in their system on the success of this competition; they are not just dumping for political purposes on world markets a surplus from a self-contained, transcontinental economy, as the Russians do.

This position in practice is so plainly absurd that the abler men who lead the Labour Party always shrink from a socialism in which their followers believe. Neither their form of socialism nor any other form of conscious and dynamic direction of industry can possibly work, if subjected to the chaos of capitalist world markets in conditions of competitive collapse. Yet the liberal internationalism which is inherent in the beliefs of the Labour Party would always tie us to that position.

The final paradox is the Labour Party's attempt to implement what Marx conceived to be the last phase of capitalism by discarding British production, which is surplus to the home market, in the form of loans to backward countries.

Marx called it imperialist aggression, and analysed with devastating effect the end of the process: Labour calls it Christian brotherhood and believes it is the means to make capitalism work forever now that its leadership is convinced socialism will not work at all.

The Labour Party neither in innate character nor in deep belief could ever possibly do what I believe is necessary to be done in the modern world. A Conservative M.P., after hearing me make a speech in the High Court, was good enough to write in an article in the Spectator the following question: Where might the Labour Party be today if Sir Oswald Mosley had not left it? He was also good enough to supply an answer: "Certainly not in the humiliating posture disclosed in the Budget debates …" I appreciate the compliment but I am afraid the real answer must be: "Finally in the same position - on its back - with all the vital forces of the coming British revival smothered underneath the tumble of the fat fellow". Meantime the victory of the more realistic Communist Party would become inevitable.

Surely it is now demonstrated by the phenomenal rise of our Movement before the war that the people desired a modern alternative. We drew from all parties and from people who were disgusted with all politicians. It required two special Acts of Parliament and a war even to delay our progress, which is now resumed with surer, firmer, more measured stride than ever to the victory which the developing situation and our proved power of appeal to every section of our people now makes certain.

Question 295. Briefly, what do you think of the Liberal Party?

Answer. You might as well ask me briefly what I think of Noah's Ark; for much the same collection came out of it. There are, of course, some good people in the Liberal Party, as there are in the other parties. But there is about the party as a whole a quite unique atmosphere of obsolescence and oddity. It is a party without any moving spirit except an agreement that each member may differ. They pick up votes, of course, from discontent in the early stages of crisis, like all cults of unreality. It is the nature of men to seek first the easy way out; this is very understandable. They are induced to turn toward reality only when they at last understand they have to do something serious to save themselves. So we may expect a little artificial progress for Liberalism in the first shock of disillusionment with the old parties. It will last only a very short time, because Liberalism has nothing real to offer, and the people will quickly grasp this in face of real problems.

The basic reason is that Liberalism, even more than the other old parties-and this is saying a lot-ties Britain to international markets, in pursuit of obsolete theories which have no relation to modern facts. Even when they advocate going into Europe, it is only as a step towards a general free trade (Times 30/9/60). And that free trade world would now include coolie labour working for a wage of a few shillings a week, but using the same modern, simplified, rationalised machines as western labour. These machines can be serviced, and the labour supervised, by very few, highly paid western technicians. For the rest, it is the level competition of a man earning a few shillings a week but using the same tools, against a man earning our wages. The factor of skill is lost in such conditions, and even the factor of physique and psychology. To stand in front of a conveyor belt with a light hammer tapping the same bit of machinery in the same place as it goes by in endless succession, is a task whose monotony is actually better suited to oriental or African than western physique and psychology. I realised this years ago standing in Ford's works at Detroit and watching some oriental workers do just that job. But the Liberals have not yet learnt the facts of modern life. Science today makes nonsense of the economics of the last century. That is why in the very brief summary appropriate to this odd case, Liberalism belongs to Noah's Ark.

Another and conclusive reason why the Liberal Party cannot succeed is that it can only gather enough support to come to power during a period of crisis, and in a crisis the last party to which anyone will turn is the present Liberal Party.

Question 296. What do you think of the small parties which spring up from time to time and disappear again?- and what are the contrary characteristics of a real movement?

Answer. There are plenty of these little parties in periods like this with a fine choice of parochial or freak programmes, which range from the simple but sensible proposal for knocking a shilling off the rates to a universal hatred of all kinds of foreigners, or any other minor or major mania which may fill an empty head to the exclusion of all else. The bob-off-the-rates lot naturally get further than the bit- off-the-head lot, but none of them get anywhere in the end. You may remember that soon after the war a party with a nice, easy, emotional little policy of Commonwealth, even got so far as winning by-elections; but it soon faded like the rest.

What then is the reason for this transient phenomenon in times like these? The answer is surely that the electorate is really quite content with things as they are, but likes to give the Establishment a prod every now and then, just to keep it awake. I suppose this accounts for the odd fact that I was able as an independent of twenty-six years old to defeat the Conservative Party by a majority of two to one in their old stronghold of Harrow, despite the utmost effort of their party machine and the visit of Lord Birkenhead and other outstanding figures to speak against me. And the performance was repeated at the next election. Then I had not a quarter of the ability or a tenth of the experience I have now. Why was it I then found it easier to win elections than I do now? The answer is not the way I have been attacked concerning the war or any other subject; my stand against the war begins already to prove an advantage as the results become clear. To be attacked is nothing; for a man who is not attacked is nothing.

The answer is surely that a vote for me as a young man in that period was just a flip of the towel, a rouser for the old gang, but a vote for me now means much more; perhaps the end of an epoch. It is one thing to send a single, bright boy back to parliament to give the old boys a bit of cheek; that is great fun. But it is quite another thing to send back a mature man, the head of a deeply serious party which stands for a fundamental change; that is a grave step. And the electorate quite naturally does not vote for a great change till it sees the need. Meantime it takes its fun in quite a variety of ways.

In contrast to some of the freak parties in easy times, you will find that serious movements and serious men in history seldom get a large popular vote until their time comes. Then they advance with extraordinary speed if they have the ideas and the men which fit the age. It matters then not a rap how much they have been previously attacked.

Take the minor case of Ramsay MacDonald, or the major case of Hitler, just for the purpose of studying this limited point. MacDonald was far more attacked on account of his opposition to the first World War than I have been for my opposition to the second; and he was assailed from much stronger ground because he had not fought in air or trenches as I had, and was just a professional pacifist. Yet within six years of the end of the war he became Prime Minister, because economic depression had arrived and the country turned to the socialist policy and to the then serious party which he represented.

Hitler was not only attacked as few men have ever been, but after ten years effort only polled 2.6% of the votes recorded in Germany in 1928. Yet five years later he was in power with 44.1% of the votes recorded. It was not his anti-Semitic policy as some imagine, nor even the Versailles Treaty, which got him there; he had been fulminating on these subjects for a decade or more, but only polled 2.6% of the votes at the end of it. It was the change in the economic situation which brought him to power.

Unemployment and his party rose together; you could see the lines rising simultaneously on a simple graph.

For better or worse a great people only change for great reasons; usually economic events which reflect profound errors in policy. Until then they may be interested in serious parties-for instance they attend our meetings in large numbers but they do not much support them by votes. At the time of writing they usually give the candidates of our Union Movement about 8% of the votes recorded. But when necessity arises the people turn to a serious movement which has done long years of preliminary work, and rapidly vote it into power. What matters to a nation in the final moment of truth is that the people should not only turn to a serious party with a serious policy but to a movement with a moral character capable of shaping the future-which is of necessity revolutionary-with full regard to the finest thoughts and noblest traditions of the past.

Question 297. When you speak of the "lunatic fringe", do you mean people in your party or outside it?

Answer. I use the phrase, but it was not invented by me. It was first uttered by Bonar Law, when he was the leader of the Conservative Party. He said that "every party has its lunatic fringe". By that he meant an extreme element which was attached to his party but made it ridiculous by exaggeration and absurdity of their attitude. Our movement, like the other parties, has a lunatic fringe. The difference is that they retain such people inside the party, and we sling them out. As explained in other answers, our party has a firmer base and a more vigorous executive capacity than the old parties. So our lunatic fringe is outside the party, because we get rid of them. But many people think they are still inside. And when they strike silly attitudes or make absurd noises, we get some of the discredit.

We were adversely affected at the time of the North Kensington election by some odd lot which had nothing in the world to do with me. Our people were circulating the constituency as polling day approached, putting through loud speakers carefully prepared slogans which appealed to the electors to vote for us without being offensive to the coloured population, such as: "Vote for Mosley and send the coloured people back to Jamaica with fares paid to a fair deal, good jobs and decent conditions at home". But another van then started to circulate which bawled crude and silly insults which no doubt lost me a lot of votes. On this occasion a well known intellectual who is a good friend of mine happened to be visiting the constituency to see how things were going. After hearing this stuff he wrote me a reproachful letter to the effect that he could not have believed it of me. If my intellectual friend fell into the error of thinking the van was mine, how many electors must have thought the same thing and how many votes must have been lost? These people advertised themselves at my expense.

So you see a lunatic fringe can be a nuisance, even when they are completely insignificant. In this way a handful of people can do much harm. For they make sounds and strike attitudes which can be mistaken for those of our people, however unlike us they are in reality. They are a walking caricature of our movement. We all know how effective it is to caricature an opponent in politics with a drawing in a newspaper. How much more effective then it is to have a walking caricature which people can actually mistake for him. No wonder these clowning antics delight our enemies and anger our friends. Although finally they prove nothing more than a minor nuisance which can no more impede the progress of a great movement than flies can stop a racehorse. In the end the truth gets through. It is our job to see it is known more rapidly.

Question 298. Why do you think that all the old party politicians are wrong, when some of them are men with fine records?

Answer. Certainly, some of them have fine records. But it is possible to be wrong even if you have a fine record, and I have given reasons for thinking them wrong which events have confirmed, or will soon confirm. And I am entitled to ask you when these men had their fine records? How many years back? And what have they been doing since? It is possible, for instance, that a man should have had a very fine record in the first World War, but be fit for nothing now if in the interval he has led the wrong kind of life. A man may be a hero at twenty and dead of drink at forty; we have all known such cases. And I can assure you that if you had been a hero at twenty but had spent the next forty years in the intrigues of a parliamentary lobby, varied only by a little baby-kissing at election time - without the system giving you any chance to do anything real, and without your having the resolution to break from the system - you would not be fit for anything much but baby-kissing by now, and anyone but a baby should have the sense to know it.

I am, of course, using the language of exaggeration to illustrate my point. But I think you get my meaning. Man must not only start good, but stay good. You may be born with the best physique in the world, yet if you spend enough years in a feather bed you will not be able to walk down the street. The old parliamentary life and the old political game just rot a man. Some of them have stayed there, but kept fit in other ways. I do not condemn them all. There are good men among them who may yet have some value to the nation. For instance, many of the best back-benchers on both sides are now coming round to our way of thinking about various matters, from European union to restricting immigration.

If you want to be fit to give great service to the country in hard times you must live in a different way. Our life of adversity and effort at least prevented us from softening up. Whatever qualities we had, have been hardened, tempered and developed by the effort of the Establishment to crush us. It was not a pleasant experience, but the real life which makes men is not all milk and honey.

Question 299. What do you think of the Establishment?

Answer. A medley of mediocrity whose malice and mendacity know no limit in pursuit of its single principle which is the maintenance of its members' positions within the country they have ruined.

Question 300. Haven't you been going a long time and not yet succeeded?

Answer. We have not been going for a fraction of the time the old parties have, and only about a quarter as long as the communists. When they had only been going as long as I have now they had got nowhere at all. I and my friends have got much further in the time.

Now the communists have won nearly half the world. And they will get the rest of the world if nothing more effective is done to stop them. By this I mean we need a higher idea and a stronger faith. Our Movement has both. As for the time business, it does not matter how long you take provided your idea is true, and that you have the courage and persistence to stick to it through thick and thin. In that event you will win in the end. And it does not matter a rap whether our idea wins before or after my death. What matters is that it shall win.

In fact it looks more and more as if the decision will come before many years are past. The present system always returns to crisis, unless its rulers can escape into war. And they cannot escape into war now, because they know war will destroy the world—themselves included.

What you need in the final crisis is a tried and tested Movement which has proved itself in a long struggle, which at times has involved the bitter unpopularity that tests character.

Question 301. Would you have won by now if the war had not come?

Answer. Even opponents have admitted we should have won long before now if the war had not come, notably the leading journalist of the Left at the time. But in the end it will not be a bad thing that our effort has been longer and our test of character has been harder. You will already have noticed that it is the men and the movements with quick successes who fail soon afterwards. The great value of a long, hard test such as we have endured is that it proves men and forms character. You know where you are with men who have been through so much for their beliefs. They are not just telling you they are honest, they have proved it. When you elect them, they will neither sell out on you, nor crack up in crisis. In the days to come our people will need to serve the men who are proved steel true.

Question 302. As some of your chief opponents admit that you would have won if the war had not come, why then did you at first not make more rapid progress after the war?

Answer. The war was an escape for our rulers from the situation which then confronted them, particularly their unsolved economic problem. But after the war the pent up demand caused full employment and a strong position for Labour to demand better wages on a buoyant market. The war, therefore, postponed crisis at the expense of making it still worse at a later date. In that situation the people naturally saw no need to change. During a long period they felt that "they had never had it so good". Very few people see far ahead, and the mass of our very stable English people never move before they must. In fact this calm, stolid quality, which can be a virtue, becomes a menace when they will not move until the house is on fire. No wonder we did not make such rapid progress in a period when few people could see any need for change. The wonder is that during that time our Movement not only lived but made considerable progress. This showed the strength of our idea; it was a near miracle.

We also at first had to contend with a certain prejudice created against us on account of our opposition to the war. It is only now that this disadvantage is being turned to a great advantage-as I always knew it would be in the end - because the development of the situation is proving both the truth we spoke and the need for men with character enough to face unpopularity for a period.

The benefit of our protracted, hard experience was that it gave time to develop clearer, better, higher ideas, and that the character of our people was tested and proved in that long adversity. A great policy and a firm character will be a sound basis for the rapid progress which is now beginning, and for our ultimate and inevitable victory.

Question 303. When you die, what arrangements are made for the leadership and further conduct of Union Movement?

Answer. After my death, Union Movement will be conducted by a council until a new leader emerges. In all movements of reality facing a serious situation, leadership is not made but makes itself. We should always remember this.

In the old parties during normal times some amiable gentleman is elected as bellwether by some committee or party conference, or sometimes to some extent by the influence of family or inheritance. When real things have to be done men emerge by reason of their ideas and personality in response to the situation.

We believe that it is better in the event of my death for the Movement to be conducted by a council until a new man emerges to show clearly by reason of his proved leadership capacity that he will undoubtedly secure the united support of our members. Inevitably, new men in new movements are unknown until time has given them a chance to make their reputation. We have many young men developing splendidly, but it is too soon for any of them to reach a point where he would clearly be my successor. The ultimate emergence of such a man is a certainty, because history - like nature - allows no vacuum, while a great people still retain the will to live.

Composition of Government

Union Movement and How to Help It

Question 304. If you formed a government, would it be composed of new, largely unknown men?

Answer. A good proportion of our new men would certainly be in the government, because we have men of first-rate ability. But a new style government shall include men of ability from all branches of national life: science, the services, business, trade unions and also, in one or two posts, the arts. I refer, of course, to the British government which would have to be formed to solve our immediate national problems and to take us into Europe after the British people have so decided at a general election. After that it would be a matter of European government, elected by all the people of Europe.

Question 305. Do you want to be Prime Minister of Britain?

Answer. No, I did once, but I do not any longer. It seems to me that I can best serve my country, first by helping to arrange the complete, the real entry of Britain into Europe, and then, if the British people so desire, by being a representative of Britain in the team of equals drawn from all the main countries, which in the early years will, I believe, be the only acceptable form of European government.

From about 1950 onwards I spent some ten years in becoming a European; this was the necessary equipment for the task. It was necessary for the future that some Englishman should become a European. This is why I believe that I can best serve in this way when Britain takes the final and inevitable decision fully and completely to enter Europe. I wish to do this, rather than be Prime Minister; that is my personal desire.

Needless to say I will always serve my country in any capacity which may be necessary and which our people may desire. It may be, for instance, that we find ourselves excluded for a period from Europe by reason of the errors of present governments, and have to take special and strenuous measures to live at all. In that event I would always do what I was wanted to do. But I remain sure that the policies I have conceived, the knowledge and friendships in Europe I have formed, will always in the end open the way into the real Europe fully and completely to the British people. It is in this respect that I believe I can best serve them, and personally desire to serve them.

Question 306. When you talk of Europe being run by a team of equals, do you not think that any government must have some chief even if he is only "primus inter pares" like the British Prime Minister?

Answer. No, I think in the case of European government it is much better to have no titular chief. Anything of that kind may make difficulty and jealousy between the nations coming together to make the new and greater nation of Europe. The early English idea of a round table is practical as well as romantic. After all, nature rules everywhere. At a round table the natural leaders emerge. Men with the best and most constructive ideas, the strongest and finest characters and the greatest capacity for influencing their fellows always emerge as leaders, if they have an equal chance with the others. This is particularly true in periods of crisis. It is only in easy times that everyone is jostling for the leading jobs; there is not so much hurry to take responsibility when things are really tough. And the birth of Europe might be accompanied by the pains of crisis. You will observe in world history, and even in recent history, that the men with most influence on events have moved mankind and made history only, or chiefly, by the force of their ideas and their personalties. Any man worth anything asks only an equal chance with the others to persuade his fellows that he is right.

Question 307. Do you encourage suggestion and criticism in your party, and how does your Constitution and method compare with that of the other parties?

Answer. Yes, we always welcome suggestion and criticism in our party. The only thing to which we object is a man not expressing any criticism he feels. More opportunities are provided for this than in the old parties. We do not have just one annual conference a year for general discussion, but at least three conferences a year in each area of the country during which every member has the right to make his criticism and suggestions.

I think that you will find in practice that the authority conferred on me in formulating policy and in party management by our Constitution does not exceed the power of the Conservative Leader as defined in R. T. McKenzie's British Political Parties pages 61 to 68. But the method of action in our organised team system is far more effective than Conservative methods. Also our method brings members of the Party into far closer contact with me and other leaders, and with the shaping of the Movement's policy.

As already suggested, we are in every sense a team. I am the leader in the sense that no effective team can work without a leader. And the Movement produces not one leader but many leaders, because a leader of some team is required for every one of our very diverse activities. Our Movement is a big team which is the aggregate of many teams. That is why it is such a fine instrument for the effective action, which the people will soon require.

Question 308. What should we do if we sympathise with you but do not agree with the whole of your policy?

Answer. Well, I should feel that you are with me if you agree with, say, 80% of the policy. After all, no two men who think a lot can ever agree about everything. But I do not press you to commit yourself to joining the Movement, if you do not feel able to do so at present. If you agree with us to that extent you will come to us in the end, at the moment of decision. Our opponents will be surprised to find the number of fine people who are at present just in this position, and also the remarkable quality and well-known achievements of many of them. In fact, today even in membership our chief strength is hidden. Like the iceberg our main bulk is under water. There are many things which keep many people from joining at all in the present situation, which we well understand. But many of them are in close touch with us, and greatly help us. At a moment which may not be very far ahead the situation will change decisively. Then our hidden support can emerge - perhaps all at the same time - and the old world will be very surprised.

Question 309. What can we do to help if we join Union Movement?

Answer. You will then be welcome as one of our companions in the hard struggle of these days. You will be valued among us today, and will be honoured in the future which our fight side by side will bring to our country. There are many ways in which you can help. If you join, please be an open member and declare your convictions if you can, because nothing so much helps our cause. This is the vital service to the beliefs which inspire us. If you are in a position to become one of those open members, you can work either in team or constituency organisation. I will describe first the team work.

You can join a team or form your own team. Our principle is "Let him lead who can". Our whole organisation rests on individual initiative. Any man or woman can join with a group of friends, and at once become a team leader. There is no limit to the size of the team. If someone joins with an outstanding gift of leadership, he or she can at once come to the forefront of our Movement. The activities of the team may vary greatly with the initiative and ideas of the team leader. The normal activities are sales of papers on the streets, mass canvass for sales or membership, and mingling with the mass of the people on popular occasions at all times to establish contact and friendship with them and finally to develop the leadership of the people.

But teams need do nothing of the kind. They can do very different things. They can also engage together in diverse activities, ranging from athletic clubs and established debating societies to forming their own discussion groups in order to debate Movement policy with friends and opponents, and to assist in its development by informing us of their conclusions.

Beyond this, any method the initiative of the team leader can devise to mix with the people and convert them to our cause is good, and gives proof of his ingenuity and leaders capacity. Men and women team leaders can use any method they like, so long as they keep the law and advance only the policy of the Movement.

Where a constituency organiser has been appointed, team leaders are subject to his direction, but only in that constituency. Elsewhere, in constituencies where a constituency organiser has not been appointed, the team leaders are entirely free to work as they wish. They are also quite free to choose where they will work. They are the spearhead of the Movement's propaganda, and of the service it offers to the people.

Question 310. Will you describe your constituency organisation and method of fighting elections?

Answer. Constituency organisation is separate and different from the team organisation. In broad definition, teams open up new territory and constituency organisation then consolidates it with a political machine designed to prepare for the winning of elections. But these two sides of the organisation help each other in between elections as well as in the election periods when Movement work is set aside.

If you prefer to act as an individual in direct political work, you will be very welcome in this side of the organisation. We are developing it to a greater extent than ever before, and regard it as absolutely vital to the Movement's future, We aim finally at building everywhere an organisation in which an individual is responsible for a block of houses in a particular constituency.

The job is to get to know the people, and to establish friendship with them by giving help when needed in their daily lives. Then to enroll members and collect their subscriptions, and to sell the journal supporting the Movement regularly to them and to find other customers as well. And finally to acquaint all who can be interested with our work and policy of the Movement. In short, to be the representative of Union Movement among the people.

At election time, when the normal organisation is temporarily dissolved and a candidate is adopted, you become responsible for canvass among the same people.

Anyone doing this work is responsible to a ward leader, who in turn is responsible to the constituency organiser. As always in our methods of organisation, we believe in a clear chain of individual responsibility. If you have political experience, so much the better. If you have no such experience but desire to do this work, you can be trained by men or women who have had the experience. The constituency organiser should arrange this and should assist you in every possible way. As stated, we regard this work as really vital to the future of the Movement. We are still far from achieving a complete network of constituency organisation. But we have made a start. And if the principles are clear and the pioneers work hard, the task can be completed rapidly when crisis brings a great inflow of new workers who are without the ties and preoccupations of today.

Question 311. What can a member do who cannot work either in a team or in constituency organisation? Are members welcome who cannot do anything active?

Answer. You are certainly welcome as a member even if you can do nothing at all, because you help by just being a member. You may be able to become an active member, but unable to work in the ways described already. In that event we ask you in your own way and time to do what you can to convince people you know and any others you can contact, on every possible occasion. Some people make a surprising number of members in this way.

Again, if you are obliged to be a secret member you are still very welcome, and many such members have greatly helped.

Question 312. What morality do you expect from your members?

Answer. First, as individuals and as a movement we believe in keeping our word. A word of honour must always be kept, whether it is given to a friend or a foe. Our word is our bond. Without that moral attitude society in the end dissolves. The absence of this morality is one of the chief dangers of today.

A communist will always believe that any lie or trick is justified to advance his cause. In the end that morality came near to destroying their own party. They started lying to and tricking each other. Then they started murdering each other in the so-called state trials. They even concluded a party argument with a shot from behind in the back of the neck; the way they settled Beria. They themselves swallowed the moral poison prepared for others.

I do not believe the end justifies the means. A noble end is not reached by ignoble means. You do not create with dirty instruments. The first principle, and the basis of all true European values, is to keep faith with friend and foe.

For the rest, we ask our members to do nothing which can impair their minds or bodies and thereby diminish their capacity to serve the cause in which we believe. This is all that a political movement should ask of its members. Keep your word and preserve your fitness to serve the cause. The rest is a matter of private life and conscience in which we should not intrude.

Beauty and Truth

Question 313. Have you sometimes suggested that the search for beauty was in some way a duty of government?

Answer: Yes, I wrote in one of my books that a civilised society - which had solved the basic material problems - should give some gifted people the means to discover how beautiful life could become. For at a certain point beauty becomes the most vital thing on earth. The present system sometimes gives some ungifted people the means to show how silly life can be. The future should rather choose people of greater sensibility to develop new and ever higher forms of beauty in living.

Question 314. Should government do more to assist the arts?

Answer: The creative artists in all spheres are chosen by nature alone, and have to prove themselves. Often posterity alone can recognise them. They should be free from all interference of government. But government can make their way easy in the future, rather than hard as in the present. Always give any form of creative talent the benefit of the doubt. The society which has resolved the basic needs should be ready to endow with the means of life people who have shown any form of creative gift in literature, music, or the plastic arts. Let them come from any school, however novel or odd it may appear at present. Be prepared to make mistakes, do not mind if you do. If you can save one genius from premature destruction, it will be worth keeping a few dunces in sterile idleness. These things will all be possible when science, in a new system, has completely solved the ordinary problem of poverty.

And in the public sphere, remember always there is no set limit to "demand" once men have really learnt to live. Directly the new production has satisfied all normal needs and has begun to outstrip demand, let us not only build new amenities - the means of pleasure and amusement for the people - but also beautify our cities on a scale and in a degree inconceivable today. Then men can feel again with the classic Greeks, and can say with Euripides: "But shall not loveliness be loved for ever?"

Question 315. Do you suggest in some of your other writings some search for a higher value, a new way of thinking, almost a higher form of man?

Answer: You refer to writings and interest which I did not really mean to consider here, as I am dealing with more immediate, practical problems. But as I suggested in the preface, the "deeper debate" must "underlie all controversy".

This was the theme of an introduction to Goethe's Faust that I wrote some years ago, and also of an essay on Wagner and Shaw and a review of Professor Heller's interesting but controversial book The Disinherited Mind, as well as some other writings not directly connected with politics. The idea of higher forms, of which I first wrote in 1947 in *The Alternative*, is dealt with in the last chapter of *Europe: Faith and Plan* (1958). Here it is mentioned briefly in the preface and in an answer on communism where I postulate that the discernible process of life is a movement from lower to higher forms. This concept has a basic simplicity but differs as completely from the main principle of current opinion as a tower does from a mine shaft.

In brief summary of this idea in relation to the coming situation, I believe that some definite concept of a higher form, for the next phase, is beginning to emerge from the turmoil of modern thought. It was slow in developing, like most ideas which matter. This particular stage of the process probably began with Goethe and the German Neo-Hellenists, was reflected in the English Neo-Hellenists and carried further by Nietzsche, and also in a new impulse to historical analysis by Spengler - from whom Toynbee in turn derives much - until in the continuous interaction of English and German thought, I hope and believe it may attain some culmination in the new English thinking. The whole process was vitalised from a new scientific source with the pervading influence of the English biologists. At all stages French thinking and the lucidity of the Latin mind have illuminated the path of Europe.

Is then some definite concept of a higher form yet discernible? What a question! How many books it would require in a calm sequestered from the dust of this arena. But if you think in terms of the eternal process of synthesis which is necessary to all really creative thinking, you may perhaps already dimly discern - rising from the clash of Hellenism and Christianity-a new synthesis at the point where the missing quality, compassion, was added to the values of the classic Greeks which remain the original and continuing inspiration of Europe. The seers and the prophets sense these things almost unconsciously long before others - Goethe with his "soul yearning for that Grecian land", yet recoiling in horror before a glittering beauty which had no compassion, until he found his synthesis in the apotheosis of Faust, and with it his "Olympian" calm: Wagner in Parsifal when his Hellene (not the simpleton, naif never meant that) learns compassion and weeps both for the death of beauty and for human pity, thus acquiring the synthesis which fits him for the highest achievement-but it is left for this age to attempt the bringing of a great new reality to consciousness, a higher form.

Yet all this is really none of my business. This belongs to the future, to a new generation. My task is to secure that there shall be a European future. Quite enough, without presuming further!

Question 316. You sometimes say you prefer the search for truth to debate, but it leads for always to Union?

Answer: I mean that if we love our country our continent, and humanity, we really all want to discover what is the best thing to do. The best way is surely not the slapstick debate - just scoring off each other - which you see so often on T.V., or even in parliament. Serious debate, in which each man strives strenuously but fairly for his point of view, is a better way of arriving at truth. But even then truth only emerges in haphazard fashion from a battle of wits.

What I really like is the kind of discussion in which we pool our Intelligences and experiences and together search consciously for truth. After all the age is serious, deadly serious. Big mistakes now can mean the end of man. You would not find a general staff behaving in this manner on the eve of a battle in which all may lose their lives. They would not even indulge in serious debate in the sense of arguing just for the sake of controversy. You would find them rather with concentrated seriousness working together to discover the best plan of action. Men in moments of dark danger and great decision ask - how together can we survive the morrow? Cannot we have something of that spirit in this great age of politics on which the future of the world may depend? Cannot we sometimes now search for truth together, even if we have disagreed in the past on lesser occasions? That is what I mean by the search for truth.

The question of this age is how Britain and Europe can now live? And world survival too may well depend on the answer to this question. Nothing matters except to find the true answer. Let us find truth together, and then act in union.

www.ingramcontent.com/pod-product-compliance
Lightning Source LLC
Chambersburg PA
CBHW071049280326

41928CB00050B/2043